# Learning
# in Action

# Learning in Action

A GUIDE TO PUTTING
THE LEARNING ORGANIZATION
TO WORK

## David A. Garvin

HARVARD BUSINESS SCHOOL PRESS
Boston, Massachusetts

Printed in the United States of America

07      5 4 3 2

978-1-59139-190-6 (ISBN 13)

**Library of Congress Cataloging-in-Publication Data**

Garvin, David A.
Learning in action : a guide to putting the learning organization to work /
David A. Garvin
p. cm.
Includes bibliographical references and index.
ISBN 1-57851-251-4
1.  Organizational learning. 2. Organizational learning—Case studies. I. Title
HD58.82 .G37 2000
658.4'06—dc21                    99-048911

ISBN 1-59139-190-3 (pbk)

*To my parents,*
*who taught me to love learning,*
*and to my wife and daughters,*
*who keep me learning every day*

# Contents

# Preface

By now the value of organizational learning is widely recognized. Managers view knowledge as a key corporate asset, to be leveraged and exploited for competitive purposes. They see best practices as sources of superior productivity and growth, to be disseminated as quickly as possible. They consider creative ideas and innovative thinking essential to success in emerging, rapidly changing markets. For all of these reasons, it is hard to find a manager today who does not give at least lip service to the importance of building a learning organization.

Yet despite this apparent acceptance, progress has been slow. Learning organizations have been embraced in theory but are still surprisingly rare. Managers find them easy to imagine but hard to create and sustain. The reason, in large part, is the lack of guidelines for practice. Past discussions of the subject have paid little or no attention to the gritty details of implementation. They have presented a compelling case for learning and painted a tempting picture of the desired endpoint but have left many questions unanswered. Most are operational and action-oriented: How do I, as a manager, get started? What tools and techniques must I master? What processes must be in place? When and how is each approach best used? What do I need to do personally to lead the learning process? And how will I know when my company has truly become a learning organization?

The aim of this book is to provide answers to these questions and, in the process, to help managers build more effective learning organizations. The analysis that follows has four distinguishing features. First, it is comprehensive and synthetic. In exploring the landscape of learning, I have drawn on research from many fields, including anthropology, cognitive science, economics, education, engineering, management, organization theory, philosophy, political science, and psychology. My goal is to provide a broad, integrated view of the topic that is grounded in scholarship. Much of the evidence I cite has deep practical importance yet has never before been assembled in one place or translated into terms that are accessible to managers. Together, the findings from these studies present a compelling picture of the drivers of organizational learning, the practices that contribute to success and failure, and the behaviors required of managers and employees.

Second, the book is filled with a wealth of examples. They take two forms: detailed case studies and brief snapshots. The case studies provide in-depth profiles of successful learning processes at organizations such as Xerox, L.L. Bean, the U.S. Army, GE, Timken, and Allegheny Ludlum Steel. They are based on extensive field research and include a wide range of quotations, tips and techniques, instructions, and lists of dos and don'ts. Each is a complete, composite picture of learning in action. The snapshots are more tightly focused; each singles out a particularly effective program or policy or else highlights an error that could be easily avoided. They do not attempt to present a complete learning story. But they do broaden the range of companies covered and show how learning can be applied in extremely diverse settings. Among the companies featured are Banc One, Boeing, British Petroleum, Corning, Disney, Emerson Electric, Intel, Microsoft, Motorola, Nike, Pepsi, Target, Time Life, and Wal-Mart, as well as a host of lesser-known firms.

Third, the book has a distinctive point of view. I argue that at the heart of organizational learning lies a set of processes that can be designed, deployed, and led. These processes need not be left to chance. They can—and, according to the main argument of the book, should—be managed. This is not to suggest that learning always arrives through planning or systematic analysis. Serendipity—in the form of unexpected connections or unanticipated events—clearly plays a role. The focus here, however, is on increasing the odds of success and improving the breadth, depth, and speed of learning by following well-crafted processes and procedures. Learning will always remain something of an art, but even the best artists can improve their technique.

Fourth, and perhaps most important, the book has a strong practical bent. Many managers remain uncomfortable with the soaring, high-minded prose of past discussions of organizational learning. They are driven by far more immediate concerns. Their focus—and the one that I have adopted in this book—is getting things done. Whenever a critical learning process is described, it is accompanied by a concrete discussion of the policies, programs, and procedures that are required for success. Whenever a tool or technique is featured, it is accompanied by a set of instructions for applying it in real organizations. Whenever a mind-set or environment is cited as conducive to learning, it is accompanied by a list of supporting steps and activities. And whenever the challenge of leading learning is discussed, it is accompanied by specific suggestions for creating opportunities, sharing knowledge, setting the proper tone, and shaping the discussion process.

The book is divided into three broad sections. The first, which consists of chapters 1 and 2, is introductory and provides the foundation for all that follows. It describes the basic elements of learning organizations as well as the primary processes. Chapter 1 begins by contrasting individual and organizational learning, then offers a precise definition of learning organizations, several litmus tests for evaluating progress, and a few simple questions that managers can ask to help them get started in raising learning higher on the corporate agenda. Chapter 2 describes the basic steps in every learning process—acquiring, interpreting, and applying knowledge—and examines the challenges posed by each one. It also introduces the notion of learning disabilities—common biases and errors that impede effective learning—and suggests ways that they can best be overcome. The chapter concludes with a discussion of the defining characteristics of supportive learning environments and presents examples of policies and programs that encourage them.

The second section, which consists of chapters 3, 4, and 5, examines different modes or processes of learning. Each involves the same basic steps of acquiring, interpreting, and applying information, but applies them in different ways. Each draws data from different sources and involves a different set of challenges. Chapter 3 discusses intelligence, the collection and interpretation of information that exists outside the organization. Interviewing and observational techniques are examples. Chapter 4 discusses experience, the accumulation of knowledge through action. Postproject reviews and action learning programs are examples. Chapter 5 discusses experimentation, the manipulation of variables or changing of conditions to draw inferences. Prototypes, exploratory designs, and tests of competing theories are examples. In each chapter, the basic characteristics of that mode of learning are first described, the necessary supporting conditions and essential steps for success are then discussed, and several variations or alternative approaches are examined. Each major alternative is accompanied by an extended case study that shows the process in action.

Together, these three chapters present a set of processes that collectively provide companies with virtually all they need to know to create a learning organization. The processes fit together neatly, since each has a different orientation. Intelligence gathering is aimed at the present; it ensures that organizations attend to currently available information. Experiential learning is aimed at the past; it ensures that organizations draw lessons from activities that have already taken place. Experimentation is aimed at the future; it ensures that organizations look ahead, trying out new designs or theories to test their validity. Present, past, and future—the coverage is comprehensive and complete.

The final section of the book, which consists of chapter 6, shifts the focus from organizations to individuals. It explores the leadership challenge that confronts executives wishing to build learning organizations. How can they personally stimulate inquiry, prompt debate, and encourage deeper thinking among subordinates? The chapter provides several answers. It begins by describing learning forums—settings and events, such as systems audits and meetings with customers, whose primary purpose is fostering learning—and shows how managers can create and support them. It then discusses the importance of setting the proper atmosphere and tone—a mix of challenge and testing on the one hand, and collegiality, collaboration, and security on the other—and highlights the ways that executives can maintain this delicate balance. Special attention is paid to the most effective use of questioning, listening, and responding, for they are the primary tools that leaders have for shaping discussions. The chapter concludes with a discussion of how executives can become better learners themselves. If they hope to build learning organizations, they too must become more open to divergent views, more aware of their personal biases, and more comfortable with raw, unfiltered data. Otherwise, they will never be able to lead others in learning.

Throughout, the book is guided by a simple premise: learning organizations are built from the gritty details of practice. Sweeping metaphors and grand themes are far less helpful than the knowledge of how individuals and organizations learn on a daily basis. The key to success is mastery of the details, coupled with a command of the levers that shape behavior. This book shows managers how they can use that understanding to create learning organizations that work.

David A. Garvin
December 1999

# Acknowledgments

I have learned a great deal writing this book and have had the benefit of many teachers. I would like to offer my thanks.

First and foremost, I wish to thank the managers and military leaders who consented to interviews, provided explanations, contributed data, and otherwise generated the raw material that lies at the heart of this book. They are the true heroes of the project, for they serve as inspirations and models, offering living proof that learning organizations do in fact exist. All of the people I spoke with were candid and cooperative, committed to telling their stories accurately and completely. Without their help, this book would not exist.

Equally helpful were my academic colleagues, who provided insightful comments on an earlier draft of the manuscript. I would like to thank Robert Burgelman, Roland Christensen, Michael Cusumano, Donald Hambrick, Morten Hansen, Gary Klein, Michael Roberto, and Michael Tushman for adding so much to my understanding of learning organizations. They posed penetrating questions, made me think hard about the underlying concepts and frameworks, suggested relevant literature and examples, and ensured that my arguments were tight and easy to follow. The final manuscript is vastly improved as a result.

Many of the detailed examples in this book first appeared in two Harvard Business School Video series, *Putting the Learning Organization to Work* and *Working Smarter.* Many people participated in their development, and I have drawn heavily on our work together. I am especially grateful to William Brennan and Jane Heifetz of Harvard Business School Video, Ed Gray of David Grubin Productions, Joe Blatt of River-Run Media, and the directors Thomas Ott and Eric Stange for their many contributions.

A number of others helped move the project along. My editor, Marjorie Williams, was a source of endless good advice; her suggestions and support have been invaluable. My research associates, Artemis March, Janet Simpson, Donald Sull, and Jonathan West, helped research and write the case studies that appear as examples throughout the book; they were active, insightful collaborators. My secretary, Andrea Truax, typed and retyped endless charts and tables; she also ensured that the final manuscript was polished and error free. Aimee Hamel of the Word Processing Center saved the day several times, finding ways to make my word processing program behave as requested.

But, as always, the greatest contributions came from my family. My parents taught me to cherish and love learning; they pointed me toward many of my current pursuits. My wife, Lynn, listened and led in equal measure; she has been and continues to be my source of inspiration. My daughters, Diana and Cynthia, showed me the true meaning of learning; they keep me grounded while teaching me something new every day. These five special people represent the very best of learning in action, and I dedicate this book to them.

# I

# FOUNDATIONS

# 1

## From Individual to Organizational Learning

Learning is the most natural of activities. It is an essential part of the human experience, and something that we as individuals do throughout our lives. Yet more often than not, our progress as learners goes unrecognized or unheeded. It happens as if by magic: one day we are ignorant, then time passes and suddenly we possess a wealth of new knowledge.

Children provide the most obvious example, for they are instinctive, intuitive learners. Much of childhood is spent expanding one's horizons and acquiring new perspectives, abilities, and skills. But the work of development does not end in childhood. Countless studies have shown that individuals continue to adapt and grow as they age.[1] Self-directed learning projects, for example, are quite common. According to pioneering research conducted in the early 1970s, the average adult engages in approximately eight learning projects per year, and roughly 90 percent of adults can cite at least one such project that they pursued in the previous year.[2] Typically, adults devote one hundred hours annually to each learning project, even though fewer than 1 percent are undertaken for credit.

3

Moreover, these projects are extremely diverse, ranging from general oc-cupational skills, such as accounting, shorthand, and tool design, to spe-cific job knowledge, such as advertising strategy and the needs of dis-advantaged adolescents, to personal interests and home-related responsibilities, such as cooking skills, child and baby care, and playing a musical instrument. Most projects are motivated by a major life transi-tion either at home or on the job, are problem-focused, and are intimately linked to a desire for self-renewal and personal growth.

Today, corporations face similar needs. They too are in the midst of massive transformations requiring renewal and growth; for this reason, many have jumped on the learning bandwagon. The most obvious mani-festation of their commitment is company-sponsored education and training. In the U.S. alone, spending on corporate education has grown at 5 percent a year for the past decade; it now totals nearly $60 billion annually.[3] A number of leading companies, including Motorola, General Electric, and McDonald's, have established their own corporate "univer-sities," offering a wide range of technical, business, and remedial courses. Others, such as Intel and Andersen Consulting, now spend as much as 6 percent of payroll on education and training, while requiring two weeks of class time per year for all employees.[4]

Yet even with these commitments, most managers remain surpris-ingly ambivalent about learning. Many give lip service to its importance, voicing strong public support for efforts to broaden employees' knowl-edge and skills. But when pressed, they usually express very different feelings. For all too many managers, learning is of questionable value because it diverts employees' attention from "real work."

Executives are action-oriented, and their goal is to get things done. Any activity that does not produce immediate, tangible results is there-fore viewed with a certain degree of suspicion. Programs to stimulate learning frequently fall into this category, especially if they require time for reflection, synthesis, and review. The result is a clash of values, as a leading proponent of learning has observed:

> The most difficult challenge is developing a culture that values . . .
> learning. A colleague once . . . told me of a dialogue with a loading
> dock foreman who, in great frustration, finally said to him, "Look, I

can either ship product or talk about it. Which do you want me to do?" The correct answer can only be "Both," but it is hard to make that answer a reality.[5]

The implicit analogy is to academic scholarship, with its overtones of bookishness, ivory-tower impracticality, and leisurely reflection. Professors are devoted to the life of the mind; they have chosen lives that give them ample opportunity to hone their arguments to a razor's edge. Managers see themselves at the opposite end of the spectrum: doers rather than thinkers, pressured for time and thus willing to rely on workable rather than ideal solutions. This view is well represented by a story that Charles Handy, the British futurist, tells about a presentation he made sketching out the organization of the future, which stressed the importance of intelligence, information, and ideas. "Increasingly," he said to a group of chief executives, "your corporations will come to resemble universities or colleges." "Then God help us all," one of them replied.[6]

In the same spirit, learning is seen by many managers as a New Age phenomenon, whose goal is releasing human potential rather than improving the bottom line. Here, scholars are partly to blame, for their discussions of learning organizations have often been reverential and utopian. Peter Senge, who popularized learning organizations in his book *The Fifth Discipline,* describes them as places "where people continually expand their capacity to create the results they truly desire, where new and expansive patterns of thinking are nurtured, where collective aspiration is set free, and where people are continually learning how to learn together."[7] Ikujiro Nonaka, a Japanese scholar, uses similar language, characterizing knowledge-creating companies as places where "inventing new knowledge is not a specialized activity . . . it is a way of behaving, indeed, a way of being, in which everyone is a knowledge worker."[8] These descriptions, while uplifting, lack a framework for action, and thus provide little comfort to practical-minded managers.

An additional source of unease comes from managers' quest for stability and predictability. At most companies, efficiency is a hallowed goal, best served by well-established routines. Yet learning demands constant questioning and repeated reevaluations of established practice. Skepticism and open-mindedness are essential. But because many managers

"cannot bear to have their cherished beliefs challenged . . . on a continuing basis . . . evaluation and organization . . . are to some extent contradictory terms."[9]

For all these reasons, learning has yet to establish a secure beachhead
at many corporations. It occurs, of course, but more often through benign
neglect than active support. All too many managers continue to regard
time spent learning as a necessary but unproductive evil. Such views are
unfortunate because they reflect an extraordinarily narrow conception of
the potential impact of learning. Nor do they recognize the many guises
in which new knowledge appears. Far from being academic, philosophi-
cal, and inefficient, corporate learning is much more likely to be practical, applied, and intimately linked to the bottom line.

## LEARNING IN ACTION

Consider the following examples:

- Thirty continuous casters, all designed by the same supplier but
  installed at different steel makers, took widely varying times to reach
  anticipated production levels. Start-up periods—the elapsed time
  from the first pouring of steel through a caster until the unit was
  producing at full capacity—varied from 7.5 months to over 6 years.
  The median start-up took 24 months. A rough calculation suggested
  that the lost contribution from these delays totaled $137 million,
  primarily because of slow and inadequate learning.[10]

- In industries as varied as banking, computers, health care, and oil,
  the typical intrafirm transfer of a best practice—from first identification of the practice to successful performance at the receiving unit—
  took nearly three years. The primary barriers were not motivational (a
  bias against ideas "not-invented here") but knowledge-related: limited understanding of the elements of successful practice and
  difficulty in absorbing new knowledge and insights.[11] The associated
  costs were significant. A study of intrafirm transfers of manufacturing
  technology found that over 50 percent experienced severe productivity problems. The initial productivity loss at the receiving plants
  averaged 34 percent, with a low of 4 percent and a high of 150

percent. The time to recover the lost productivity ranged from 1 to 13 months; at 20 percent of the facilities, the original levels were never regained.[12]

- When radical or disruptive technologies are involved, conventional marketing research is of little help. This is especially true if current customers are the primary sources of information. The disk-drive industry provides a telling example. As the industry shifted from 14-inch to 8-inch to 5.25-inch to 3.5-inch drives, virtually all of the leading firms were displaced. Each time, they failed to shift to the next-generation technology, largely because their current customers were expressing satisfaction with existing products while demand was coming from newer organizations that they were neither serving nor surveying. The failure was one of learning, not technological prowess.[13] Much the same displacement occurred in the semiconductor industry as it shifted from vacuum tubes to semiconductors to microprocessors.[14]

- In late 1994 Intel discovered a flaw in its Pentium processor. The problem, due to a design error in the chip, caused a rounding error in division once every nine billion calculations. The company knew of the problem early, considered it to be minor, and developed a policy of reassurance and occasional replacement. But it vastly underestimated the ensuing public reaction. Once the problem was publicized, the press was highly critical, as were customers and industry experts. After several months of analysis, reflection, and review—in other words, intensive learning—Intel announced a completely new policy: it would replace the offending part for anyone who wanted it changed. The cost? A $475 million write-off.[15]

At first glance, these examples involve seemingly unrelated challenges: installing new equipment, transferring best practices, responding to technological changes, and interpreting customer feedback. But at a deeper level, they are remarkably similar. Each illustrates the difficulties of effective implementation and, by implication, the power and potential of improved organizational learning.

There are several common denominators. First, in each of these cases success requires additional knowledge. Whether the task is operating an unfamiliar piece of equipment or understanding an emerging market, learning is essential to achieving desired results. Sometimes the knowledge is new and has to be created from scratch; at other times it already exists and has to be transferred elsewhere in the organization. Either way, the required insights are practical, applied, and focused on the task at hand. Learning is not desired for learning's sake, or for abstract, academic purposes. It is needed to get the job done.

Second, in each case improved learning has direct links to the bottom line. Both costs and revenues are affected. On the cost side, smoother transfers of best practices yield impressive gains in productivity. A sense for the size of the payoffs can be obtained by comparing the best and worst transferrers of manufacturing technology, whose productivity losses differed by a factor of 40. On the revenue side, better processing of customer and market information would undoubtedly improve the odds of succeeding with next-generation products, leading to more accurate market positioning and increased sales. The continuous caster example shows that where capacity is a constraint, more rapid ramp-ups to full production yield large increases in sales and contribution. Again, a sense for the payoffs can be gained by comparing the best and worst performers; their startup periods differed by a factor of 10.

Third and perhaps most important, managers seldom use the term learning when describing these situations. Typically, they reserve it for other purposes, primarily discussions of education and training programs or workshops where knowledge sharing is the stated goal. When learning is embedded in real work, managers normally use other language; frequently, they overlook learning's role completely. Yet situations like these—where learning is essential for completing a task, yet is neither recognized nor publicly acknowledged—are extraordinarily common. Entrepreneurship, for example, invariably involves new skills and behaviors, as do most business development projects. Effective mergers and acquisitions demand learning on both sides of the table. The same is true of most cost-reduction and quality-improvement programs, where process and operating knowledge must be deepened and expanded.

Because these situations arise so frequently, all organizations learn at some point in their lives. A few learn repeatedly but largely by happenstance. Long-successful companies, however, such as IBM and Johnson & Johnson, are invariably committed, conscientious learners.[16] In fact, it is almost a truism to say that such organizations learn, for they have prospered for decades while facing diverse and varied conditions. Revolutionary technologies, shifting markets, and unanticipated competitors have all required innovative responses. How else would these companies have survived if they were not continually learning something new?

One implication of this argument is that we need to view organizational effectiveness through a different lens. Corporate success is best judged by adaptability and flexibility, not the usual short-term measures of profitability and productivity. The latter present mere snapshots in time; a more appropriate metric would take into account long-term survival and growth:

> If we view organizations as adaptive, problem-solving, organic structures, then inferences about effectiveness have to be made, not from static measures of output, but on the basis of the processes through which the organization approaches problems. . . . The measure of health is flexibility, the freedom to learn through experience, the freedom to change with changing internal and external circumstances. . . .[17]

Examples include Microsoft's 1995 shift from operating systems and applications software to Internet offerings, which required a wholly new strategy as well as the broadening of programming and software skills, and 3M's continued outpouring of new products, often far removed from its base in adhesives and abrasives. Such adaptability is common in learning organizations.

## LEARNING ORGANIZATIONS

Surprisingly, a clear definition of learning organizations has proved to be elusive over the years. Organizational theorists have studied learning for a long time, but as the quotations in Table 1-1 suggest, there is still considerable disagreement.[18] Most scholars agree that learning is a process that unfolds over time and link it with knowledge acquisition, deeper understanding, and improved performance. But they differ on other important matters.

Some, for example, believe that behavioral change is required for

## TABLE 1-1

### DEFINITIONS OF ORGANIZATIONAL LEARNING

Organizational learning means the process of improving actions through better knowledge and understanding.[a]

Organizational learning is defined as increasing an organization's capacity to take effective action.[b]

An entity learns if, through its processing of information, the range of potential behaviors is increased.[c]

Organizational learning is a process of detecting and correcting error.[d]

Organizational learning is defined as the process by which knowledge about action-outcome relationships between the organization and the environment is developed.[e]

Organizations are seen as learning by encoding inferences from history into routines that guide behavior.[f]

Organizational learning occurs through shared insights, knowledge, and mental models . . . [and] builds on past knowledge and experience—that is, on memory.[g]

a  C. Marlene Fiol and Marjorie A. Lyles, "Organizational Learning," *Academy of Management Review* 10 (1985): 803.
b  Daniel H. Kim, "The Link between Individual and Organizational Learning," *Sloan Management Review* (fall 1993): 43.
c  George P. Huber, "Organizational Learning: The Contributing Processes and the Literatures," *Organization Science* 2 (1991): 89.
d  Chris Argyris, "Double Loop Learning in Organizations," *Harvard Business Review* 55 (September/October 1977): 116.
e  Richard L. Daft and Karl E. Weick, "Toward a Model of Organizations as Interpretation Systems," *Academy of Management Review* 9 (1984): 286.
f  Barbara Levitt and James G. March, "Organizational Learning," *Annual Review of Sociology* 14 (1991): 319.
g  Ray Stata, "Organizational Learning—The Key to Management Innovation," *Sloan Management Review* (spring 1989): 64.

learning; others insist that new ways of thinking are enough. Some cite information processing as the mechanism through which learning takes place; others propose shared insights, organizational routines, even memory. Some see the interpretative process as central to effective learning; others focus on the detection and correction of errors. And some think that organizational learning is common, while others believe that flawed, self-serving assessments are the norm.

Practitioners, of course, are less interested in academic fine points than in having a definition that is clear, compelling, and actionable. How, then, can we distinguish between these competing voices, yet build on the insights of other scholars? As a first step, consider the following definition:

*A learning organization is an organization skilled at creating, acquiring, interpreting, transferring, and retaining knowledge, and at purposefully modifying its behavior to reflect new knowledge and insights.*

This definition begins with a simple truth: new ideas are essential if learning is to take place. Sometimes they are created through flashes of insight and creativity; that is frequently the job of research centers such as Bell Laboratories and Xerox PARC. At other times they arrive from outside the organization, gleaned from technical articles, knowledgeable experts, or tracking studies. But even an abundance of new knowledge does not ensure that a learning organization exists. As the story of the Pentium processor makes clear, raw unfiltered information is of limited value. Managers must also be skilled at giving meaning to the data they have assembled. Without the ability to interpret unfamiliar knowledge accurately, even the best ideas will remain unutilized.

Nor does the process end with interpretation. Knowledge must also be shared collectively, rather than limited to a privileged few. New ideas must diffuse rapidly throughout the organization, extending from person to person, department to department, and division to division. Eventually, they must become embedded in organizational "memory," appearing as policies, procedures, and norms to ensure that they are retained over time. Purely local knowledge is valuable, but it does not mark the existence of an organization that has learned.

These activities provide the foundation for learning organizations. But they are no guarantee of success. Without accompanying changes in the way that work gets done, only the potential for improvement exists. According to this definition, learning requires action. But that action cannot be uninformed; it must be tied in some way to prior reflection. For this reason, neither book knowledge alone—collecting facts, without putting them into practice—nor spur-of-the-moment activity—doing something, without a clear rationale—meets the standard.

This is a surprisingly stringent test, for it rules out a number of obvious candidates for learning organizations. Many universities fail to qualify, as do many consulting firms. Even such a diligent student of modern management as General Motors is found wanting. All of these organizations have been effective at creating, acquiring, and interpreting knowledge but notably less successful in applying that knowledge to their own activities. Total quality management, for example, is now taught at many business schools, but the number using it to guide their own decision making is very small. Organizational consultants advise clients on social dynamics and small-group behavior but are notorious for their own infighting and factionalism. And GM, with a few exceptions such as New United Motors Manufacturing, Inc. (NUMMI), its highly productive assembly plant in Fremont, California, has had great difficulty mimicking the manufacturing practices of industry leaders like Toyota, even though its managers have carefully studied just-in-time production methods.

Organizations that do pass the definitional test—Xerox, L.L. Bean, and the many other examples cited in later chapters—have, by contrast, become adept at translating new knowledge into new ways of behaving. These organizations actively manage the learning process so that it is focused and purposeful. Learning occurs by design and in pursuit of clearly defined needs, rather than for its own sake. GE provides an instructive example. In 1989 Jack Welch, the company's CEO, launched Work-Out, a problem-solving process modeled after a New England town meeting. Welch was determined to improve productivity while streamlining the company's slow, cumbersome decision-making process. His learning agenda was quite explicit:

> Work-Out has a practical and an intellectual goal. The practical goal is to get rid of thousands of bad habits accumulated since the creation of General Electric. . . . [T]he intellectual part begins by putting the leaders of each business in front of a hundred or so of their people, eight to ten times a year, to let them hear what their people think. . . . Ultimately, we're talking about redefining the relationship between boss and subordinate. I want to get to the point where people challenge their bosses every day.[19]

To that end, Work-Out combined three days of off-site discussion by groups of thirty to one hundred hourly and salaried employees, aimed at fleshing out departmental or divisional problems and developing possible solutions, with a final intense session, at which the boss returned, was bombarded by the group's proposals, and was forced to make instant, on-the-spot decisions. For each recommendation, his or her only alternatives were to say yes, no, or I need more data. Welch made this process a virtual requirement at GE and personally pressed managers to get involved—he was determined to share the learning widely and retain it in organizational memory—and by mid-1993 over 85 percent of the work force had participated. By all accounts, the process was a huge success; not only did productivity improve, but managers' responsiveness increased as well. For these reasons, Work-Out provides a perfect example of a learning organization in action, for it shows how the creation, interpretation, and retention of knowledge can be coupled with changes in behavior to produce meaningful results.

## LITMUS TESTS

By this point readers will be wondering, How will I know if mine is a learning organization? Are there any obvious clues? There are, in fact, a few simple litmus tests that can be applied to determine whether or not a company qualifies.[20] Each is framed as a question that probes for evidence of distinctive behaviors. The presence of these traits does not guarantee the existence of a learning organization—specific practices and processes are also required—but their absence certainly raises grave doubts.

*Does the organization have a defined learning agenda?* Learning organizations have a clear picture of their future knowledge requirements. They know what they need to know, whether the subject is customers, competitors, markets, technologies, or production processes, and are actively pursuing the desired information. Even in industries that are changing as rapidly as telecommunications, computers, and financial services, broad areas of needed learning can usually be mapped with some precision. Once they have been identified, these topics are pursued through multiple approaches, including experiments, simulations, research studies, post-audits, and benchmarking visits, rather than education and training alone.

*Is the organization open to discordant information?* If an organization regularly "shoots the messenger" who brings forward unexpected or bad news, the environment is clearly hostile to learning.

Behavior change is extremely difficult in such settings, for there are few challenges to the status quo. Sensitive topics—dissension in the ranks, unhappy customers, preemptive moves by competitors, problems with new technologies—are considered to be off limits, and messages are filtered, massaged, and watered down as they make their way up the chain of command. Senior managers are likely to remain out of touch because they will be confronted with little of the conflict and contrast that are so essential to effective learning.

*Does the organization avoid repeated mistakes?* Learning organizations reflect on their past experience, distill it into useful lessons, share the knowledge internally, and ensure that errors are not repeated elsewhere. Databases, intranets, training sessions, and workshops can all be used for this purpose. Even more critical, however, "is a mind-set that . . . enables companies to recognize the value of productive failure as contrasted with unproductive success. A productive failure is one that leads to insights, understanding, and thus an addition to the commonly held wisdom of the organization. An unproductive success occurs when something goes well, but nobody knows how or why."[21] There is a peculiar logic at work here: to avoid repeating mistakes, managers must learn to accept them the first time around. They must adopt the philosophy of John McCoy, the chairman of Banc One, who observed: "I don't remember my successes. It's the mistakes that I . . . learned from."[22] This mind-set is rare in corporate America, because it requires a tolerance for error and a willingness to view failures as a necessary by-product of experimentation and risk taking.

*Does the organization lose critical knowledge when key people leave?* The story is all too common: a talented engineer (or marketer or production supervisor) leaves the company, and critical skills disappear as well. Tasks that were previously routine become impossible, for the required know-how can no longer be found. Why? Because crucial knowledge was tacit, unarticulated, and unshared, locked in the head of a single person. Learning organizations avoid this problem by institutionalizing essential knowledge. Whenever possible, they codify it in policies or procedures, retain it in reports or memos, disperse it to large groups of people, and build it into the company's values, norms, and operating practices. Knowledge becomes common property, rather than the province of individuals or small groups.

*Does the organization act on what it knows?* Learning organizations are not simply repositories of knowledge. They take advantage of their new learnings and adapt their behavior accordingly. Information is to be used; if it languishes or is ignored, its impact is certain to be minimal. By this test, an organization that discovers an unmet market need but fails to fill it does not qualify as a learning organization, nor does a company that identifies its own best practices but is unable to transfer them across departments or divisions.

## FIRST STEPS

Learning organizations are not built overnight. As later chapters will show, most successful examples are the products of carefully cultivated attitudes, commitments, and management processes that have accrued slowly and steadily over time. Still, some changes can be made immediately. Any company that wishes to become a learning organization can begin by answering three simple questions.

- What are our most pressing business challenges and greatest business opportunities?

- What do we need to learn to meet the challenges and take advantage of the opportunities?

- How should the necessary knowledge and skills be acquired?

The first of these questions is the most common. In most companies the answer already exists in the output of annual retreats, monthly review meetings, and strategic planning exercises. At some point, virtually all companies require that their managers identify the unit's strengths and weaknesses and develop an associated list of opportunities and threats (SWOTs). These SWOTs typically provide the basis for the company's annual plan, as well as the goals for individual managers.

The second question is much rarer. Most managers move immediately from identifying an opportunity or problem to developing an action plan; they seldom pause to ask what needs to be learned if they are to proceed in an informed fashion. Yet new knowledge is invariably required if real progress is to be made. Consider, for example, a consumer goods company that has decided to begin selling its products in China. To succeed, it must develop knowledge on several fronts: an understanding of the role of government officials, the nature of existing supply networks, how to distribute products effectively, the required adaptations of designs and formulations to local needs, and how to advertise and price competitively. Such information is crucial to moving forward but is unlikely to be readily available and on tap. It must be actively assembled and acquired.

Alternatively, consider a steelmaker experiencing problems with a new generation of materials. Yields are low, and defects are multiplying. Again, the company's learning needs can be clearly specified: deeper knowledge of the cause-and-effect relationships governing the production process, and identification of the critical process variables (temperature, pressure, time) that must be controlled for superior performance. Without this knowledge, improvement is likely to be impeded by false starts and misdirected efforts. Or consider an airline planning to upgrade its fleet by acquiring more modern planes. Its learning needs cover a broad sweep: new approaches to routing and scheduling to accommodate the faster, more flexible jets, and new skills for those pilots, mechanics, and flight attendants who will service and use the new equipment. Here too learning is an essential intermediate step on the road to effective action.

The explicit identification of learning needs leads naturally to the third question, which is rarer still. New ideas do not materialize of their own accord; they must be actively pursued. Managers must learn to ask, What is the best way to acquire the necessary knowledge and skills? Organizations have a wide range of learning tools at their disposal; in any given situation, some are likely to provide more leverage than others.

The consumer goods company, for example, could learn more about the Chinese market by relying on a consulting firm with expertise in the region, forming a joint venture with a Chinese partner, hiring a manager from another company who has already built a successful Chinese subsidiary, sending benchmarking teams and study missions to China, or establishing a small-scale pilot operation to gain practical knowledge firsthand. The steel maker could conduct shop-floor experiments to identify critical operating variables, send metallurgists back to the library or the laboratory to carry out further investigative research, or collaborate with academic scientists to diagnose and solve the problem. The airline could develop software programs to optimize routing and scheduling, collect competitive intelligence to identify the scheduling practices used by airlines that had modernized earlier, purchase simulators as part of its own education and training program, or send employees to outside vendors or established flight academies to acquire needed skills.

In each case, the most effective learning strategy depends on the situation. There is no stock answer, nor is there a single best approach. But by asking these questions, managers are taking an important first step: they are agreeing that learning can be managed. New knowledge need not materialize by magic, nor through sweeping metaphors or grand themes. The roots of learning organizations lie in the gritty realities of practice.

# 2

---

# The Learning Process

Organizational learning demands inquisitiveness and openness—a willingness by managers to challenge assumptions and tackle conventional wisdom. Otherwise, behavior will continue to be ruled by habit, and the status quo will remain undisturbed.

Unfortunately, most organizations have been designed with the status quo firmly in mind. They accomplish their work through what scholars call "routines," commonly accepted practices and procedures that are uniform, unvarying, and performed without thinking.[1] Repetition and consistency, rather than new insights, are the primary goals. Examples include McDonald's strict standards for cooking burgers and fries, timed tasks on an assembly line, and rules for processing travel vouchers in a busy office. In most cases, the associated activities are programmed and automatic, and soon become accepted as "the way we do things around here."

Managers are equally vulnerable to habit, especially when processing information and interpreting events. They are continually bombarded by facts, opinions, and forecasts; to avoid overload, many rely on time-tested categories and filters.[2] Often, these categories are implicit and unstated; like most routines, they are invoked without conscious thought. Examples include assumptions about market boundaries—who is a potential competitor, and who is not—and the underlying economics of a business. Even when industry environments are changing rapidly, these assumptions continue to influence the way that managers think about customers, competitors, and required competencies.

The goal of these routines is laudable: improved efficiency through standardization. Time is saved in both operations and information processing because the same approach is used repeatedly—and often unconsciously. Unfortunately, the side effects can be severe. Learning requires new knowledge and approaches—as a pioneering scientist has put it, "discovery consists of seeing what everybody has seen and thinking what nobody has thought"—and habitual, preset responses leave little room for fresh perspectives or innovative ways of thinking.[3] In the presence of routines, the wonder of organizational learning is that it occurs at all. To ensure that it does, managers first need to develop a better understanding of the learning process—the stages through which learning unfolds, the biases and disabilities that so often stand in the way, and the enablers and supporting conditions that allow new ideas to flourish. Only then will they be able to combat ingrained routines and actively cultivate learning.

## STAGES OF LEARNING

Virtually all studies of organizational learning divide the process into three or four stages. The terminology varies, but the same basic steps appear again and again.[4] For learning to occur, organizations must first *acquire* information, assembling facts, observations, and data. At this stage, the raw material of learning is gathered, and the crucial questions include, What information should we collect? From where? How should it be obtained, and by whom? Next, organizations *interpret* information, producing perspectives, positions, and refined understanding. At this point, the raw material is processed and reviewed, and the crucial questions include, What does the information mean? What categories should we apply? What cause-and-effect relationships are at work? Finally, organizations *use* or *apply* information, engaging in tasks, activities, and new behaviors. At this time, analysis is translated into action, and the crucial questions include, What new activities are appropriate? What behaviors must be modified? How do we generate a collective response by the organization? Not surprisingly, each of these stages brings its own distinctive tasks and challenges.

## Acquiring Information

It is easy for managers to be overwhelmed in today's information-rich economy. The number of business books, journals, conferences, and Web sites with up-to-the-minute insights continues to grow at an alarming rate. Is it any wonder that most organizations find themselves drowning in data? In such settings, acquiring information is easy—too easy, in fact. The real challenge for managers is to distinguish relevant from irrelevant information, while remaining open to unexpected, and occasionally unwelcome, surprises.

In technical terms, the first task involves separating "signals" from "noise." Both terms are drawn from modern information theory but have commonsense definitions. A signal is the true impact or evidence associated with an activity or event; noise is any contradictory, confusing, or random information that obscures the message.[5] Effective organizational learning demands clear signals and minimal noise, as well as the ability to share critical insights so that they do not remain isolated or unacknowledged. Unfortunately, in many settings, especially those involving rapid change and multiple sources of data, the combination is rare. Low signal-to-noise ratios are a pervasive problem, as the following examples suggest:

- The Japanese raid on Pearl Harbor was preceded by a number of clear signals, including the famous message "East Wind Rain," drawn from the top-secret code MAGIC, suggesting that an attack was imminent. As a leading historian has observed: "Our decisionmakers had at hand an impressive amount of information on the enemy."[6] Yet at the same time, there was a welter of conflicting evidence, especially from European sources, that pointed to different conclusions. No single analyst had a complete, integrated picture because critical intelligence information was not widely shared. The Japanese were also maintaining strict secrecy about the attack, while announcing a number of false targets. All told, the noise in the system was simply too great for a clear message to get through. According to the same historian: "We failed to anticipate Pearl Harbor not for want of the relevant materials, but because of a plethora of irrelevant ones . . . [I]t is much easier *after* the event to sort the relevant from the irrelevant signals . . . Signals that are characterized today as absolutely unequivocal warnings of a surprise air attack on Pearl Harbor become, on analysis, not merely ambiguous but occasionally inconsistent with such an attack."[7]

- The explosion of the space shuttle *Challenger* is often cited as a preventable disaster resulting from failure to heed clear signals of potential danger prior to launch. But those signals were extremely difficult to read in real time; many of them, on careful analysis, were mixed, weak, or routine. "A mixed signal was one where a signal of potential danger was followed by signals that all was well, convincing engineers that the problem had been successfully diagnosed [and] corrected . . . A weak signal was one that was unclear, or one that, after analysis, seemed such an improbable event that working engineers believed there was little probability of it recurring . . . Routine signals are those that occur frequently. The frequent event . . . loses some of its seriousness as similar events occur."[8] In particular, damage to the *Challenger's* O-rings, which sealed the solid rocket booster joints and were later implicated in the disaster, had been found on a number of previous flights but were not regarded as a serious concern. Why? Because the known sources of the problem had already been fixed; cold temperatures, which produced much of the deterioration, were rare in Florida and not expected to recur; and previous flights had weathered the damage without problems. Here, too, fuzzy signals resulted in critical problems being overlooked.

- Semiconductor manufacturing is a business where rapid learning is essential for commercial success. Manufacturing yields are typically quite low when a new semiconductor is introduced; they must be raised quickly if the product is to become profitable. Experimentation is therefore common during the first few months of production; the goals are to identify critical operating parameters and setpoints, to better understand the underlying manufacturing process, and to increase yields. Unfortunately, these experiments do not always produce the desired learning. Studies of VLSI (very large scale integration) integrated circuit fabrication have found extremely high levels of process noise, making improvements difficult to identify. In most cases, there was so much variability within and across production lots that experiments were of limited value. For example, in four of the five plants studied the "probability of overlooking a three percent yield improvement was over twenty percent." At times, noise levels were so high that the likelihood of identifying critical variables was "little better than pure chance."[9]

These examples suggest that acquiring information is surprisingly difficult. Valuable signals are frequently accompanied by worthless noise. Critical insights remain in isolated pockets and are not always connected or pulled together. Even when all the necessary data have been obtained, the underlying message often remains obscure. The implications for managers are obvious. To enhance learning, they must improve signal-to-noise ratios, develop mechanisms for pooling information, and work to craft an integrated, unbiased picture of events.

As if these challenges were not enough, there is a further complication. Unlike instruments or electronic equipment, which are programmed to record all incoming data, managers are more selective. They do not attend to all information but instead rely on "processes that amplify some stimuli and attenuate others, thus distorting the raw data and focusing attention."[10] A hypothesis is first formed, or a perspective established; information is then collected with these frameworks in mind.[11] As social psychologists have observed, the results are predictable: "much of what people would label as information only reaffirms old news."[12]

In fact, it is extremely difficult—and, at times, impossible—for organizations to assemble pure, unvarnished facts, especially if they are unexpected. Most people are drawn to the familiar, and managers are no exception. Market research provides a good example. Studies show that managers typically use market research for confirmatory purposes—to reduce uncertainties, fill information gaps, and generate support for decisions that have already been made—rather than as a source of new insights.[13] Open-minded inquiry is seldom the goal. Instead, data collection is normally limited to current customers, known competitors, and a narrow set of questions. Surprises are shunned, and unforeseen or counterintuitive findings, which could produce deep learning, usually have the opposite effect: they upset managers and receive little attention. Here, as in many other settings, effective organizational learning requires a more open and accepting process for acquiring information.

## Interpreting Information

Even if organizations were able to acquire all essential information, they would still have to interpret it. Industry environments are seldom tidy or orderly; most are in constant flux. Unadorned facts and opinions are therefore of limited value. They become useful only after they have been classified, grouped, or placed within a larger context. For this reason, scholars have observed:

> Organizations must make interpretations. Managers must literally wade into the swarm of events that constitute and surround the organization and actively try to impose some order. . . . Interpretation is the process of translating these events, of developing models for understanding, of bringing out meaning, and of assembling conceptual schemes.[14]

To evaluate the impact of a new product, for example, managers must first make assumptions about industry rivalry and customer needs; the same is true when assessing the consequences of a complex, cross-border alliance. In both situations, they rely heavily on what cognitive scientists call "schemas," deeply rooted mental structures that organize knowledge and give it form and meaning. At an abstract level, schemas consist of categories, models, classification schemes, and assumed cause-and-effect relationships that together give shape and texture to independent, unconnected observations. They play a variety of roles: organizing and classifying new information, filling in missing data, assigning probabilities to events, and providing rationales and explanations for behavior. To the extent that the underlying frameworks are shared, members of an organization will think along similar lines.[15]

Peter Drucker, for example, has observed that all companies have an implicit "theory of the business," a set of shared assumptions about markets, customers, competitors, technology, and the organization's mission and competencies.[16] These theories provide consistent, cohesive frameworks for interpreting events and guiding behavior. Unfortunately, they also have a critical weakness: they eventually become obsolete. The theory on which a business was built does not always accord with current realities; when the two diverge, problems are inevitable. IBM's fall from grace in the 1980s is representative. At the time, managers were unable to harmonize the company's long-standing theory of the business, which was based on a dominant presence in mainframe computers, with the growing demand for PCs, which required a very different competitive logic.

Interpretative frameworks thus present two challenges for managers. First, as the IBM example illustrates, they must be tested and updated continually. Without active scanning of the environment and an openness to contradictory information, frameworks can quickly become irrelevant. Second, managers must recognize that their frameworks are invariably sketchy and incomplete; they are approximations of reality that are "reasonable rather than right."[17] In most cases, the underlying cause-and-effect relationships are difficult to specify, and data can be viewed in more than one light. Supporting evidence is often fragmentary. The same facts may well produce conflicting interpretations, with considerable room for disagreement and debate. Do a competitor's price cuts, for example, imply that a price war is imminent, or are they an innocuous attempt to reduce excess inventory? When does rising demand signal a turnaround in the economy, and when is it a mere seasonal correction? Are the latest technologies fads that will soon disappear, or do they signify fundamental shifts in product requirements?

Each of these questions lacks an obvious, factual answer, and each can be addressed only by invoking an interpretative framework. For this reason, interpretation lies at the heart of decision making. As Dean Stanley Teele of the Harvard Business School was fond of telling students: "The art of management is the art of making meaningful generalizations out of inadequate facts." But which generalizations should managers use? And on what basis should they choose? The goal, of course, is to select the most accurate interpretation, the one whose categories, constructs, and cause-and-effect relationships best match reality. But because accuracy can be determined only after the fact, managers must rely on proxies when making comparisons, judging competing frameworks by their richness and degree of detail. In general, more effective frameworks are better grounded in concrete data, include more comprehensive taxonomies, are tied together by stronger, more fine-grained causal linkages, and are more widely shared by key actors.[18] Xerox, for example, was far more successful in marketing its copiers after it expanded its original two broad categories of customers—large and small accounts—to six—large- and small-customer major accounts, large and small named accounts, general markets, and government/education. Predictive power improved because the new categories were more differentiated and better able to discriminate between actors and their needs.[19]

## *Applying Information*

Because learning is usually associated with thinking rather than doing, this stage is not always considered to be part of the learning process. But according to the definition and litmus tests of chapter 1, action is essential; if an entity does not purposefully modify its behavior to reflect new knowledge and insights, it does not qualify as a learning organization. Two steps are required. Managers must translate their interpretations into concrete behaviors and must then ensure that a critical mass of the organization adopts the new activities.

The first task is often difficult. Interpretative frameworks classify and organize data; they do not always have obvious implications for action. Agreeing on the meaning of events still leaves open the question of what to do about them. Recall, for example, Intel's difficulties with the flawed Pentium processor. Even after managers recognized that their "Intel Inside" advertising campaign, coupled with the company's vast size, had transformed the firm into a highly visible consumer marketer, they remained unsure how to respond. According to Andy Grove, Intel's chairman and CEO:

the old rules of business no longer worked. New rules prevailed. . . . The trouble was, not only didn't we realize that the rules had changed—what was worse, we didn't know what rules we now had to abide by. . . .

It's like sailing a boat when the wind shifts on you. . . . [T]he boat suddenly heels over. What worked before doesn't work anymore; you need to steer the boat in a different direction quickly before you are in trouble, yet you have to get a feel of the new direction and the strength of the wind before you can hope to right the boat and set a new course.[20]

Even when the behavioral implications of a new interpretation are obvious, employees may still not take the required steps. Habits and routines are difficult to dislodge. To overcome inertia, managers must first send clear signals but, even more important, must offer opportunities to practice new behaviors. Hands-on experience is usually the best teacher, and managers must make the time for employees to learn new behaviors: "If you really want people to spend time doing something new, give them the time to do it. Take away old activities, provide released time, ask them to work overtime—somehow demonstrate that time allocation patterns are to change."[21]

It is essential to eliminate unnecessary or outdated tasks at the same time that new ones are added. Otherwise, overload is inevitable. Most companies, unfortunately, only understand the concept of addition; they are much weaker when it comes to subtracting work. Continental Airlines is a notable exception. In the mid-1990s, it studied a competitor, Southwest Airlines, to learn how to cross-utilize personnel (to have the same people perform multiple tasks such as loading baggage and boarding customers at the gate). Initially, employees objected to cross-utilization, fearing that workloads would increase. But they were soon persuaded, after management asked them to list all the "dumb, non-value-added things" they did each day and then eliminated many of these useless chores. The result was a much speedier adoption of cross-utilization because time was now available for learning.[22]

Time to practice, however, is seldom sufficient by itself, especially if new competencies are required and members of the organization must broaden or alter their skills. Then, resistance is likely to reflect deeper forces—personal values, a sense of identity, preferred work styles—and forceful action is often necessary if behavior is to change. Software providers, for example, have long preached the gospel of customer service. But their help lines still suffer from technical jargon and poor communication because employees continue to identify with the technology, rather than with unskilled users. To overcome the problem, a new breed of customer service representatives may be needed, and financial incentives may have to be tied directly to customer satisfaction scores. Only then will a critical mass of the organization make the desired behavioral shifts.

## LEARNING DISABILITIES

At first glance, the acquire-interpret-apply process is a model of simplicity. Each of the three stages brings challenges, but they appear to be predictable and easy to identify. With attention and forethought, managers would seem to face few difficulties in cultivating learning.

Unfortunately, a wide range of learning disabilities impede the process. They are a common and often unavoidable by-product of the way people think and act, and occur at every stage in the learning process. Acquisition problems arise from oversights, omissions, and errors in the way information is collected; they result in slanted or incomplete data. Interpretation problems arise from distortions in the way that information is processed by preexisting frameworks; a large number occur because managers are imperfect statisticians and make flawed judgments about the likelihood and probability of events. Application and use problems arise from corporate risk aversion and the difficulties people have in recognizing that their actual behavior often deviates markedly from their espoused behavior. Together, these problems conspire to undermine learning and reduce its effectiveness. Managers must tackle them aggressively if they want accurate inferences and appropriate action to result from new information.

### Biased Information

When acquiring information, organizations suffer from three primary disabilities: blind spots, filtering, and lack of information sharing. Blind spots arise when scanning and search activities are narrow or misdirected, resulting in areas where managers "will . . . not see the sig-

nificance of events . . . at all, will perceive them incorrectly, or will perceive them very slowly."[23] They normally reflect mistaken or incomplete
assumptions. A common error is misjudging industry boundaries and
expecting that competition will continue to come from traditional
sources. Newspapers, for example, long underestimated the threat posed
by cable TV and the Internet, as did the major networks. Only after
audiences declined steadily did both groups begin to reexamine their
definitions of the industry. The rise of biotechnology had a similar impact
on pharmaceutical firms, who initially overlooked chemical companies as
likely competitors because they failed to see the similarities between the
requirements for success in biotechnology and chemical companies'
long-established competencies and skills.[24]

Blind spots are especially likely to arise during times of crisis. Stress
and anxiety typically lead to restrictions in the amount and type of information that managers process, as well as a tendency to search for data
that confirm preexisting views.[25] The result is a narrowing of focus and
attention. Nike, for example, after a decade of extraordinarily rapid
growth, faced slowing sales in the early 1980s. Reebok had entered the
market with an innovative new design, a soft, comfortable aerobics shoe
made of garment leather that required no break-in period. Sales quickly
took off. Yet managers at Nike were slow to respond, largely because of
their traditional focus on athletes and performance-oriented shoes.
Many, in fact, found it so difficult to accept customers' changing preferences that they deemed the first prototype, made of soft leather, as
"simply unsuitable" for a Nike product. According to a senior executive:
"We could still be purists and talk about shoes that were for runners and
athletes. And anybody who didn't make it the way we made it was a fool.
We also had the idea that everything we sold . . . was used by an athlete
to perform, which was absolute bull."[26]

Nike's difficulties are closely related to another bias in acquiring
information: filtering. Filtering occurs when critical data are downplayed
or ignored because they do not accord with preexisting schemas or frameworks.[27] In a revealing set of experiments, psychologists found that expos-
ing supporters and opponents of capital punishment to *identical* evidence
led them to diametrically opposed conclusions.[28] Polarization actually
increased, and established positions became more entrenched. Why?

Because each group read the findings selectively, allowing assumptions to drown out facts. They discounted surprises and minimized the importance of contrary evidence. Such problems are especially likely to occur under stress, when expectations are high, existing hypotheses or interpretations serve as a defense against anxiety or threats, attention is focused elsewhere, and attentiveness decreases because a period of intense concentration has come to an end. In the Tenerife air disaster, for example, two jumbo jets collided on takeoff with a loss of 583 lives. Among the causes were a series of miscommunications in which pilots heard distorted messages yet did not raise questions, filled in missing information in ways that confirmed their assumptions about clearances and lack of obstructions, were preoccupied with flying their planes rather than monitoring radio traffic, and relaxed momentarily after completing difficult maneuvers.[29] The parallels to management are painfully clear. Like the pilots at Tenerife, managers under pressure often hear what they want to hear.

Lack of information sharing only compounds the problem. Undiffused, local knowledge is of limited use, for it is seldom available when needed. To ensure effectiveness, critical incoming data must quickly become common property, woven into the organization's collective consciousness. Otherwise, as the attack on Pearl Harbor illustrates, it will remain unheeded, without the visibility needed to impact decision making.

Unfortunately, such sharing is easier said than done. Information hoarding is a fact of organizational life, especially in political settings or where information is highly valued.[30] Functional fiefdoms contribute to the problem, as do departmental loyalties and narrow, issue-oriented coalitions. But even when the problem has been recognized and independent competitive intelligence or environmental analysis groups have been established, difficulties remain. Especially when they are freestanding, these groups often find themselves isolated and unable to tie into the decision-making process. They remain vulnerable because they lack well-defined roles and power bases and are not tightly integrated into the line organization. As one director of environmental analysis described the problem: "It doesn't help to have a 16 cylinder engine, if it isn't connected to the wheels."[31]

## Flawed Interpretation

Disabilities are common during interpretation because the underlying processes are complex and poorly understood. Interpretation involves judgment and a certain amount of inspired guesswork; both are easily swayed by factors other than logic or reason. In particular, human beings are subject to a wide range of interpretative errors because they are notoriously poor statisticians. Few people understand the strict requirements for inferring causation; fewer still are well versed in the laws and limits of probabilistic reasoning.[32] Even the most sophisticated managers make these mistakes.[33] Despite the best of intentions, they routinely develop interpretations, causal connections, and probability estimates that are seriously biased.

Scholars have identified a number of distinctive problems. The best known include the following:

- *illusory correlation*: viewing events as related simply because they have appeared together;
- *illusory causation*: ascribing causality to events that occur in sequence and seem to be linked;
- *the illusion of validity*: increasing confidence in one's judgment, especially with larger and larger amounts of information, even though the accuracy of judgment remains unchanged;
- *framing effects*: different responses to identical, uncertain payoffs that have been framed as potential gains rather than potential losses;
- *categorical bias*: the use and persistence of stereotypical categories for classifying people and events, even when faced with conflicting information;
- *availability bias*: assessing the probability of events by the ease with which examples come to mind, rather than their actual frequencies or likelihoods;
- *regression artifacts*: ascribing causality to actions that change a variable from an extreme (high or low) level to an average level, even though the change is really due to chance (i.e., the greater likelihood

that an average score will be obtained rather than an extreme value);
and

- *hindsight bias:* the systematic biasing of probability estimates toward actual outcomes.[34]

At first glance, many of these errors seem esoteric and even irrelevant
to the task of management. But they have very real implications. Consider two examples: the illusion of validity and hindsight bias. The former
is simply a fancy way of describing an age-old problem: *hubris,* or excessive confidence in one's ability to form accurate judgments. Unfortunately, such confidence is seldom warranted, especially when information
is incomplete or ambiguous. A study of clinical psychologists, for example, found that their ability to answer questions about a subject's personality type changed relatively little as they received more data, increasing
from being 26 percent to 28 percent correct. But their confidence in their
accuracy rose far more dramatically. Initially, psychologists estimated that
they would answer 33 percent of the questions correctly; once they had
complete background information, they estimated that they would be 53
percent correct. As the author of the study concluded: "The judges'
confidence ratings showed that *they become convinced of their own increasing understanding of the case* . . . entirely out of proportion to the
actual correctness of those decisions."[35] Is it at all difficult to imagine
managers reacting similarly to increasing amounts of information about
customers, competitors, or employees? Is there any reason to believe that
their self-assessments will be any more accurate than psychologists'?

Hindsight bias is an equally pervasive problem. It too describes a
familiar phenomenon: the tendency to look back on events and assume
that one "knew it all along." When presented with information about
historical situations and asked to judge the probability of different outcomes, individuals systematically bias their estimates in the direction of
the outcomes that actually occurred. They appear, on reflection, to have
been inevitable. The process works unconsciously and is difficult to overcome, even when subjects have been warned in advance. Retrospective
assessments are therefore quite different from those made in real time.

In a revealing experiment, M.B.A. students were divided into groups
and asked to analyze a complex investment proposal. Each group was
provided with identical facts about the project but was given different

information about outcomes. "When told, but then asked to ignore, the results . . . they were unable to do so. . . . [T]hose who were told of favorable outcomes rated the project as more promising, less risky, more likely to succeed, and more attractive for a personal investment than did others told of less favorable results; subjects given no outcome information fell in between."[36] The implications for managers are disturbing. Because of hindsight bias, it is extremely difficult to judge the appropriateness of past decisions and draw inferences for the future. To learn from experience, managers must be able to evaluate situations as they appeared at the time that choices were made. They must ask, "Considering what I knew then, how likely did the event seem?"[37] Unfortunately, because of biases in remembered or reconstructed evaluations, the answers that emerge are seldom accurate.

## *Inaction*

At the third stage of the learning process, the primary problem is passivity—an inability or unwillingness to act on new interpretations. Inertia is partly to blame, as are continued efforts to justify the past. Most individuals and organizations are also risk averse; they do not like to experiment with unfamiliar, untested approaches. In part, this is a problem of incentives and the frequent lack of support for new initiatives. As Jack Welch of GE put it: "Change has no constituency."[38] At times, however, the problem runs deeper and reflects the very human tendency to overlook personal shortcomings.

A certain level of self-awareness is essential if changes are to be made. Current practice must be clearly understood; only then is it possible to take remedial action. Yet all too often, the required understanding is lacking. People are surprisingly unaware of their own behavior; they do not always act the way they think they do. In technical terms, the problem is one of distinguishing "espoused theories" from "theories-in-use":

When someone is asked how he would behave under certain circumstances, the answer he usually gives is his espoused theory of action for that situation. This is the theory of action to which he gives allegiance and which, upon request, he communicates to others. However, the theory that actually governs his actions is his

theory-in-use, which may or may not be compatible with his espoused theory; furthermore, the individual may or may not be aware
of the incompatibility of the two theories.[39]

The examples are legion: the autocratic manager who claims that he is
already using participative approaches, the surly saleswoman who asserts
that she is only responding to customer needs, the arrogant consultant
who insists that he avoids dictating to clients. All firmly believe that
they are acting in the manner described and are usually unaware of any
discrepancies. Learning is extremely unlikely in such settings because
people remain unconvinced that changes in behavior are actually
required.

## SUPPORTIVE LEARNING ENVIRONMENTS

Learning disabilities are common and predictable. Like competition, they
are a fact of organizational life. But that does not mean they have to be
paralyzing. Companies can take a number of steps to minimize these
disabilities and cultivate more accurate, effective learning. To begin, they
need to create supportive, stimulating environments. Four conditions are
essential if learning is to flourish: the recognition and acceptance of
differences; the provision of timely, unvarnished feedback; the pursuit of
new ways of thinking and untapped sources of information; and the
acceptance of errors, mistakes, and occasional failures as the price of
improvement.

### *Recognize and Accept Differences*

Differences are crucial to learning because they provide energy and motivation. Without them, lethargy and drift are likely, and prevailing schemas and frameworks are almost certain to remain in place. Questions
arise only when we become aware of inconsistencies, contradictions, and
competing perspectives; the resulting tensions produce discomfort and
lead to a search for solutions. In business settings, inconsistencies frequently take the form of gaps or unfilled promises—gulfs between aspira-

tions and reality or expected and actual performance. Divergent opinions, especially among powerful managers, are an equally strong force for change. But these differences must first be acknowledged and brought into close proximity if learning is to occur.[40] In many organizations, the difficulty lies not in creating differences—they are invariably widespread and deeply rooted—but in ensuring that processes exist for bringing divergent points of view together, airing them fully, and resolving the resulting tensions productively.

Boeing, for example, has developed a system of checks and balances that serves precisely this purpose. The development of a new airframe is a several-billion-dollar bet, and the task is dauntingly complex. A typical 767 contains over three million parts and eighty-five miles of wiring. Because the potential for error is so great, Boeing has long used audit teams to inject diverse views into the design process. When the 767 was still on the drawing board, teams of experienced managers were asked to review every significant element of the program, including technology, finance, manufacturing, and management. Teams acted as devil's advocates, introducing competing perspectives and questioning all aspects of the work. A typical audit took three months. To preserve autonomy, all teams were isolated organizationally and given a direct reporting line to the chairman.[41]

Emerson Electric has used a similar approach in strategic planning. Each fiscal year, senior corporate officers meet with the management of every division to discuss their plans. A few basic charts are presented summarizing historical trends, financial targets, sales goals, and expected sources of growth and cost savings, but the real focus is the discussion that follows. Differences are highlighted and even created when necessary. According to Charles (Chuck) Knight, the company's long-term CEO:

The mood is confrontational—by design. Though we're not trying to put anyone on the spot, we do want to challenge assumptions and conventional thinking. . . . Often, a manager will give a logical presentation on why we should approve a plan. We may challenge that logic by questioning underlying assumptions illogically. The people who know their strategies in detail are the ones who, after going through that, are able to stand up for the merits of their proposal.[42]

Although the settings differ, both Boeing and Emerson Electric are pursuing the same goal: encouraging learning by battling complacency. Conflict and debate are invaluable for this purpose; both result from differences that have been brought into close contact. The same ends can be achieved by other means. Heterogeneous management teams, made up of individuals of diverse ages, genders, functional backgrounds, and industry experiences, are helpful, as are attempts to develop multiple alternatives, options, and scenarios before settling on a single course of action.[43] Occasionally, the decision-making process itself can be re-designed. Techniques for introducing differences include "dialectical inquiry" and "devil's advocacy"; the former breaks teams into subgroups to develop competing positions, while the latter institutionalizes criticism by assigning the responsibility and role to an individual or subgroup.[44] Both approaches have been judged to produce superior outcomes in a wide range of experimental settings. Both have also proven themselves under fire. After his disastrous experience with the Bay of Pigs, President Kennedy redesigned the process of national security decision making to explicitly include these techniques and used them to great effect in the Cuban Missile Crisis.[45]

## Provide Timely Feedback

Timely, accurate feedback is equally important in encouraging learning.[46] By compressing the learning cycle into a brief period and then coupling it with revised, updated information, organizations can more quickly as-similate new observations; can more easily compare predicted and actual behaviors; and can more readily identify problems and disabilities. Com-panies can obtain these benefits even with simple feedback processes. Skilled managers, for example, often float trial balloons to get a quick reading on their organizations' receptiveness to new proposals. Effective product developers rely heavily on prototypes—small models, mock-ups, or simulations, built quickly and inexpensively—to uncover potential design conflicts and manufacturing problems. Shop-floor employees calibrate their skills by visiting customers' factories and discussing their work.

More elaborate systems can have even greater impact, especially if they introduce detailed, comparative data. Such systems create immediate pressures to learn because the facts are difficult to deny. Flawed interpretations are far more likely to be questioned, as are inertia and failure to act. Banc One, for example, a large bank-holding company, for many years used its financial reporting system for this purpose. After a new bank was acquired, it was immediately converted to a standard IT system to ensure apples-to-apples comparisons. All banks then received a monthly "peer report," based on asset size, which compared their performance to comparable banks on measures of revenue, income, balance sheet quality, productivity, and liquidity. The culture was one of "share and compare," and both were expected. As the chairman observed at the time: "[E]veryone has access to everyone else's numbers. They can see who is the best, who is the worst. If you see you're the worst, you pick a better bank and see what's happening there. It's friendly peer competition, but not deadly . . . [because you're] . . . not competing in the same market."[47] The result? Banc One consistently increased the return on assets of acquired banks by a spectacular 62 percent, well above industry norms.[48]

Other companies rely more heavily on external feedback. Both Wal-Mart and GE use a process called Quick Market Intelligence (QMI) to stay in close touch with the field. The typical cycle is one week. From Monday to Thursday, Wal-Mart's regional managers fan out to collect information on competitors' stores, as well as their own. On Friday, they reconvene, accompanied by buyers, functional heads, and vice presidents, to discuss their findings about prices, merchandise, and sales. Decisions are made on the spot and are then communicated immediately to store managers through video.[49] GE Appliances devotes equal attention to staying in touch with the market. Weekly teleconferences and video conferences link top executives with their counterparts in Europe, Asia, and South America; the same process is used to connect field salespeople with headquarters and plant personnel. The goal, according to a vice president, is real-time learning and responsiveness: "QMI . . . circumvents layers of bureaucracy. . . . [Salespeople] get on the phone for an hour and talk about what happened that week, what are the big opportunities they can go after, and people pick up assignments then and there. The following week they go through it again, so the most they can be off on anything is a week."[50]

## Stimulate New Ideas

Such feedback is powerful but has an important limitation. It is primarily corrective, a way of resetting a wayward course rather than generating fresh insights. Effective learning also requires a steady flow of new ideas. Some companies focus externally; their approach, like Milliken's, is to "steal ideas shamelessly." Chaparral Steel, one of the world's most productive minimills, sends its first-line supervisors on sabbaticals around the globe, where they visit academic and industry leaders, develop an understanding of new work practices and technologies, and then bring what they have learned back to the company and apply it to daily operations.[51] GE's Impact Program originally sent manufacturing managers to Japan to study factory innovations, such as quality circles and kanban cards; later, Europe was the destination, and productivity improvement practices were the target.

Other companies focus internally. Their goal is to foster creative cultures by introducing forums and processes that ferret out ideas, incentives that encourage risk taking, and targets that spur employees. Disney, for example, believes that ideas for successful animated films are everywhere in the organization; they need only be drawn out and developed. Three times a year senior managers, including the chairman, vice chairman, and president of feature animation, attend a Gong Show, at which any employee, from secretary to senior executive, is permitted to pitch concepts and story lines. Pitches are limited to five minutes, and managers respond immediately—and bluntly—to all proposals. If the pitch is accepted, the presenter gets the normal fee for a first treatment, usually $20,000. The results? An extraordinary esprit de corps, not to mention the central concepts for *Hercules* and other animated features.[52]

Disney's approach works well when ideas are already bubbling and prodding is unnecessary. At times, however, more aggressive approaches are required. Toshio Okuno, the plant manager of Higashimaru Shoyu, a Japanese soy sauce manufacturer, devised one of the most unusual: the *hangen* (cutting in half) game. To improve productivity, Okuno repeatedly cut work groups in half, then asked the remaining workers, including those observing the process, to identify any unnecessary or noncritical tasks that could be eliminated. Based on their suggestions, work flows were redesigned, and extraneous employees were reassigned elsewhere in the plant. The most spectacular results were achieved on the bottling line, where a twenty-five-person group was quickly reduced to thirteen line workers, plus three roving troubleshooters. Okuno's explanation? "[T]o become more efficient, it is necessary to continuously review one's job to ensure that every task is absolutely necessary. Unfortunately, it is impossible to do so under normal conditions. There simply isn't enough pressure to allow creative thinking to occur."[53] The *hangen* game's bold targets stretched employees by providing the stimulus to pursue break-throughs rather than the usual marginal improvements.

## *Tolerate Errors and Mistakes*

Pressure alone, of course, will not produce bold thinking. The environment must also encourage risk taking. Employees must feel that the benefits of pursuing new approaches exceed the costs; otherwise, they will not contribute. Such settings are termed "psychologically safe." They have five distinguishing features: "(1) opportunities for training and practice, (2) support and encouragement to overcome fear and shame associated with making errors, (3) coaching and rewards for efforts in the right direction, (4) norms that legitimize the making of errors, and (5) norms that reward innovative thinking and experimentation."[54] Both culture and incentives play pivotal roles. IDEO, for example, the largest product design consulting firm in the United States, has built its entire culture around brainstorming. Sessions occur daily, and freewheeling discussions are the norm. Civility and praise are encouraged; interruptions and criticism are not. Designers are urged to treat the process as a game; the goal is to generate "wild ideas" and "defer judgment" as long as possible. The result, according to a careful anthropological study, is that at IDEO "there is little cost for suggesting a bad idea as long as a person occasionally comes up with a good one."[55] A sense of psychological safety has clearly been built into the culture.

3M has long worked to create similarly supportive settings for its scientists. Resources are clearly part of the story. Funds are readily available for experiments, and researchers are encouraged to invest 15 percent of their time on projects of their own choosing. But even more important are deliberate attempts to create an atmosphere that encourages fresh thinking. Early in their career, new employees attend a class on risk taking. They come with their supervisors and are regaled with stories about products that survived despite the opposition of bosses. Thinsulate, the wildly successful insulating material, is featured prominently; the project was killed five times by the CEO, only to rise phoenixlike on each occasion. Students then participate in an exercise in which they are given real money to wager. They first walk a long plank laid on the floor to collect a small amount of money at the other side. Then, they are asked if they would cross the same plank for a larger payoff, but under slightly different conditions—the plank is now seven stories high, stretched between 3M's headquarters buildings. Most immediately complain of the risk, at which point instructors respond, "What risk? You already proved you could do it."[56] The message is clear—risk is in the eyes of the beholder.

Yet even with a supportive culture, employees will resist new ideas if they believe that they will be penalized for anything less than perfection. Errors, mistakes, and occasional failures must be accepted—embraced even—if learning is to occur. Especially when flawed information, biased interpretations, or differences between espoused and actual behavior exist, corrections will be suggested only if employees are certain that managers will not "shoot the messenger" bringing unwanted news. This is perhaps the most important condition supporting learning and the most difficult to implement. The problem is human nature: the fact that "everyone wants to learn, but nobody wants to be wrong."[57] Unfortunately, it is seldom possible to have one without the other.

Organizations thus face a difficult dilemma. Candor is needed on precisely those topics that people prefer to avoid. Moreover, the problem must be met head on, for there is no way around it: "You cannot solve your problems until you know what they are. And you will not know what they are unless you create an environment where people feel free to tell you."[58] Three conditions are essential: a culture that does not demand infallibility and perfection; freedom to fail without punishment or penalty; and systems or incentives that encourage the identification, analysis, and review of errors. IBM's legendary founder, Thomas Watson Sr., apparently understood the first condition well. Company lore has it that a young manager, after losing $10 million in a risky venture, was called into Watson's office. The young man, thoroughly intimidated, began by saying: "I guess you want my resignation." Watson replied: "You can't be serious. We just spent $10 million educating you."[59]

As Watson recognized, demanding infallibility is a prescription for paralysis. Business environments are inherently uncertain; it is the rare manager who makes all calls correctly. Those who do are invariably risk averse and plodding. They collect excessive amounts of data, eschew innovation, and stick to the party line. Learning is seldom high on their, or their subordinates', agendas. Freedom to fail creates a different mindset. It opens up possibilities and creates opportunities to improve. In such settings, there may be mistakes, but they will be acknowledged and discussed—and seldom repeated. A recent study of errors in administering drugs in hospitals, in fact, found higher *reported* error rates in units with greater openness and more sympathetic management. When environments were less supportive and errors were associated with blame or discipline—a search for the guilty, rather than a search for solutions—errors were much more likely to be hidden or suppressed.[60] Fear does little to encourage learning.

At times, supportive cultures must be coupled with changed incentives if mistakes are to surface. Employees who see themselves at risk must occasionally be granted anonymity and immunity. The Federal Aviation Administration (FAA), for example, established the Aviation Safety Reporting System (ASRS) to ensure that pilots voluntarily report "incidents" or "near misses"—deviations from required altitudes, headings, or spacing between planes that might constitute FAA violations. As long as pilots file safety reports—confidentially—with the ASRS within ten days of an incident's occurrence, they are granted partial immunity by the FAA.[61] Within hospitals, weekly morbidity and mortality conferences serve a similar purpose, allowing doctors to debrief confidentially, discussing errors or problems they encountered without fear of liability.[62] The same approach could easily be applied to safety violations in a factory, refinery, mine, or nuclear power plant or data processing errors in a back office.

Some readers may find this argument disturbing, for it appears to

## TABLE 2-1

### LEARNING BARRIERS AND FACILITATORS

| Stage of Learning | Barriers to Learning | Facilitators of Learning | Tools and Techniques |
| --- | --- | --- | --- |
| Acquiring | Reliance on a few, traditional data sources<br><br>Difficulty separating signals from noise<br><br>Biased, filtered data collection<br><br>Limited pooling of available information | A broad base of contributors and data sources<br><br>A process for sharing diverse perspectives and points of view<br><br>A willingness to embrace contradictory, unexpected findings | Forums for brainstorming, generating new ideas, and stimulating creative thinking<br><br>Regular benchmarking and peer comparisons<br><br>Quick feedback and market intelligence |
| Interpreting | Biased, incorrect estimates<br><br>Improper attribution of cause and effect<br><br>Overconfidence in judgment | A process of conflict and debate that tests prevailing views<br><br>The provision of timely, accurate feedback | Probing, challenging review sessions<br><br>Dialectical inquiry, devil's advocacy processes<br><br>Audit teams |
| Applying | Unwillingness to change behavior<br><br>Lack of time to practice new skills<br><br>Fear of failure | Incentives that encourage new approaches<br><br>The creation of space for learning<br><br>A sense of psychological safety | Linking promotion, pay, and status to the development of new ideas and skills<br><br>Eliminating unnecessary, obsolete work when new tasks are added<br><br>Acceptance of mistakes due to systems problems, unanticipated events, or inexperience<br><br>Partial immunity when reporting errors |

encourage permissiveness and a lack of accountability. But there is an important distinction. Freedom to fail should not be confused with a license to commit foolish mistakes. Accountability remains essential for effective performance, and no organization should embrace fuzzy or wrongheaded thinking. At GE, the difference is well understood. According to the head of leadership development: "If your decision made sense, given the database you had at the time, you won't be hanged for it. If you made a bad decision and anyone could have foreseen it, nobody's very forgiving at GE. We don't tolerate mediocrity."[63] Other organizations would be wise to follow the same rule. Safety nets are no excuse for low standards.

But they remain essential. Learning, after all, is a delicate and difficult undertaking. There are many barriers to overcome, and stimulating environments must be consciously created (see Table 2-1). Routines are ever present, and it is far easier to accept current practice than to question prevailing views or experiment with untried approaches. Disabilities frequently impede the process. If learning is to occur, individuals must feel comfortable taking on the status quo. They must be encouraged and supported, especially when events do not turn out as planned. Mistakes and errors are humbling, but they are also extraordinarily effective teachers. As the old saying goes: "Good decisions come from wisdom, knowledge, and experience. And wisdom, knowledge, and experience come from bad decisions."

# II

# TYPES OF LEARNING

# 3

## Intelligence

There is no single best approach to learning. Successful managers possess a portfolio of skills and apply them selectively, based on the information available and issues to be addressed. They are pragmatists, not purists, who share the scientist's goal of solving problems "by finding ways of getting at [them]."[1]

The choices are seldom easy or obvious. Managers may glean information on product requirements through focus groups or field observations, may improve work processes through hands-on experience or designed experiments, and may monitor competitive moves through press clippings or private databases. Each of these methods employs the same basic steps of acquiring, interpreting, and applying information. Each suffers from similar disabilities and responds to similar supporting conditions. Each also has distinctive strengths and weaknesses and requires vastly different sensitivities, systems, and skills. The challenge for managers is to become more knowledgeable about the range of techniques available, so that they can tailor their learning strategies to the tasks at hand.

This chapter addresses the first of these methods: the collection and interpretation of information that exists outside the organization. Chapters 4 and 5 discuss the accumulation of knowledge through experience and the manipulation of variables and experimental conditions to draw inferences. In general, the progression is from less to more active modes, from techniques that accept the environment as given to those that engage or alter it to create insights. The discussion thus begins in this chapter with incremental learning and small-scale improvements and moves gradually to radical changes, including breakthroughs and dramatic innovations, in chapter 5.[2]

## GATHERING INTELLIGENCE

Few companies could survive today without accurate, up-to-date information on the external environment. Competitors, customers, technologies, regulations, and social and demographic trends must all be understood for effective decision making. This, in the broadest sense, is the purpose of intelligence: "the selection, collection, interpretation and distribution of . . . information that has strategic importance."[3] Typically, the emphasis is on publicly available data, information that can be collected directly—and legally—from individuals or organizations. But there are disagreements on whether other approaches to intelligence gathering are acceptable, and managers vary in their openness to less direct methods and their willingness to pursue confidential material.

In part, the reasons for these disagreements are historical. The concept of intelligence has both military and diplomatic roots.[4] The Chinese were early proponents, as were the Swedes and Prussians; all viewed espionage as an instrument of statecraft and the primary tool of intelligence. These approaches came later to the English-speaking world. The British Army created a formal intelligence branch in 1873; the U.S. Army followed suit twelve years later but long lacked uniform standards of operation. Sporadic efforts to standardize methods of intelligence gathering followed, but it was not until World War II that the process was centralized and consolidated in this country. In fact, for many years leaders resisted covert intelligence activities because they felt that they violated standards of fair play. During World War I, for example, the War Department established a cryptanalysis section, called the Black Chamber, to decipher critical codes. It later served the State Department, intercepting and decoding messages from other countries to their ambassadors.[5] But when Harry Stimson, the secretary of state, learned of the unit in 1929, he ordered it dismantled, noting that "gentlemen do not read other gentlemen's mail."[6]

The surprise attack on Pearl Harbor, widely regarded as a failure of intelligence, led to more intensive efforts. In its aftermath, the Office of Strategic Services was created; in 1947 its successor, the Central Intelligence Agency, was formed. Both groups were charged with collecting information on the enemy through a variety of means, ranging from library research to reconnaissance flights to agents dropped behind enemy lines. Later, the National Security Agency was formed and engaged in even more clandestine activities.

Because of this history, intelligence gathering has long had unsavory, and often unethical, overtones. Especially during the Cold War, spying and subterfuge were accepted parts of the game, regarded as necessary because of the issues at stake. All too often, business intelligence has been viewed as little more than a commercial version of the same cloak-and-dagger activities. The titles of two recent reviews in the popular press—"I Spy, You Spy" and "They Snoop to Conquer"—are representative.[7] But there is no necessary connection between these activities and the illicit or covert. The primary goal of intelligence is securing salient, current information about the environment; in most cases, the necessary data are readily available or there for the asking.

Data can be gathered in three ways: through search, inquiry, or observation. Search relies on public sources or documents; the primary skills are careful analysis and research. Inquiry relies on interviews or surveys; the primary skills are framing and asking insightful questions. Observation relies on direct contact with users; the primary skills are attentive looking and listening. Surprisingly, the underlying process of intelligence gathering remains the same. In each case, managers decide what information to look for, figure out where to look, assemble the raw material, determine its meaning and implications, and then disseminate their findings to relevant parties.

# SEARCH

For most managers, this form of learning is part of the daily routine. Their success, after all, requires staying a step ahead of competitors; to do so, they must remain current and well informed. The credo of Frederick the Great—"it is pardonable to be defeated, but never to be surprised"—is as pertinent to managers as it is to statesmen.[8]

Much of the resulting activity, which scholars call "viewing" or "monitoring," is virtually automatic.[9] Managers collect and process information in a steady, unbroken stream, drawing on a host of formal and informal sources. Strategic planners, for example, regularly read the Wall Street Journal, skim the trade press, and surf company Web sites to gain insights about competitors. Brand managers routinely track product sales, pricing, and market shares through Nielsen and SAMI audits. R&D scientists stay abreast of the latest technologies by studying patent filings and attending specialized conferences and symposia. All also rely heavily on "soft" information gained through personal contacts—hearsay and tidbits plucked from conversations with insiders and outsiders—to ensure ready access to late-breaking news.[10]

At times, however, the desired information is complex, difficult to access, or squirreled away in assorted nooks and crannies. Then, automatic approaches are unlikely to be effective, and more active search is required. Managers must seek out specialized reports or comb through databases to produce a complete, coherent story. Both primary and secondary sources are helpful.[11] They range from the obvious—annual reports, SEC 10-Ks, newspaper and magazine articles, trade shows, and databases such as DIALOG, INVESTEXT, and NEXIS—to the obscure. Environmental Protection Agency (EPA) and Uniform Commercial Code (UCC) filings, for example, are little known but surprisingly comprehensive sources of basic operating information, especially when combined with creative judgment. Coors used Anheuser-Busch's reports of wastewater discharges to determine its brewing capacity in the Denver area, while a food-packaging company used UCC filings, which are posted by lenders and list all goods that have been purchased, leased, or pledged as collateral, to estimate the equipment in a competitor's facility and the associated depreciation charges.[12]

A particularly effective technique is to draw on knowledge that has

*Soft Data - personal Contacts*

already been accumulated internally. Salespeople are an obvious source, but there are many others, including managers themselves. The trick is to organize an orderly collection process. Motorola, for example, assigns one member of its intelligence unit to debrief company executives after they have returned from overseas, and occasionally domestic, trips. The resulting information is then collated, distilled, and mined for insights.[13] AT&T has benefited from similar discipline. In the mid-1980s it established a program called "Access to AT&T Analysts" that put company experts on-line, allowing employees to pose questions directly to those in the know. The program came with a unique feature, a flagging system that routinely tracked the ten companies attracting the most attention from employees. Most of the time, the list included the same set of suspects; on one occasion, however, a new name appeared. Further research showed that the company had just entered one of AT&T's lines of business, providing an early warning that would not otherwise have been available.[14]

## Approaches to Search

Whatever the sources of data, competition and the market are the primary topics of interest. Regulatory and technical issues rank a distant second and third. A summary of studies of search activity in several U.S. industries—chemicals, farm equipment, financial services, meat packing, and diverse multinationals—found that managers devoted 49 percent of their total search time to securing market information, 19 percent to regulatory information, 16 percent to technical information, 11 percent to resource-related information, 8 percent to broad environmental conditions, and 7 percent to acquisition leads. The proportions for Korean managers were strikingly similar. Both groups also relied more heavily on external sources (at least 55 percent of total search time) but varied considerably by industry in their use of passive and active modes of search.[15] Other studies have found that viewing and monitoring are more likely to be used when the industry is predictable and relatively homogeneous, while active, directed modes of search are more effective when the environment is unpredictable, turbulent, or complex.[16] Even in those settings, however, few organizations have full-fledged intelligence units; those that do, an estimated 10 percent of all large corporations, are often firms like Kodak and Merck with an obvious, established set of competitors.[17]

## Guidelines for Effective Search

There are a number of guidelines for effective search. Companies should collect information from diverse sources, cross-check their findings to ensure reliability, shift smoothly between passive and active modes, devote considerable effort to analysis and interpretation, and connect intelligence gathering directly with decision making. The first two tasks are necessary because much intelligence is of questionable validity. Internet sites, for example, are notorious for mixing facts, opinions, and hearsay without attempting to differentiate one from the other; the same is true of unconfirmed rumors and late-breaking news. As the president of a medium-sized chemical company observed: "I can usually find more than enough information on questions of importance. The real problem is whether I can believe it."[18] Comparisons and cross-checks are vital for guaranteeing that collected data are accurate.

The next two tasks are needed because intelligence is rarely self-explanatory or obvious. Signals are difficult to distinguish from noise, and critical insights often spring from barely noticeable differences. In most cases, routine monitoring provides an effective early warning but not a complete picture of events. Follow up is needed to flesh out and broaden the story, and some mechanism must be available for triggering the shift from automatic to targeted search. Effectiveness is often closely linked with the ability to "switch cognitive gears" and probe further once a novel event or unanticipated discrepancy has been recognized.[19] This is precisely what happened at AT&T when the top-ten list generated an unexpected company name. Analysts must also take care to develop the business implications of their findings. Managers are action-oriented; they view data without recommendations as unhelpful and incomplete. Many environmental analysis units, for example, devote far more time and attention to collecting information than to interpreting it. Even at firms with highly regarded units, senior executives were sharply critical: "The straight reporting of environmental 'facts' by staff, without connection to plans or policies, was often seen as worthless."[20]

Interpretation, however, does not complete the learning process. If search activities are to have real impact, executives must internalize the information they receive and apply it where appropriate. Eventually, they must move from analysis to action, the second to the third step in the acquire-interpret-apply cycle. Yet all too often, critical intelligence is communicated to the top of the organization, only to remain unacknowledged or ignored. Effective search processes overcome the problem by linking important insights directly to decision making, ensuring that they will have an immediate impact.

## XEROX'S SEARCH PROCESSES: SPURRING STRATEGIC CHANGE

Xerox provides a dramatic example of effective intelligence gathering.[21] In the 1980s and 1990s the company engaged in a series of intelligence exercises: Xerox '92, Xerox '95, Xerox 2000, and Xerox 2005. Each was designed to scan the environment, predict trends a decade ahead, and provide a foundation for long-term strategy.[22] Xerox '92, conducted over a seven-month period, was the most traditional study, a high-level "strategic reconnaissance" prepared by the corporate strategy staff. It was designed to answer a single, broad question using the techniques of systems and environmental analysis: How might Xerox's revenues grow over the coming decade?

The assessment was based on six factors—economics (e.g., expected growth of the global economy, on a region-by-region basis), demographics (e.g., expected number of factory versus office workers), social forces (e.g., the proportion of employees working at home versus the office), technology (e.g., trends in miniaturization and digital versus analog technology), government policy (e.g., public regulation and trade policy), and competition (e.g., profiles of key competitors and their expected behavior)—and information was collected largely from public sources. The data were then combined using a simple conceptual model to derive estimates of Xerox's likely revenues and market share.[23] The resulting 300-page report was highly visible; it was presented to the company's top 250 managers in a half-day session and was even made "required reading." Yet the results were discouraging. According to Roger

Levien, vice president of corporate strategy and the initiator of the project: "Xerox '92 was widely recognized as an excellent piece of work. But it had zero impact on the strategic direction of the company."

There were two basic problems. First, Xerox '92 was a staff exercise; there was little direct involvement of senior managers and limited incentive for them to apply the results. The search process was careful and complete but was not driven by a compelling business need or linked to an upcoming decision. Second, the conclusions remained distant and abstract; while the data were carefully massaged by analysts, they were not processed firsthand by senior managers nor tested against their personal theories and experiences. Not surprisingly, few managers identified with the study's findings or drew on them for insights.

Xerox '95 differed in both method and impact. It was a far more participative process, involving the top fifteen corporate managers as well as the strategy office, again over a seven-month period. Intelligence gathering now had a clear purpose; the goal, set by David Kearns, the CEO, was to determine a broad strategic direction for the company. Most important, the process included a heavy hands-on component, with senior managers actively weighing in at critical junctures with their own observations, experiences, and opinions.

To begin, members of the strategy office conducted lengthy interviews with participating managers. Each time, they asked the same broad questions:

- What is the desired future state for Xerox (including size, financial performance, the way we work, worldwide/geographical presence, staff/people, and reputation)?

- What are expected trends in technology, economics, politics, competition, and emerging opportunities/threats?

- What are the business implications (including current businesses, extensions of current businesses, and new areas)?

- What are the required competencies?

- What are current weaknesses? Current strengths?

- What are the imperatives for Xerox?

- What are the desired outputs of the Xerox '95 process?

The strategy office then collated the answers and fed them back to participants; they provided the foundation for a day-long discussion of the company's long-term goals and critical success factors. The results were disappointing. Both the interviews and discussion revealed huge differences in perspective, so much so that at the end of the session a frustrated Kearns concluded: "It's absolutely clear to me that we don't even agree on what business we're in."

Members of the strategy office were therefore assigned responsibility for collecting further information and imposing order. They developed questionnaires, with more detailed questions about competitive positioning, customer segments, company size, and functional strategies, and distributed them to all participants. After reviewing the responses, analysts identified four alternative strategies. Each was framed as a "pure tone," a distinctive, differentiated strategy that was easy to describe and discuss. Together, the tones mapped out the entire "strategy space" and covered the spectrum of possibilities. Each was given a code name, based on a representative company that followed a similar approach, and was described in a single brief sentence, using the Hollywood notion of a "high concept." The choices included:

- *Boeing:* "sticking to the knitting" and remaining a first-class copier and printer business;

- *Chrysler:* facing off against IBM in the systems business and becoming a strong number two or three;

- *Sears:* focusing on distribution and expanding the company's offerings to include as many products as possible;

- *BMW:* focusing on financial performance and exiting businesses that did not provide superior short-term returns.[24]

These alternatives were discussed by senior managers at a second day-long meeting. Participants were assigned to small groups and asked to develop a single strategy in detail; each group included at least one supporter and one critic. The full team then reconvened to discuss the alternatives; again, there were sharp disagreements. For the most part, the disputes hinged on different underlying assumptions—the likely role of paper in the office of the future, the expected growth of Asian versus

North American markets, the anticipated moves of key competitors—rather than disagreements about the strategies themselves. As Levien observed: "Where you stood on a strategy was determined by your view of the world."

The strategy office was asked to resolve the differences. It began by conducting further economic and political research. Within a month, analysts produced a list of forty major trends that might impact Xerox's future; each was framed as a "view-of-the-world" assumption about the expected social or competitive environment. At the next off-site meeting, senior managers spent three days reviewing the assumptions and assessing alternative strategies. Initially, they were assigned to small groups to discuss the forty trends and select the ten that they felt were most important to Xerox. Then, the full team reconvened to discuss the pared down list. Using a Consensor, an electronic device that allows individuals to vote anonymously by entering their preferences on a keypad or numbered dials, participants rated each assumption in turn, eventually reducing the list to fourteen. These assumptions were then used as a filter for reviewing the four pure strategies. At the end of the discussion, Kearns asked each participant for a recommendation; this time, votes could be cast for mixed strategies. Kearns reviewed the comments overnight and announced his decision the next morning, a "modified Boeing" strategy that eventually led to Xerox's becoming "the document company."

Xerox '95 was a major advance over its predecessor. Throughout the process, senior managers were actively engaged in evaluating intelligence, testing it against their personal schemas and experiences. The resulting frameworks became theirs, not the staff's, and insights were that much more likely to be internalized and accepted. Search activities were linked directly to decision making, providing additional motivation and momentum. Moreover, the four pure tones ensured that the interpretative process was both disciplined and broad. The tones provided a lens for screening data, yet kept the group from settling prematurely on an easy solution, improving both clarity and differentiation.

But Xerox '95 was not without weaknesses. Much of the initial intelligence was drawn solely from internal sources. External search was limited, and at no time did senior managers directly confront the envi-

ronment. The critical view-of-the-world assumptions were generated independently by the strategy office, with little input from line managers.
They appeared relatively late in the process and were based on quick,
cursory research. Activities were also poorly timed and sequenced, with
considerable meandering up front and a rush to judgment at the end.

Xerox 2000 was designed to overcome these weaknesses. Unlike its
predecessors, it stretched over a full year and included eleven meetings,
each roughly a month apart. Eight of the meetings were designed to
assess the environment and develop view-of-the-world assumptions; the
remaining three were to set strategic direction. The process was initiated
by Paul Allaire, Kearns's successor as CEO, who had participated in
Xerox '95 and believed that a similar exercise would be useful in generating a shared vision of the company's future. A core group of Allaire plus
four senior managers, handpicked for their strategic skills, participated
in the entire exercise; they were joined by five operating officers during
the later stages of decision making. The corporate strategy office again
provided staff support, supplemented by outside consultants and subject matter experts.

This time, senior managers participated personally in intelligence
gathering. The group also paid far more attention to external search.
View-of-the-world meetings, for example, drew heavily on firsthand information—unfiltered, unprocessed, and occasionally contradictory—so
that managers could assess trends and critical assumptions directly.
Each meeting was a full-day affair, with required reading prior to the
meeting—a twenty-page white paper, prepared by the strategy office or
outside consultants, that reviewed the most current published research.
Discussions were videotaped and transcribed, and topics were carefully
sequenced. They became increasingly focused over time, moving from
broad trends in the economy and society to specialized information
about the industry and key competitors. All, however, drew on a wide
range of experts, sources, and sites (see Table 3-1).

After each topic was covered, members of the strategy office met to
review the discussion and write up view-of-the-world assumptions. They
produced sixty in all, approximately fifteen per topic. Each assumption
was stated as succinctly as possible and included, when appropriate,
implications for action. For example, a critical assumption in the area of

## TABLE 3-1
### XEROX 2000: VIEW-OF-THE-WORLD MEETINGS

*Economy and Society*

1. Discuss Europe 2000 and Asia 2000 with an expert presenter for each topic; held at the Japan House.

2. Discuss the global corporation with a leading academic expert and the chief editorial writer of the *Financial Times*; held at the New York Stock Exchange.

*Technology and Organization*

3. Explore advances in computer science with experts in the field; held at the MIT Media Laboratory.

4. Explore imaging and documentation technology with experts in the field; held at the Association of Image and Information Management trade show.

*Markets and Customers*

5. Discuss customers' needs after hearing presentations by the IT directors of four major customers.

6. Explore diverse channels and customer needs after attending COMDEX (the computer trade show), visiting a local CompUSA store, and meeting with a systems integrator.

*Industry and Competition*

7. Discuss industry trends after hearing presentations by industry association consultants.

8. Discuss competitors after hearing presentations by an academic expert and the IT director of Fuji-Xerox, who provided data on Canon, the company's chief competitor.

economy and society was that "trends will continue toward increased globalization, simultaneously with increased regionalization and localization; successful global competitors will combine global integration with 'insider status' in each major market."

Once the complete list was in hand, senior managers were asked to rank all sixty assumptions by their level of agreement and perceived strategic importance. Questionnaires were used for the purpose; they were distributed, collected, and summarized by the strategy office prior to the first direction-setting meeting. The senior team then met to discuss the rankings; eventually, after extensive debate and voting, they reduced the list to twenty-eight shared assumptions. These assumptions, plus prior work on the strengths and weaknesses of the organization, led to a series of "strategic imperatives." Each flagged an important area for development, using the phrase "Xerox must . . . " The group then used these imperatives, plus prior work on the company's strengths and weaknesses, to analyze and assess alternative strategies, businesses, and organizational architectures before selecting a final proposal. It was implemented a year later and led to dramatic improvements in performance, including sharp gains in profitability and stock price.

Xerox 2000 represents intelligence gathering at its best. Because senior managers engaged directly in search activities, vital information was processed without screening or filtering by intermediaries. Because research reports were combined with firsthand exposure to customers, technologies, and subject matter experts, biases were minimized and a wide range of perspectives were explored. Because meetings were spread over an extended period, time was available for careful and complete analysis—before choices were made. And because interpretation was followed immediately by decision making, new understandings were incorporated into action.

Xerox 2000 also built on the lessons of its predecessors (see Table 3-2). The major categories for collecting and presenting information— economics and society, technology and organization, markets and customers, industry and competition—were elaborations of those first used in Xerox '92. The process of articulating and ranking view-of-the-world assumptions was a refinement of the methods pioneered in Xerox '95. Those methods, in fact, were vital to the success of the entire effort.

Unresolved debates can frequently be traced to unstated perceptions or beliefs that lie just below the surface. Without a common, articulated foundation—a conscious effort to bring these differences into the open—groups often find it difficult to move forward.[25] Xerox 2000 tackled the problem directly by devoting the entire front end of the process to debating and clarifying assumptions. As Levien observed, the stimulus was Xerox '95: "We discovered that the more time you invest at the senior management level in agreeing on where the world is going, the more likely you are to get agreement on strategy."[26]

There was another associated learning. In the early stages of Xerox 2000, managers cast their nets widely, generating and debating a long list

# TABLE 3-2

## THE EVOLUTION OF INTELLIGENCE GATHERING AT XEROX

| | Xerox '92 | Xerox '95 | Xerox 2000 |
|---|---|---|---|
| **Purpose** | Estimate the company's revenue growth over the next decade | Determine a broad strategic direction for the company | Develop a shared vision of the company's future |
| **Participants** | Corporate strategy staff | 15 top managers, including the CEO, supported by the corporate strategy staff | 5 top managers with strategic skills, including the CEO, later joined by 5 top operating officers, supported by the corporate strategy staff and outside experts |
| **Duration** | 7 months | 7 months | 1 year |
| **Process** | All analysis performed by staff, final report presented to top 250 managers | Alternating periods of interviewing and surveying of managers by staff, followed by discussion of findings; strategic alternatives and lists of underlying assumptions for review by managers created by staff; voting by all managers before final decision by the CEO | Intense focus up front on developing a shared set of assumptions about the external environment, drawing on firsthand experience, white papers, and meetings with experts; divergence to develop a broad set of perspectives before narrowing the list; only at the end consider strategic imperatives, alternatives, and organization design |

# TABLE 3-2 (CONTINUED)

## THE EVOLUTION OF INTELLIGENCE GATHERING AT XEROX

| | | | |
|---|---|---|---|
| **Critical tasks** | Data collection from primary and secondary sources; trend analysis; modeling and estimation | Interviewing and surveying managers; creating "pure tone" strategies and "view-of-the-world" assumptions | Collecting market intelligence through visits, discussions, and external search; interpreting findings and applying them to strategic choices |
| **Strengths** | Careful, systematic analysis | Complete airing and comparison of differing views; open discussion of assumptions and strategic alternatives; high involvement of top managers | Direct involvement of top managers in intelligence gathering; systematic development and review of assumptions |
| **Weaknesses** | Little or no impact on decision making | Little external intelligence; too much reliance on staff for analysis; poor sequencing of activities | Time-consuming |

of alternative assumptions. They strove for breadth, seeking out multiple possibilities rather than gravitating immediately to the most likely prospects. Diversity of this sort avoids the common trap of premature closure—settling too quickly on an easy, obvious solution. Only after they had developed a complete set of assumptions did managers vote to narrow the list and establish priorities. This approach—first "diverging" to create multiple alternatives, then "converging" on a smaller set—has long been associated with effective problem solving, intelligence gathering, and decision making.[27] Unfortunately, far too many groups are content to pursue the second step without the first.

Xerox's search for intelligence did not end with Xerox 2000. Five years later, Allaire launched a follow-on exercise, Xerox 2005, using many of the same techniques. Seventeen managers participated; they ranged from young high-potentials to senior officers. The goal was to identify, by businesses and geographical regions, the areas of greatest opportunity for Xerox; once again, the process began with a critical evaluation of underlying assumptions. This time, however, the strategy office had already prepared an overview of thirty major competitors, as well as an assessment of the company's strengths and weaknesses. Discussion was therefore highly focused, and the process moved quickly to action. After briefly reviewing likely competitive scenarios, participants decided on a number of concrete steps, most of them extensions of existing businesses. Xerox 2005 thus continued the company's tradition of using search to spur strategic change.

## INQUIRY

Despite its appeal, search has an important limitation: the required data must already exist. Information is collected, not constructed or created, and there is little effort to generate new raw material. At times, a more probing process is required, for certain information cannot be found through search alone. How often, for example, do families buy a new car? How long is the average business trip? What activities are most in demand at health clubs? Because published information is sketchy or incomplete, questions of this sort must usually be answered through inquiry, using interviews or questionnaires to draw data directly from users. This approach is common in market research, where it has long been used to acquire information about consumers' behavior and preferences.

## Guidelines for Effective Inquiry

Since we all use questions on a daily basis, inquiry would seem to demand few special skills. But the process can easily derail, and careful planning is required. The choice of respondents is crucial; even small changes in mix can produce vastly different results. Predictions are especially sensitive to these choices. In 1936 the editors of *Literary Digest* tried to predict the outcome of the upcoming presidential election by using a sample of voters drawn from telephone books and club memberships, groups that tended to be far more Republican than the population at large. Not surprisingly, their projection—a victory for Alf Landon, the Republican candidate—was way off the mark. Franklin Roosevelt, the Democratic incumbent, won in a landslide.[28]

Questions must also be carefully framed, since subtle, almost indistinguishable, differences in wording can cause wide swings in responses. Perceptual data must be treated with caution, since most individuals lack the self-awareness needed to articulate latent feelings and needs. Even when people are able to respond to a proposal or concept, their stated views may not be accurate harbingers of the future. When asked during market tests for their reactions to the concept of a film about "a professor who fights Nazis to rescue a sacred relic," consumers were uniformly negative. Yet *Raiders of the Lost Ark* went on to become one of the biggest moneymakers in Hollywood history.[29] Test groups were equally unenthusiastic about the proposed title of *Star Wars,* noting that they had little interest in either science fiction or war movies.[30]

Stories like these suggest that inquiry remains very much an art. Nevertheless, there are a few broad guidelines. Respondents must be representative and appropriate; otherwise, the results will be meaningless. It makes little sense, for example, to ask baby boomers about the latest rock bands, or seniors about snowboarding. Refusal rates must be carefully monitored; if certain groups cooperate while others do not, there will undoubtedly be biases.[31] Sampling procedures and research methods must be rigorous, with sound, thoughtfully constructed designs.

Perhaps most important, questions must be worded to avoid slanting results. Common errors include leading the witness ("Do you prefer our brand for its taste, or for some other reason?"), loading the dice ("Do you believe that preschool children should be allowed to learn at their own rates?"), false precision ("Exactly how many mail-order catalogs did you receive in the last six months?"), and fuzzy language ("Are you a strong or weak supporter of the proposed amendment?").[32]

## Forms of Inquiry

There are two basic approaches to inquiry: descriptive and exploratory.[33] Descriptive approaches are the most traditional; they involve precise, focused questions and targeted information collection. Usually, the goal is to determine frequencies or patterns of use, or to compare one's products and services with competitors'. Most surveys and questionnaires employ this approach, as do focus groups and structured conversations with users. There are obvious advantages, including well-defined methodologies, easy-to-summarize results, and little ambiguity in interpretation. Marketers have used these techniques to generate facts of dizzying detail. Coca-Cola knows how many ice cubes we put in a glass, Frito-Lay knows whether we eat broken or whole pretzels first, and Timex knows when we received our first watches.[34] Yet despite these insights, the approach has several limitations. With targeted questions, it is extremely difficult to generate unexpected ideas, tease out unmet needs, or discover something fundamentally new about consumers' likes and dislikes.[35]

Exploratory approaches overcome many of these problems. They use open-ended questions to elicit users' perceptions and needs. Frequently, stories and firsthand experiences are sought because they are thought to embody larger truths.[36] Clinical and ethnographic techniques therefore play important roles, and interpretation becomes a more challenging task. Among the required skills are the ability to conduct unstructured, far-reaching interviews (beginning with what anthropologists call "grand-tour questions"), follow up and probe discretely, suspend judgment, keep an open mind, and listen empathically.[37] These techniques are designed to ensure that respondents say what is really on their minds, rather than answering well-meaning but possibly irrelevant questions. Robert Galvin, the CEO of Motorola, used this approach to great effect in the 1980s when he launched the company's quality process. Galvin insisted that all members of the Operating and Policy Committee—including himself—personally visit customers and ask a single question: "What do you like about doing business with Motorola, and what don't you like?" The result, he observed, was invariably a sobering conversation and at least fifteen pages of notes.

Occasionally, questions must be framed less directly. Latent needs are difficult to extract; when sensitive subjects are involved, even open-ended questions may fail to produce the desired insights. The underlying feelings may be hard to identify; at times, they are recognized but kept from view because they are "socially unacceptable."[38] In a classic study published in 1950, people were asked if they used Nescafé, an instant coffee. Those who did not were asked why; most responded that they did not like the flavor. But when projective techniques were used instead, a different picture emerged. Such techniques present subjects with ambiguous or unclear material and then ask for interpretations. Rorschach tests are a well-known example. In the Nescafé case, people were shown two hypothetical shopping lists and asked to characterize the women who made the purchases. The lists were identical, except that one included Nescafé while the other included Maxwell House. The responses, however, were dramatically different. Forty-eight percent of respondents described the woman who purchased Nescafé as lazy, 48 percent described her as failing to plan household purchases and schedules well, and 16 percent described her as not a good wife; the corresponding percentages for the woman who bought Maxwell House were 4 percent, 12 percent, and 0 percent.[39] In the 1950s, at least, instant coffee triggered deep feelings about a woman's responsibility for home and hearth that could be unearthed only through indirect techniques.

To be successful, these techniques must be accompanied by attentive listening. Inquiry, after all, is a two-way street. There is little learning if questions are posed but answers fail to register. Unfortunately, sensitive, supportive listening is extremely hard work.

> It requires, first, that the listener focus carefully on what is being said—and *how*. . . . The tone and music of the speaker's voice, the perspective from which she speaks, the degree of authority or confidence invoked or projected, the speaker's emotional attach-

ment to the ideas, and the emotional force of the ideas on the listener—all these elements are integral to the full meaning of a message.[40]

In addition, most managers view the task as thankless, with little personal payoff. Talking is vastly preferred to listening because it offers visibility and exposure. Those who talk hold onto the spotlight; listeners remain largely offstage. The results are predictable but hardly conducive to learning. As a leading executive has observed, only partly in jest: "One often hears the remark 'He talks too much,' but when did anyone last hear the criticism 'He listens too much?'"[41]

## L.L. BEAN'S CREATIVE INQUIRY: CONVERSING WITH CUSTOMERS

L.L. Bean, the direct-mail marketer of outdoor clothing and equipment, has long relied on inquiry as a source of learning.[42] The process can be traced to the company's earliest years. Legend has it that the original L.L. sold one hundred pairs of his first product, the Maine hunting boot, only to have them all returned as defective. He talked with customers and listened carefully to their complaints, fixed each and every boot without charge, and created a sense of commitment and responsiveness that pervades the company even today. L.L. Bean continues to draw on this legacy, deepening its understanding of customer needs by combining its own creative techniques with traditional methods of inquiry.

Field testers, for example, are used extensively as a source of descriptive information. Rather than collecting impressions second- or thirdhand, L.L. Bean goes to those in the know—experienced users who have lived with the product, often under demanding conditions. Over time, it has developed a database of more than 1,200 testers. The selection process is rigorous—the original model was the Yale Medical School application—and applicants must submit a series of essays, profiles, and product evaluations before they are accepted. After testers have evaluated several products, they are assigned to one of three categories, allowing Bean to select the right mix of testers for any project. *Lead users* are those who spend enormous amounts of time researching their purchases; typically, after taking them home, they personally modify and improve them. These users have two identifying characteristics: they "face needs that will be general in the marketplace—but face them months or years before [others] . . . and . . . are positioned to benefit significantly by obtaining a solution to those needs."[43] Frequently, their livelihood or safety depends on the products they buy. At L.L. Bean, lead users include mountaineering guides, Outward Bound instructors, and park rangers; at a software firm, they might be computer-savvy telecommuters or road warriors. *Demanding users* are as informed and committed to an activity as lead users but do not modify products or make a living from them. Examples would be dedicated hunters and hikers, who spend much of their spare time in the woods. *Happy customers* are satisfied but intermittent users, the once-per-season backpacker or the family that camps out every other summer.

Testers are selected not only for their experience, but also for their articulateness and candor. The combination is rare, and Bean goes to great lengths to cultivate the individuals it finds. Many have developed close, multiyear relationships with developers. Trust is essential. Testers must feel free to call them as they see them, without concern for repercussions or hurt feelings; at the same time, they must have faith in the company that has supplied them with products. Bean is well aware of this delicate line. According to David Bennell, manager of research and testing:

> We don't ask them to do more than is appropriate. We don't put them in dangerous situations. We don't send them products that we know will fail. We encourage them not to use a product if they're going to be out for three months in Antarctica, and they have to absolutely rely on it. We want them to be safe.

Normally, testers are sent several samples, one from L.L. Bean and at least one from a competitor, to use for three months. These side-by-side comparisons are considered essential to stimulate learning. As Tom Armstrong Jr., director of outerwear and footwear, observed: "It's hard to test something in a void. What we're really interested in is the Bean, but the foil of a competitor seems to elicit more ideas from our testers."

Often, testers will be asked for their assessments of particular attributes—the fit of a garment, the traction of a boot, the durability of a fly
rod—as well as general impressions.

To maximize learning, Bean requests extensive feedback. Communication is encouraged in all forms, including telephone, letters, and
e-mail. Testers are provided with data logs for recording information and
are asked to complete a number of surveys. But the process is flexible,
and feedback sometimes comes in unexpected packages. One tester
traveled the Australian outback for several months, camping out each
night in an L.L. Bean tent. Rather than carrying logs or rating forms,
which would have added weight to an already overburdened pack, he
simply scrawled his observations on the ceiling and walls. When the trip
was over, he sent the annotated tent back to the company for all to read.

Bean solicits formal feedback at three points: when the product is
first received (to assess first impressions, "out-of-box quality," and initial
fit), at the midpoint of the test (to identify design opportunities and
obvious problems), and at the end of the test (to collect a comprehensive, comparative assessment, including recommended changes). This
format keeps cycles short and ensures that little learning is lost. Midpoint evaluations are often especially revealing because of the creative
approach that the company employs. Typically, Bean structures these
sessions as group conversations and builds them around an outdoor
activity such as hiking or cross-country skiing. Fifteen to thirty field
testers attend, as well as developers, marketers, and occasionally vendors and manufacturers.

Perhaps the best example of this process is the Cresta Hiker. Bean
introduced the boot in 1987; for many years, it was a best-seller. In the
early 1990s, however, sales began to decline because of advances in
competitive boots. After extensive interviewing and testing, Bean developed an upgraded version of the Hiker, using new designs and materials,
and sent it to a broad mix of testers for evaluation. Two months into the
process, the group was invited to Pinkham Notch, New Hampshire, at
the base of Mt. Washington, to discuss their experiences. But first they
went for a hike—not just any hike but one artfully designed to stimulate
learning.

To begin, participants were divided into groups by foot size. One group consisted only of men who wore size nine; another consisted only of women who wore size seven. Each participant was given two or three pairs of boots—the new Cresta Hiker, as well as the very best competitive offerings—and was instructed to hike for one and a half hours in one pair, then to switch to another brand, continuing the process up and down the trail. Hikers were urged to take notes, share observations, and trade boots. One group waded through streams to check the boots' water resistance; another briefly wore mismatched pairs to assess comfort and fit. As Bennell observed, this approach was dramatically different—and far more effective in eliciting insights—than traditional modes of inquiry:

> The old way would have been to bring a group of customers together in a focus group and ask them what are their likes, dislikes, and experiences. The problem is that what they say and what they do could be very different, not because they're trying to lie to us but just because it's difficult in a focus group environment to clearly understand the customer.
>
> We decided to go out into the end use environment. We wanted to bring the vendor/manufacturer in. We wanted to bring product developers together, and we wanted to really see customers behaving with hiking boots. About every hour, we'd switch footwear products. Meanwhile, developers are watching all of this happen, and they're doing the switch as well, so everybody, including the manufacturer, is evaluating footwear in the place where people hike.
>
> We're also very, very much interacting with each other. Developers are asking customers questions. Manufacturers are asking customers questions. Testers are asking each other questions. It's very different from a focus group. This is behavior in the making and in the watching.

The next day, the entire group reconvened to reflect on the process and craft recommendations. In addition to obvious design changes, developers sought information on preferences and trade-offs: "If we made these design changes, would you be happy? Suppose we could only make two changes—which should they be? Suppose these changes added $x to the price, would you still buy the boot?" After returning to Bean, the design team immediately debriefed and extracted key learnings. They used the insights they had collected to make further changes in the boot's sole, toe, and side panels. Prototypes were quickly developed and sent to testers for their reactions. They approved, and the new Cresta Hiker was launched in 1996. The learning process was given top billing and became a potent marketing tool. According to Pat Murtagh, product developer for active footwear:

> We actually introduced the boot by talking about the process—the fact that changes came directly from the customer. In the catalog we've been able to tell that story, using photography from our testing days up at Mt. Washington, and pointing to some of the specific requirements that customers brought to us and saying this is how they translate into the changes that are built into the shoe.

The results were stunning. Sales rose 85 percent over the previous year, and the initial shipment sold out within weeks.

Bean's approach to the Cresta Hiker offers several lessons for effective inquiry (see Table 3-3). They include the power of conducting conversations in context rather than in artificial settings; the importance of conversing with users while they are carrying out activities rather than sedentary or bored; the benefits of conducting comparative tests rather than assessments in isolation; the usefulness of side-by-side comparisons and short feedback cycles rather than drawn out, extended processes; the importance of cultivating long-term associations with users rather than holding brief, once-and-for-all meetings; the benefits of categorizing users by type rather than mixing them indiscriminately; and the value of employing a diversity of methods rather than a single, unvarying technique. The last point is particularly important.[44] Traditional methods of inquiry, such as focus groups, surveys, and laboratory tests, have much to offer, and Bean uses them extensively to collect information on products and customers. The Cresta Hiker was no exception. But by combining these techniques with its own innovative approaches, the company generated much richer insights and vastly increased its learning.

## TABLE 3-3
### TECHNIQUES FOR DESCRIPTIVE INQUIRY:
### LESSONS FROM THE CRESTA HIKER

1. *Rely on experienced field testers.*

- Use a rigorous screening and selection process.
- Categorize by type and intensity of experience (e.g., lead users, demanding users, happy customers).
- Cultivate long-term relationships based on trust.
- Encourage candor and honest feedback.

2. *Collect information at multiple points and in multiple ways.*

- Include first impressions, midpoint evaluations, and overall assessments.
- Encourage communication by phone, letters, and e-mail.
- Keep cycles short so that information is not lost.
- Combine qualitative and quantitative data.

3. *Encourage conversations that maximize learning.*

- Group users with similar characteristics.
- Conduct conversations in the settings of use.
- Mingle users with designers, marketers, and suppliers.
- Provide competitive products as a basis for comparison.

4. *Validate all findings.*

- Conduct a systematic debriefing process.
- Probe for trade-offs and value judgments.
- Check back with users to ensure that new designs accurately reflect their recommendations.
- Use large-scale surveys to confirm initial qualitative results.

This same spirit of innovation can be found in the company's exploratory methods. To generate radical redesigns or develop deep knowledge about a product category, Bean now uses a technique called "concept engineering."[45] It has three basic elements, which mirror the stages of learning: open-ended interviewing to acquire data, collaborative interpretation and synthesis to define user needs, and unfettered brainstorming to generate prototypes and new designs. The process begins with the formation of a cross-functional team, consisting of product developers, marketing managers, and product testing assistants. At their first meeting, the team establishes a learning agenda by defining the scope of the project. In some cases, the task is obvious—for example, to develop a new hunting boot or an innovative "sleeping system"—and discussion is relatively brief. In other cases, the mission is unclear, and a complex scope statement is required. After considerable wrangling, the parka and outerwear team eventually decided that its goal was "to develop a complete, compatible apparel layering system for a variety of active, outdoor, four-season activities with components suitable for everyday use."

Once the scope has been determined, the team develops interview questions. Typically, no more than five or six questions are involved; all are broad and reflective. Wording is crucial because the team is seeking windows into the customer's world. They are looking for ways to get people to tell their stories and relate personal experiences. As one developer put it, the goal is to "find questions that will prompt people to speak." The hunting boot team, for example, created the following list:

- In what kinds of conditions do you find yourself hunting? Can you describe a situation in the field where your hunting footwear let you down?

- Where do you store your hunting equipment? If you were to show me your sporting goods closet/storage area, what would I see? What footwear equipment do you have there?

- Describe what went through your mind when you purchased your last pair of boots. Please describe the experience.

- If you could build your own custom hunting boots, what would they look like? What features of other footwear or sporting products would you like to incorporate into your current hunting footwear?

- What haven't I asked you about your footwear that you'd like to discuss?

Such questions are designed to elicit "thick descriptions"—rich, nuanced pictures of the environment that allow researchers "to draw large conclusions from small, but very densely textured facts."[46]

At the same time, the team is selecting interviewees, drawing on the company's database of field testers. They strive for a mix of characteristics, combining lead users, demanding customers, and happy customers, men and women, young and old, and people from different parts of the country. In addition, a small number of noncustomers are included; usually, they are former Bean customers culled from the company's master file, or experts known to prefer other brands. Novices or first-time users are deliberately excluded because they lack needed experience. As one developer put it: "It's an empathy thing; they have to have suffered." The final list is small, with approximately fifteen to eighteen names, but broadly representative, giving the team confidence that the results will be meaningful.

All interviews take place at users' homes or workplaces. Typically, they last for 1¼ hours and are conducted by two people, an interviewer and a scribe. The interviewer poses questions, asks for clarification, follows up on topics of interest, listens attentively, and generally keeps the process moving. The scribe serves as a human tape recorder. According to Bennell:

> That person is just writing as quickly as they can exactly what the customer says—and I mean *exactly*. The metaphor we use is that the customer's voice goes in your ear. It bypasses your brain. It goes right to your pen or your pencil, and you get it down. You're not trying to filter. You're not trying to guess at what they said. You're trying to capture their words verbatim.

Both roles require practice, and team members generally simulate interviews before heading out to the field. The process is quite different from the usual, targeted interviewing (see Table 3-4).

Immediately after completing an interview, the interviewer and scribe meet to debrief. First, they reconstruct the interview and fill in gaps in their notes; then, using yellow Post-Its, they write up a long list of "voices" and "images," one item per Post-It. A *voice* is a verbatim quote—in Armstrong's words, a "sound bite"—taken directly from the interview (e.g., "at the end of a day of hiking, I come into camp and strip off my jacket"); an *image* is an evocative picture or scene that may or may not have been stated directly (e.g., "dripping with sweat"). Together,

## TABLE 3-4

### L.L. BEAN'S GUIDELINES FOR EXPLORATORY INTERVIEWING

1. Go to the user's environment; do not use an interview room or focus group facility.

2. Conduct the interviews yourself; do not farm them out to a market research firm.

3. Be as open-minded as possible; do not begin with specific hypotheses in mind.

4. Let users tell their stories; do not interrupt.

5. Listen for understanding; do not judge.

6. Ask "why" and "how" questions for clarification; do not rely on unstated assumptions.

7. Follow the interviewee's lead; do not rush from topic to topic.

8. Take down all comments verbatim; do not summarize or paraphrase.

these vignettes produce an almost visceral identification with the environment and a deep understanding of the activity or experience. They also signify a subtle shift in perspective. According to Pete Gilmour, product manager for footwear: "We're looked to be the experts on our products. We develop them, we come up with the concepts, and we have this kind of expert opinion about everything we do. And what this process is all about is throwing that out the window, and letting the customer be the expert."

After all interviews have been completed, the interpretative process begins. At this stage, the goal is to develop a shared understanding of the customer's world, as well as agreement on the most important product requirements. Because the team is seeking common ground, intense concentration is required, and meetings are often difficult and drawn out. The first project team spent five days in discussion and named the process "Hell Week"; meetings have since been reduced to three days, but the nickname remains.

To begin, the entire group meets to share voices and images. Each interviewing team, after all, has talked with different users and has developed a slightly different picture of the customer's world. They exchange Post-Its and listen to one another's findings. Then, the team engages in several rounds of voting, reducing the number of images from several hundred to thirty-five or forty. By grouping, categorizing, and connecting the Post-Its that remain, they develop a single, composite diagram that presents an integrated picture of the activity and the environment in which it takes place.

The process involves two distinctive steps. First, all Post-Its are placed on the wall, and team members silently arrange and rearrange them to form categories. Individuals are not permitted to speak; they simply move Post-Its in a silent dance, creating their own connections as others do the same.[47] The goal is to force synthetic thinking and broaden perspectives. According to Murtagh:

> There are some connections that are very clear, very linear, and very easy for everyone to see. Part of the exercise is getting past them, expanding connections so that we walk away with some significant insight. The process of moving things around without speaking forces us to think about connections that we would not make individually, connections that other people are making that are not obvious to us. So there's a great learning that goes on, and it forces you to learn in your own world because there's no discussion about it.

Once consensus has been reached—the team can tell because the Post-Its remain in place and are no longer being moved—discussion resumes. The team tries to summarize succinctly each cluster of images, taking great care to distinguish and clarify categories. This step is called "scrubbing the stickies"; the goal, according to Murtagh, is to ensure that there is genuine agreement and understanding:

> We have to be clear as a group that these little Post-It notes are capturing exactly the things we think they are, that the language within them is accurate. Often, we're in our own worlds, and we write things down and think that everybody else understands them. The scrubbing process gives us the opportunity to be precise with our language. It gives us the opportunity to discuss what each one means. Ultimately, it allows us all to agree on what is up on the wall.

A similar process is used to define customer requirements. The team combines concrete voices and images to create more general ideas, translating them into explicit needs. The process is one of progressive abstraction. The apparel team, for example, generated one of its requirements by moving from voice ("I walk into camp and strip off my jacket") to image ("dripping with sweat") to driving idea ("need two shirts") to requirement statement ("layer next to the skin that can dry within ten minutes"). After producing a lengthy list, the team distills, synthesizes, and "scrubs" the requirements. They reduce the number by voting, then group the remaining items into categories. Again, they silently arrange and rearrange Post-Its, then discuss appropriate category headings or titles. Because the ranking of requirements is crucial, the final list is carefully validated. To ensure representativeness, the team develops a written questionnaire and sends it to one thousand customers.

With these rankings in hand, team members begin the search for solutions. Brainstorming and wild ideas are encouraged, and no proposal is out of bounds. A particularly effective technique is borrowing—taking a technology or feature from one product category and applying it to another. Gaiters, for example, are used to keep snow out of boots when cross-country skiing. Why not use the same approach to seal the tops of hunting or fishing footwear? Analogies like these stimulate creativity; they also ensure that the group has fun. Eventually, however, the team applies a rigorous test: how well do the new ideas match up against customer requirements? At times, there are disagreements. The sleeping system team generated seven potential designs, then narrowed the list to two. Each had zealous supporters. To resolve the debate, the team divided itself in half; each group took one option and assessed it against the best competitive offerings. When the groups reconvened, the solution was obvious: the "Burrito Bag," so named because it came with multiple layers of fleece that could be wrapped and unwrapped to regulate temperature. It was a nearly perfect match with the top customer requirements. But to be certain, the team sent prototypes to five of its original interviewees, asking "Does this solve the problems you told us about?" The answer was a resounding yes, and the bag was launched in spring 1997. Within weeks, sales were 200 percent above forecast, and vendors were struggling to keep up with demand.

This approach to product development puts a premium on learning. Inquiry takes center stage, interpretation is carefully structured, and solutions are deferred until the very end. As one developer put it, the goal is to "bubble up deep knowledge to the point where it is actionable." The resulting process is unusual in two respects: the amount of direct contact between designers and customers, and the time spent developing a shared understanding of customer needs. At times, the payoff is a single "Aha" like the Burrito Bag; more often, the insights are applied in bits and pieces over the years. According to Armstrong:

> There are usually some twenty to twenty-four customer requirements that get adopted at the end of a project and provide learnings that go on season after season. Ultimately, that's the real power of this approach. Individual products come and go, but if you can leverage those requirements against all of your future developments—using them as a touchstone—chances are you're going to be on track with the customer.

## OBSERVATION

At times, even the most thoughtful questions will be ineffective. When knowledge is tacit or unarticulated, known only at a subconscious or nonverbal level, individuals are likely to have trouble communicating clearly. Examples include latent, untapped feelings or needs; processes or practices that have been internalized and are performed without thinking; and shortcuts, workarounds, and rules of thumb that are the product of years of experience.[48] In such cases, a leading philosopher has observed, "we can know more than we can tell."[49] The resulting knowledge is difficult to extract, even if questions are artfully and sensitively framed. Companies seeking this kind of information often have only one option: direct observation.

Designers of office equipment, for example, must first understand the realities of white-collar work. Yet formal office procedures often bear little resemblance to employees' actual behavior. When researchers at Xerox asked accounting clerks to describe their jobs, they received an-

swers that corresponded reasonably well with the formal procedures described in the company's job manual. But when they observed clerks in
action, they found that they were behaving quite differently:

> [T]hey relied on a rich variety of informal practices that weren't in
> the manual but turned out to be crucial to getting the work done. In
> fact, the clerks were constantly improvising, inventing new methods
> to deal with unexpected difficulties and to solve immediate prob-
> lems. Without being aware of it, they were far more innovative and
> creative than anybody who heard them describe their "routine" jobs
> ever would have thought.[50]

The problem is particularly acute when new or unfamiliar technologies are involved. Then, all learnings unfold in real time, and adaptations
are often subtle and difficult to identify. Designers must usually observe
users directly to ensure that important insights are not lost. Steelcase has
used this approach to collect data on its new office system, Personal
Harbors, which was designed to encourage collaboration and group
work.[51] The system combines innovative, adjustable personal work
spaces, equipped with a full array of computer and communication technologies, with a large, open commons area. To better understand the
resulting interactions and flows, researchers conducted field tests at
three companies. Each firm agreed to use Personal Harbors for at least
several months and to share its experiences with Steelcase. To collect
information, researchers used traditional methods of inquiry, such as
questionnaires, focus groups, and user journals, plus time-lapsed videotape. By mounting cameras unobtrusively at each site, they developed an
objective visual record, ensuring that users' perceptions were supplemented by observed patterns of behavior.

## Guidelines for Effective Observation

Anthropologists and sociologists have long relied on these techniques to
conduct field work.[52] Together with the Xerox and Steelcase examples,
their experiences suggest several guidelines for practice. Observation
should be carried out in context, in real rather than artificial settings.

Observers should immerse themselves in the local scene, watching individuals and groups as they conduct their daily work. At times, this may require that they become "participant observers," simultaneously involved in and detached from the activity at hand. Yet even then they should remain as unobtrusive as possible—the proverbial flies on the wall—to preserve natural patterns of behavior and avoid distortions due to their presence. Learning is most effective when observers blend into the background and others are onstage. But observation must still be public and aboveboard. To avoid breaches of trust, observers should identify themselves and explain their goals, especially when lengthy periods of immersion are required to obtain sensitive information. Deeply rooted ways of thinking, feeling, and acting should not be discovered through subterfuge or disguise.

Several skills are essential. Surprisingly, the initial requirement is political savvy and negotiating ability. Every observer, after all, must first obtain access and acceptance. In most organizations, permission is required to videotape or observe individuals or groups. Tact and persuasiveness are essential for gaining entrée, and anonymity and confidentiality must usually be guaranteed. But all too often, inexperienced observers assume that this stage has been completed once guarantees have been made and a senior member of the organization has agreed to serve as host or has signed off on the project. In fact, "entrée is a *continuous* process of establishing and developing relationships, not only with a chief host but with a variety of less powerful persons. . . . [T]here are many doorways that must be negotiated."[53] The deepest learnings often occur only after observers have been fully accepted by the local community and people feel free to behave naturally.

Once entrée has been obtained, the most important skills are attentive looking and listening. In the immortal words of Yogi Berra: "You can observe a lot by watching."[54] The best observers keep detailed records and are scrupulous in pursuing accuracy and fidelity. They work hard to keep personal biases and preconceptions at bay, while constantly seeking out anomalies, exceptions, and contradictory evidence. This is more difficult than it first appears, for "not only do observers frequently miss seemingly obvious things . . . they often invent quite false observations."[55] Charles Darwin, the father of evolutionary theory and one of the finest observers of all time, went so far as to keep a separate record of all observations that contradicted his theory "because he knew they had a way of slipping out of the memory more readily than the welcome facts."[56]

Skilled observers also suspend judgment and postpone analysis as long as possible; they strive to do more "'sponging up' (of sights and sounds) than 'spewing out' (of interpretations)."[57] Curiosity and receptivity are essential to success, as is the ability to retain and muse on information without immediately sorting or classifying it. According to a prominent scientist:

> Novices . . . worry too soon about developing salient categories for final analysis, about developing brilliant concepts, and about establishing "patterns of interaction." . . . Not so our model researcher; he is quite content to experience the ambiance of the scene. He has great patience, as well as a tolerance for ambiguity and for his own ignorance. . . . [H]e is genuinely busy being a learner.[58]

This is especially important during the initial minutes, hours, and days of observation. First impressions are usually the most powerful teachers; they come at a time when observers are most sensitive to subtle distinctions and cues. As familiarity and exposure increase, most people find it more and more difficult to separate themselves from the environment and make fine discriminations.

In most cases, observation involves listening as well as watching. Sometimes, the required skill is nothing more than a well-tuned ear, for conversations are often within earshot or accompany videotapes. On other occasions, information must be elicited, through either casual, incidental questioning or formal interviewing. Both techniques demand sensitivity and restraint. As a sociologist investigating inner-city behavior discovered after his blunt questions about illegal gambling stopped a promising discussion cold: "One has to learn when to question and when not to question as well as what questions to ask."[59] It is equally essential to use the language of participants when posing questions, both to create comfort and to avoid forcing responses into artificial categories.

Eventually, researchers must couple observation with interpretation to form meaningful insights and connections. One approach is to begin early to develop collection plans to target observations and provide focus.

The alternative is open-minded immersion, with sorting and sifting performed after the fact. In general, the choice depends on the clarity of goals and on how precisely the learning agenda can be defined before the process begins. Either way, however, it is essential to have a classification scheme that is broad enough to encompass the full range of observed behaviors and experiences.

## Approaches to Observation

Approaches to observation are distinguished primarily by the degree of involvement or participation required.[60] Passive observation lies at one extreme. Observers are silent and unobtrusive; there is no interaction, and the goal is simply to record experiences for later review. The advantages of this approach are ready access to users and limited difficulty securing permission; the disadvantages are an inability to pose follow-up questions and clarify meaning. The process can be performed by unacknowledged or identified observers, and in natural or constructed settings.

Honda, for example, sent a floundering design team to Disneyland, where they spent the entire day in the parking lot, "watching how people in the United States used their cars, what they put in their trunks, and noting which design features made each activity easier or more difficult."[61] U.S. designers, by contrast, frequently invite users to staged clinics, where they interact with mock-ups and prototypes. Appliance manufacturers use test kitchens for similar purposes, while computer firms employ usability laboratories. Occasionally, the process can be conducted remotely, using cameras, recording equipment, or other instrumentation. Hoover became suspicious when it found, in response to surveys, that people claimed to be vacuuming their homes one hour per week. To be certain, the company attached timers to a few models and exchanged them with users' current machines. They showed that people spent a little more than half the stated time actually vacuuming.[62]

Observation becomes more probing when it is coupled with modest amounts of participation and interaction. Observers are no longer mute but limit their discussions with users to clarifications and on-the-spot attempts to refine understanding. Critical skills include the ability to convey interest, probe discretely, and intervene without disruption. The advantage of this approach is that it often leads to deeper insights than passive observation; the disadvantage is that observers' questions will distort, to some degree, the natural flow of activities. Questions may be informal or scripted, and interventions may be more or less structured.

Milliken, for example, has created "first-delivery teams" that accompany the first shipment of products; team members follow the product through the customer's production process to see how it is used, pose occasional questions along the way, and then develop ideas for further improvement. Digital Equipment, by contrast, developed a structured, interactive process that was used by software engineers to observe users of new technologies as they went about their work.[63] Called "contextual inquiry," it included a defined learning agenda, planned interviews, and targeted questions. Still, most interventions were broad and general, designed to keep users focused on the task and technology at hand. Sample questions included: What are you doing? Why are you doing that? Is that what you expected? Tell me about the problem you just encountered? How do you work around it?

Participant observation lies at the other end of the spectrum from passive techniques. Observers are fully engaged in activities and are accepted as insiders. Marketers at Serengeti Eyewear, a division of Corning that manufactured and sold sunglasses, for example, stayed in touch with consumers by spending at least some time every few months selling sunglasses from behind the counter of different retail outlets.[64] Here, crucial skills include gaining trust and acceptance, performing required tasks competently, "being constantly on stage . . . without dropping your guard,"[65] and, perhaps most important, maintaining bifocal vision—simultaneously participating in events while remaining a detached, objective observer. The advantages of this approach are deep, empathic understanding and insights, often in the language and categories of users, plus the opportunity to observe natural interactions and patterns. The disadvantages are difficulties in obtaining access, long periods of data collection, and observers who occasionally "go native" and lose objectivity. For these reasons, businesses have often been slow to employ this mode of learning, despite its enormous power.

Observation, it should be clear, is an invaluable technique for collect-

ing first-hand, unfiltered information. But it is not inherently superior to
search or inquiry. The three techniques are complementary. Each provides a window on the world that is best used under certain circumstances. Search is well suited to settings where needed information has
already been published or is there for the taking. Inquiry is well suited to
settings where facts or insights have yet to be collected but key sources
can be readily identified and questioned. Observation is well suited to
settings where questions are likely to produce incomplete or misleading
responses but insights can be gained by watching people at work or at
play. Independently, these three techniques have much to offer; in combination, they provide intelligence of the highest order.

## THE U.S. ARMY'S CENTER FOR ARMY LESSONS LEARNED: NOT MAKING THE SAME MISTAKE TWICE

The U.S. Army's Center for Army Lessons Learned (CALL), based at
Fort Leavenworth, Kansas, is a leader in participant observation.[66] CALL
was founded in 1985; its initial role was to capture lessons from the
National Training Centers, where troops engage in long, simulated battles to test their readiness and skills. Later, as the Army's mission broadened to include "operations other than war"—interventions in Somalia,
Bosnia, and Haiti, plus fire fighting, flood control, and other forms of
disaster relief at home—CALL was charged with learning from these
experiences as well. Today, CALL observation teams are among the first
troops on the ground in any Army operation. They collect on-the-spot
information about new practices and techniques, identify problems and
trouble spots, distinguish approaches that work from those that do not,
and share their findings with others. According to Colonel Orin A.
Nagel, director of CALL from 1994 to 1996:

> CALL stands at the crossroads of knowledge in the United States
> Army. We are both a provider of information and a collector of
> information. We like to think of ourselves as a conduit between
> what's going on in a thousand locations in the Army and what you
> need to know in your location.

CALL is the Army's institutional memory—the guy who's been around forever, the bottom drawer of your oldest employee. We are a knowledge repository, with three customers: the unit that's on the ground today, the unit that's training to replace them tomorrow, and the rest of the Army, who can use these lessons next year or whenever we have something similar going on.

Despite this broad mandate, the center is relatively small. It is divided into several divisions: a Lessons Learned Division, which develops and disseminates lessons from actual operations, major exercises, and the Combat Training Centers; an Information Systems Division, which supports CALL's hardware and software; a Research Division, which designs and maintains CALL's database and document storage and retrieval systems; the Foreign Military Studies Office, which produces high-quality military security assessments; and the University After Next Division, which provides the best practices and technologies from public, academic, private, and military sectors to the Army.

The heart of the center's activities is real-time observation and data collection. All steps are carefully planned in advance, beginning with a clear statement of learning needs. To determine "critical information requirements," the director of CALL meets quarterly with the chief of staff of the Army and even more frequently with brigade and battalion commanders. Among his questions: What do you need to know to be more effective in the future? What operations are pending that will impose new demands on soldiers? What kinds of decisions will commanders face that they have not faced before?

With the answers in hand, CALL leaders identify appropriate missions and form collection teams. Teams are of varying size, depending on the task. For small assignments, there may be as few as eight to ten participants; on large operations, there are as many as forty or fifty. In Bosnia, the observation team consisted of thirty-eight people; only six were CALL observers. For obvious reasons, every team relies heavily on borrowed manpower. Teams are headed by a line officer from an outside unit, selected for his or her rank, credibility, and access to the group being observed. A second supporting leader, skilled in observation and collection, is drawn from CALL. Several members of CALL's Lessons

Learned Division are assigned to the team; they are often supplemented by combat camera crews. Additional experts are then recruited from the various military schools to contribute their knowledge of communications, logistics, and other relevant fields. Occasionally, even more specialized skills are required. In Haiti, because of the distinctive culture, the observation team included both a minister and a linguist.

This approach has several advantages. By designating a line officer with connections to the unit being observed as leader, it overcomes the problem of access that so often plagues participant observation. By drawing on CALL's skilled observers and designating one member of CALL as coleader of the team, it ensures that the process of observation will be disciplined and accurate and that appropriate methodologies will be used. By involving camera crews, it provides for a detailed visual record that will supplement and support written observations. And by drawing on subject matter experts, it keeps CALL's staff small while introducing diverse perspectives and a cross-fertilization of ideas. The last point is particularly important, as Nagel observed:

> If you have the same people looking at the same things all of the time, you're going to get the same perspectives back. But if you have twenty different people looking at twenty different issues, then you get twenty different perspectives. And that starts to give credibility to your knowledge base. You begin to feel comfortable that what you are observing is in fact what is going on.

Specialized experts are also able to contribute immediately to units in the field. Because they are a help rather than a hindrance, with valuable knowledge to impart, they are able to overcome the natural suspicion that so often prevents observers from becoming insiders. Assimilation is quick and easy, knowledge sharing becomes a two-way street, and observers and participants become almost indistinguishable. But why would specialized experts participate in the first place? Because they are able to obtain information and insights that would not otherwise be available. Those members of the engineer school who were part of CALL's team in Bosnia were among the first to observe the crossing of the Sava River. They were able to bring critical new knowledge back to their colleagues, for study and subsequent inclusion in curriculum, training, and doctrine.

All teams begin with a collection plan, a formal document that guides the observation process. Plans are structured hierarchically, with a few overarching themes at the top and a large group of focused topics below. They begin with *issues,* which are broad areas that Army leaders have identified as targets of learning; proceed to *subissues,* which are functions and tasks that fall under a broader theme and map directly into the categories of the Army's Blueprint of the Battlefield, a generic process model that fits all operations; and conclude with detailed sets of *questions,* which specify the precise areas where data must be collected and observations must be made. All plans are constructed with the advice and input of subject matter experts, who know where current knowledge is thin and additional information is required. In Haiti, for example, an aircraft carrier, the U.S.S. Eisenhower, was used for the first time to deploy troops. Because carriers are designed for pilots and planes, not soldiers and troop-carrying helicopters, the logistics, staging, and loading of troops all presented unique problems. Questions were developed in each area to ensure that lessons were learned for use in future operations.

Occasionally, collection plans must be prepared before teams are formed. This is necessary because certain missions can be anticipated but still arrive without warning. The date of deployment is unknown. More often, time is available before operations are scheduled to begin, and teams develop their own collection plans. Subject matter experts first canvas their peers to develop an initial set of issues, subissues, and questions; then, the team assembles at CALL headquarters for a three- to five-day workshop. During the workshop, members develop and refine the collection plan, learn how to observe unobtrusively, and are taught the CALL methodology for extracting and distilling lessons.

To ensure continuity, the process begins even before troops are sent to the field. According to Nagel:

Today, when you see the Army deploying on an operation, CALL is not only there with the lead soldier, it has already been there for weeks. We work with the unit from the day they are notified, helping them in their final training, passing on the lessons learned from the last similar operation, and sorting out the information and knowledge that they're going to need as they go into that theater. Then we're right with them from the time that the first soldier goes in until the last soldier comes out.

Once units are in the field, data collection begins in earnest. Whenever possible, members of the collection team try to observe events on the spot and in real time; they supplement their observations with interviews, briefings, photographs, videotapes, and written reports. In addition to questions identified in the collection plan, they focus on emerging problems and unexpected difficulties. The team in Haiti, for example, discovered that cargo containers were arriving with their content lists inside, making routing impossible without first opening the container. The team in Bosnia discovered that untracked, snow-covered roads were especially dangerous because they were likely to be mined. At times, teams have trouble tracing problems to their source—a process called "threading the needle"—and must tap additional sources of information. Anonymity, however, is always guaranteed, and individuals are never singled out or identified by name. Quick fixes and warnings are then developed and disseminated, often at evening briefings. This rapid information sharing is an important part of CALL's role; it both enhances credibility and provides an immediate payoff to units in the field. As Nagel put it: "It would be a shame if a soldier in one battalion made the same mistake tomorrow that was made in a different battalion today."

Teams are urged to develop their observations as quickly as possible. Each day, their notes are sent electronically to CALL headquarters for review. Every team has its own dedicated analyst, who serves as editor, interpreter, and librarian. Observation is thus separated, to the extent possible, from interpretation and the development of formal lessons. But the process is highly interactive, as Nagel observed:

The analyst's job is to look at all information coming from the team and sort and evaluate it. Is it complete? Does it make any sense? Does it pass the "so-what" test? He'll make some notes and then ship that observation back to the team for more information. "Tell me a little more about this. Tell me a little more about that. I don't quite understand how this fits with what you told me yesterday." The team will then collect more information, make some changes, and send the observation back. The analyst will clean it up and begin loading it into the computer.

All observations, as well as supporting documents, photographs, and videotapes, are coded in the categories of the Blueprint of the Battlefield. Coding is relatively rapid because collection plans are designed with these categories in mind. New lessons can often be accessed through CALL's Web site within days. Moreover, because the Blueprint is a standardized indexing and retrieval system, field units know precisely where to look for needed information.

At the end of their assignment, collection teams return to CALL headquarters to prepare an Initial Impressions report. That document summarizes the most important lessons; it is immediately sent to replacement units. Later, additional bulletins, newsletters, and handbooks are developed for dissemination throughout the Army. Videotapes are prepared as well; they are valued for their immediacy and fidelity and because they provide a feel for the local setting. In addition, CALL observers participate personally in knowledge transfer. They temporarily join up with replacement units, communicate lessons directly, and contribute to training scenarios developed from observations in the field. The latter are especially powerful. Based on its observations of the 10th Mountain Division, the first group in Haiti, CALL developed twenty-four training vignettes. They covered such topics as crowd control and weapons searches. The follow-on unit built its training around these vignettes; when it returned from the field six months later, the division commander observed that he had actually executed twenty-three of the twenty-four scenarios. The only one he had not encountered was reacting to a terrorist attack.

CALL's approach is a model of effective learning (see Table 3-5). Observation is targeted and carefully planned, observers are knowledgeable and well trained, and acceptance by field units is assured through networking, added value, and assurances of anonymity. All data are col-

## TABLE 3-5
### REAL-TIME OBSERVATION: LESSONS FROM CALL

1. *Keep the unit small.*

- Combine dedicated employees with borrowed manpower.
- Focus on a limited number of strategically important operations or initiatives.

2. *Develop a plan for collecting information.*

- Establish learning needs in advance.
- Solicit input from subject matter experts.
- Proceed from broad issues to narrow, targeted questions.

3. *Form collection teams with well-defined responsibilities.*

- Assign dual leaders: a line manager and a member of the collection unit.
- Combine trained observers with subject matter experts.
- Add specialized skills (e.g., language experts, translators) when necessary.

4. *Employ a disciplined process of observation.*

- Assign collection teams to operating units before they are sent to the field.
- Ensure that collection teams are among the first individuals on-site.
- Combine observation with written reports, interviews, and on-the-spot debriefings.
- Do not attribute observations (especially mistakes) to particular individuals or units.
- Use video and still cameras to compile an objective visual record.
- Separate observation from analysis: assign the roles to different people, and ensure continuing dialogue between them.

5. *Actively disseminate results.*

- Relay critical, pertinent information to members of field units as soon as possible.
- Summarize findings in written and oral reports and send them to follow-on units.
- Participate personally in knowledge transfer by temporarily joining up with follow-on units.
- Capture and communicate lessons using vivid, easy-to-follow formats such as training scenarios.

lected on the spot, drawing on multiple sources and perspectives, and accuracy and reliability are relentlessly pursued. Objective analysts provide additional checks and balances; they also keep interpretation separate from observation. Feedback cycles are short, so that critical information becomes available while it is still useful. Diverse formats are used to package knowledge and communicate lessons, ensuring wide-spread dissemination.

The entire system rests on norms of reciprocity and on a collective commitment to learn from others. According to Nagel:

> When I talk to a soldier about CALL, I say, "You have an unlimited credit card. You can come to my data warehouse and have access to all the knowledge that I have. But one day I am going to come knocking on your door and say, 'Hey, it's Nagel. I'm here to collect. It's your turn to pay in. You've been drawing on your account, on the tens of thousands of others who have input data, knowledge, and information, and now it's time to return the favor.'"
>
> He's been using this information for years. He knows that he can't figure out where it came from, so it's pretty safe to let CALL come in and look at his operation. He knows that we've got credibility, we produce pretty good stuff, and we make sure that anonymity is preserved so that nobody else is going to be able to figure out that he's the only guy that managed to screw things up. And we always go out of our way to give credit to the people who first crack a problem.
>
> Besides, he knows we're going to be helpful. As I used to tell my kids, "You don't have to make every mistake personally. I've made plenty of them, and if you just let me tell you what they were and how you can avoid them, there's still plenty of mistakes for you to make."

As chapter 1 pointed out, one of the litmus tests of a learning organization is that it seldom makes the same mistake twice. CALL ensures that the U.S. Army passes this test.

# 4

---

# Experience

Practice makes perfect. Experience is the best teacher. Trained at the school of hard knocks. This mode of learning is so widely recognized it even has its own proverbs. All suggest that certain types of knowledge come only from participation and personal involvement—from doing things rather than studying or talking about them. We undertake new projects, carry out challenging tasks, and immerse ourselves in unfamiliar environments; then, we repeat the process, usually with considerably more success. These cycles of activity generate rich veins of information; when those veins are tapped, we learn from experience. The mining process may be unconscious or reflective, individual or organizational, spontaneous or planned; the goals, however, remain deeper understanding, increased skill, and superior performance.

This mode of learning has been studied by a wide range of scholars. Philosophers, for example, have been debating its importance for hundreds of years. Two schools have occupied center stage. Rationalists, represented by Descartes and Leibniz, argued that knowledge was based on innate ideas and principles known independently of experience, while empiricists, represented by Locke, Berkeley, and Hume, disagreed, arguing that knowledge came only from perceptions and sensory data.[1]

In the early 1900s, John Dewey, the American pragmatist, added a practical spin to this long-running debate. As an empiricist as well as a stern critic of traditional schooling, he argued that "all genuine education comes about through experience" and proposed a curriculum that drew on a steady stream of hands-on projects rather than the usual lectures and tests.[2] Practical, applied problems ensured that there was no separation of subject matter and method; they gave students "something to do, not something to learn; and the doing is of such nature as to demand thinking, or the intentional noting of connections; learning naturally results."[3] Business scholars soon adopted this same approach, coining the phrase "action learning" to describe the immersion of students in complex, multifunctional workplace problems rather than theory alone.[4]

Today psychologists have joined the chorus. Many now define learning as changes in behavior brought about by experience, with trial and error the primary mechanism at work.[5] Like Dewey, they believe that the process is most effective when it is situated and grounded, linked closely with concrete activities and past experience.[6] Unanchored ideas and concepts—techniques without a home—are difficult to grasp. They are far more likely to be understood when they are taught in familiar contexts, settings, and environments.

Problem solving, for example, can seldom be mastered as an abstract art. It must first be coupled with focused experiential knowledge—a deep understanding of relevant areas of practice, such as business, politics, science, or law—if deep learning is to occur. According to a study by the National Research Council:

> General skills such as breaking down a problem into simpler problems or checking to see whether one has captured the main idea of a passage may be impossible to apply if one does not have a store of knowledge about similar problems—or know enough about the topic to recognize its central ideas.[7]

The dilemma should be obvious. Novices lack experience, which is why they are engaged in learning. But to learn most effectively, they must already have sufficient prior knowledge. Otherwise, they will be slow to process and retain new facts and concepts because of a lack of what scholars call "absorptive capacity"—the ability to interpret and classify information based on preexisting schemas and frameworks.[8]

Practice therefore plays a large role in explaining expert performance. Elite chess players, musicians, and athletes are distinguished less by their innate talents and abilities than by the accumulated amount of time they have spent in deliberate, supervised practice.[9] Far from being naturally superior, the most accomplished performers have simply dedicated themselves to working harder and longer at mastering their craft. Typically, they begin practicing two to five years earlier than their less accomplished peers and then remain focused, capturing the benefits of experience. The process has a certain natural rhythm and cannot be rushed. Studies in a wide range of fields show that world-class performance is achieved only after ten years of effort.[10] But that superiority comes at a price. The associated mental and physical skills are highly specialized and do not transfer easily across fields.

Managers are no different. They too take years to perfect their craft and learn best from practice and hands-on experiences. But to be effective, those experiences must be diverse. When it comes to leadership, more of the same seldom produces superior results. Instead, the best teachers are varied assignments (working in a start-up, a turnaround, an international subsidiary, and a large successful domestic business); hardships and difficulties (overcoming business failures, missed opportunities, and demotions); and serving bosses with different strengths and styles (both positive and negative role models).[11] As an expert on management development has observed: "[T]he potential lessons in each kind of experience are determined by the overlap between what the experience demands and what a person does not yet know how to do. . . . [D]evelopment results from doing something *different* from one's current strengths."[12]

These arguments suggest that we learn from experience in two distinct ways: by repetition and by exposure. Repetition ensures that the same tasks are performed more efficiently over time. Skills are honed through repeated use, and the goal is refinement and depth. The adage "practice makes perfect" is as true of swinging a golf club as it is of conducting a performance review or fitting parts on an assembly line. Exposure, on the other hand, ensures that a new set of talents is developed. Skills are added through the exploration of unfamiliar environments or the assumption of new responsibilities; when coupled with personal involvement, the results are commitment and change. The target may be musical composition or management skills, but the rationale for doing something different is always breadth and expanded understanding.

## LEARNING AND EXPERIENCE CURVES

The impact of these processes is difficult to measure directly. Both repetition and exposure operate in the background; their lessons are often implicit and automatic. In fact, much learning from experience occurs without conscious thought or control. Many of the resulting rules, tasks, and procedures emerge without our awareness and cannot easily be articulated or retrieved.[13] For these reasons, engineers and economists have turned to more concrete, accessible measures of experience. Rather than trying to disentangle and evaluate the distinctive contributions of repetition and exposure, they have bundled them under a single, comprehensive umbrella: the learning curve.[14]

The concept dates back to the discovery in the 1920s and 1930s that the costs of airframe manufacturing fell predictably with increases in cumulative volume.[15] These increases were viewed as proxies for greater skill and knowledge, and most early studies examined their impact on the costs of direct labor. Later studies expanded the focus, looking at total manufacturing costs and the impact of experience in other industries, including automobile assembly, shipbuilding, oil refining, and consumer electronics. Learning rates were highly variable but tended to cluster in the 75 to 85 percent range (meaning that with a doubling of cumulative production from one to two units, two to four units, four to eight units, and so on, costs fell to 75 to 85 percent of their previous level).[16] The combined effect of these improvements could be staggering. In 1906 and 1907 Ford introduced several automobiles priced at more than $5,000. Two years later the company settled on a single, standardized design, the Model T, bringing the price down to $3,000. By 1923, after eight million units of the Model T had been produced and an 85 percent learning curve was firmly in place, the price had fallen to $900 (see Figure 4-1).[17]

## FIGURE 4-1

### PRICE OF MODEL T, 1909–1923

(AVERAGE LIST PRICE IN 1958 DOLLARS)

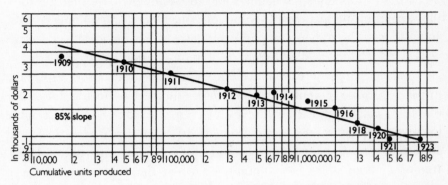

These effects are not confined to manufacturing but apply to almost any repetitive activity. Accident rates fall steadily with cumulative experience, as does the time required for parts replacement and maintenance. There is an additional, associated effect that scholars call "learning by using."[18] Often, the reliability and repair needs of complex capital goods—turbines, generators, boiler vessels, and the like—can be established only through experience. Failure rates are difficult to predict in advance; since safety may be at stake, engineers' initial estimates are usually conservative. The result is a steady expansion of knowledge through use, as well as increased efficiency. Airlines experienced this effect when they shifted from piston to jet engines. Initially, they had little idea of the proper timing of overhauls. The new engines were assumed to be more durable, but there were many unknowns. To avoid problems, engineers scheduled overhauls every 2,000 hours, just as they had with piston engines. With experience, however, their confidence in the reliability of jet engines increased, and they raised the time between overhauls to as long as 8,000 hours.

Firms like the Boston Consulting Group took these ideas to a higher level in the 1970s.[19] Drawing on the logic of learning curves, they argued that industries as a whole faced experience curves, predictable decreases in costs and prices as industries grew and their total production increased. Again, improvement rates were highly variable but tended to fall in roughly the same range as learning curves: 75 to 90 percent.[20] With these figures, consultants suggested, came an iron law of competition. To profit from experience, companies had to rapidly increase their production ahead of competitors, thereby lowering prices and gaining market share. Texas Instruments applied this approach with great success in pocket calculators, as did DuPont in titanium dioxide.

Both learning and experience curves are still widely used, especially in the aerospace, defense, and electronics industries. Boeing, for example, has established learning curves for every workstation in its assembly plant; they assist in monitoring productivity, determining work flows and staffing levels, and setting prices and profit margins on new airplanes. But other companies have floundered when they have applied these techniques. The problem, in large part, is the vast mythology that now surrounds learning and experience curves and impedes their thoughtful use.

Consider these popular but misguided views:

- *Labor learning is the primary engine driving improvement*. This assumption dates back to the original work on learning curves, which examined complex products and time-consuming assembly operations. Because parts were fitted by hand, improved labor rates were usually the target. But the lessons of experience come in many other guises. While production and service workers certainly become more skilled and efficient with practice, additional savings result from simplified processes, rationalized layouts, superior tooling, standardized products, and new forms of organization. Exposure and insight bring new ideas; with them come a wide range of improvements. According to an experienced observer: "The industrial learning curve thus embraces more than the increasing skill of an individual by repetition of a simple operation. Instead, it describes a more complex organism— the collective efforts of many people, some in line and others in staff positions, but all aiming to accomplish a common task progressively more efficiently."[21]

- *Learning rates are uniform across products, processes, firms, and industries*. Early researchers, drawing on data from the airframe industry, reported an 80 percent learning rate. That figure soon became accepted as a universal phenomenon, with great predictability.

Yet subsequent studies have uncovered widely varying learning rates and surprisingly little uniformity. Even within a single industry, there is considerable dispersion. In airframe manufacturing, curves differ by type of airplane, as well as by facility. During World War II, bombers, fighters, and trainers each had strikingly different learning rates. Moreover, the difference between the average industry learning rate for any one of those categories and the experience of a particular manufacturing facility was typically 25 percent.[22] Similar differences have been observed in other industries such as chemical processing, suggesting the danger of projecting individual learning curves from industry averages.[23] Some products, processes, and plants simply have more potential for experience-based improvements than others. They involve less customization, more frequent repetition, and greater transparency in equipment and techniques.

- *Learning curves are stable over time.* For many years, learning curves were thought to have great predictive power. Existing improvement rates were expected to remain steady, with little or no change over time. Unfortunately, such stability requires that both inputs and outputs remain constant and undisturbed; otherwise, there will be large errors. Knowledge, after all, normally depreciates with time and is easily lost. Both Lockheed and Douglas Aircraft suffered the consequences. Lockheed introduced the L-1011 TriStar in 1972, basing its price on steady and predictable cost reductions. A year later the company announced that profits would begin to flow by mid-1974. But because of widely varying production rates, learning was far less rapid than anticipated. In late 1975 managers reported that production costs were still above selling prices; they remained at that level for the remainder of the program.[24] Douglas encountered similar problems. It set prices for the DC-9 based on an anticipated 85 percent learning curve. But a few years into production, the economy boomed, and a large number of experienced workers left for other employers. Because they took their knowledge with them, the 85 percent learning rate was never obtained. Despite a massive hiring program, large losses ensued.[25]

- *Knowledge gained through experience is easily retained and transferred.* Learning curves measure the accumulation of knowledge, not its retention. But the usual assumption is that gains will be maintained over time, either because they become embodied in techniques and procedures or because they pass fluidly from one group of production workers to the next. Studies of shipbuilding and truck manufacturing suggest that both arguments are flawed.[26] During World War II, the construction of Liberty Ships was accompanied by rapid depreciation of knowledge. Continuing production was essential to learning; without it, only 3.2 percent of the stock of knowledge at the beginning of the year was available twelve months later. In truck manufacturing, knowledge was also difficult to retain and communicate. It did not transfer fully between workers on a company's first and second shifts, despite significant investments in training. These findings suggest that experience may be a wise teacher, but that its lessons are easily forgotten.

- *Learning and experience curves are universal sources of competitive advantage.* Consultants have long extolled the virtuous cycle of increasing output, reaping the benefits of experience, reducing prices, seizing market share, and then repeating the process until an unassailable competitive position has been established. There is indeed value to this approach but only if the environment is ripe. When industries are early in their life cycles and output doubles rapidly, when technologies are stable and unlikely to change, and when customers are sensitive to price changes, riding the experience curve is often an effective strategy.[27] But when cost leadership comes from sources other than experience (minimills in steel, just-in-time production in autos) or when the primary basis for competition is product or service differentiation (applications programs in software, the fit and features of running shoes), strategies based on learning or experience curves are far less likely to be successful. In fact, when it comes to acquisitions, increases in experience often lead, at least in the short run, to poorer financial performance. Why? Because "[a]cquisitions are a complex practice and lessons from one acquisition simply cannot be extrapolated to another."[28] Managers tend to generalize inappropriately from earlier efforts, drawing parallels that are incorrect and misleading.[29]

These findings have a number of practical implications. Operationally, they suggest that managers should pursue learning opportunities with indirect as well as direct labor; use experience as a catalyst for considering new methods, as well as as a form of repetitive practice; be wary of estimated learning rates, especially when drawn from other products, processes, or facilities; maintain steady, unvarying production levels rather than responding to sudden surges in demand; minimize employee turnover to capture the lessons of experience; and institutionalize and retain knowledge through training and explicit procedures. Strategically, they suggest that managers should match their use of learning and experience curves to the demands of the environment. These curves are not an all-purpose solution to competitive problems. But under the right circumstances they can provide an edge. How does one tell? By asking the following questions: Does the industry exhibit a significant experience curve? Do some facilities learn more rapidly than others? Can the sources of advantage be kept proprietary? Will price reductions lead to increased sales? Are new technologies or products likely to undermine these advantages, or will they persist over time?[30]

Perhaps most important, these findings suggests that learning from experience is an active process. Improvements must be carefully and consciously managed. There is nothing automatic about the resulting gains, and "merely expecting progress does not bring it about."[31] Quite the opposite, in fact:

> Costs do not fall by natural inclination—they rise. Almost all cost reductions are the result of concerted, and often substantial, effort. . . . Without . . . steady, significant pressure . . . the experience effect will rarely be obtained. In other words, accumulated experience does not *cause* cost reductions but rather provides an opportunity which alert managements can exploit.[32]

## REFLECTION AND REVIEW

Surprisingly, few companies take the time to reflect on their experiences and develop lessons for the future. With the repeated activities that are by learning curves, the task can sometimes be avoided, since ...ciencies and practical guidelines often emerge as a by-product of getting things done. But when activities are episodic or rare—new product launches, geographical expansions, the introduction of unfamiliar technologies or processes—conscious reflection is usually necessary if lessons are to be learned. Managers must carefully review past efforts to distinguish effective from ineffective practice; they must then record their findings in an accessible form and disseminate the results to employees. One expert has called this process the "Santayana Review," citing the famous philosopher George Santayana, who coined the phrase "Those who cannot remember the past are condemned to repeat it."[33]

Unfortunately, a wide range of barriers stand in the way. The most obvious are time pressures. Most businesses operate with little or no slack. Tasks are tightly sequenced, and milestones pass all too quickly. As a harried computer engineer observed about his company's design process: "There was no question of deadlines. You'd already missed it, whatever it was."[34] In such settings, tomorrow's tasks are far more important than yesterday's. Reflection becomes an avoidable luxury because it adds an additional step, with uncertain payoff, to an already compressed schedule. Moreover, employees seldom welcome reviews of past projects. Rather than serving as opportunities for learning, they frequently become searches for the guilty, an excuse to scapegoat. In all too many companies, there are good reasons to believe that mistakes are best kept hidden.

Yet even when the environment is supportive, reflection can be problematic. Cause-and-effect relationships are difficult to disentangle when samples are small.[35] A complex project often involves hundreds of participants and thousands of steps; how does one isolate the critical variables and determine their relative contribution? Here, failures play a vital role, especially when compared with prior expectations or successes. Failures focus attention, simplify diagnosis, help discriminate among alternatives, and provide essential operating and design information.[36] A study of more than 150 new products concluded that "the knowledge gained from failures [is] often instrumental in achieving subsequent successes. . . . [P]roducts that fail act as important probes into user space about what it would take to make a brand new effort successful. . . . In the simplest terms, failure is the ultimate teacher."[37] IBM's 360 computer series, for example, one of the most popular and profitable ever built, was based on the technology of the failed Stretch computer that preceded it. The lessons learned from the initial, unsuccessful launch were used to modify and enhance the next generation of products.

## Single Case or Comparison Reviews

Lessons may be drawn from single cases or comparisons. The former, usually written up as narratives or institutional histories, attempt to tease out insights and practical advice by combining diverse recollections and commentaries.[38] Microsoft, for example, now follows virtually every new software release with a detailed postmortem.[39] The majority involve written reports and require three to six months of work. Groups review their time together, zero in on problems, distinguish effective from ineffective processes, and make recommendations for the future. Over time, postmortems have become steadily more comprehensive and now include separate discussions of program management, development, testing, product management, and user education. They are usually sharply self-critical and "read like the recountings of disasters. If all product names were removed . . . readers would assume they were investigations of failed projects. [Yet] nearly all . . . proved to be among the best-sellers in their category."[40]

Comparisons involve side-by-side assessments of successes and failures or contrasts of superior and average performers. The presence of multiple cases highlights differences, isolates causal factors, and reduces interpretative errors. Boeing used this approach immediately after experiencing difficulties with its 737 and 747 plane programs. Both planes were introduced with much fanfare—as well as serious problems. To ensure that the problems were not repeated, senior managers commissioned a high-level employee group, called Project Homework, to compare the development processes of the 737 and 747 with those of the 707 and 727, two of the company's most profitable planes. The group was asked to develop a set of "lessons learned" that could be used on future projects. After working for three years, they produced hundreds of recommendations and an inch-thick booklet. Several members of the team were then transferred to the 757 and 767 start-ups. Guided by experience, they produced the most successful, error-free launches in Boeing's history.[41]

Whether single cases or comparisons are used, the required conditions remain the same. Reviews must be conducted immediately, while memories are fresh and data can still be verified. They must be accepted as "real work" rather than avoidable frills and consciously scheduled into work plans and projects. A disciplined, structured process is essential, as are trained facilitators; both keep discussions focused, emotions under control, and finger-pointing to a minimum. Reviews should be as objective as possible, with considerable time and effort devoted to verifying the nature and sequence of events. Facts must be clearly separated from opinions; otherwise, interpretation is certain to be difficult and divisive. Here, helpful steps include the involvement of neutral third-party observers and analysts, as well as the use of internal control groups.

Perhaps most important, the climate must be right. A supportive, tolerant culture is essential if reviews are to flourish. Most employees will cooperate only if they believe that self-assessment and critical thinking are truly valued by management. There must be room for mistakes, as well as improvement. For this reason, perfectionist cultures seldom produce active, honest reflection. Their evaluation and control systems are intolerant of error, leading employees to associate mistakes with career risk rather than learning.

## Individual, Group, or Organizational Reviews

Reviews may also focus on individuals, groups, or organizations. At the individual level, the goal is to distill and disseminate the elements of effective practice. Skilled managers, engineers, marketers, and salespeople normally employ a distinctive bag of tricks—a set of tools and techniques, learned through experience, that their less successful counterparts have yet to adopt. They also possess distinctive patterns of thought, feeling, and behavior.[42] By putting the most effective performers under a microscope, companies can identify these essential attitudes and approaches and ensure that they are shared. The resulting profiles have two primary uses: screening potential employees and developing existing talent.

AT&T's Bell Laboratories, for example, studied its own software engineers to determine why some were more productive than others.[43] Managers and engineers were first asked to identify star performers; since there was only a 50 percent overlap in the nominations of the two groups, the stars were identified as those ranked highly by both camps. They were then interviewed in depth about how they went about their work and, specifically, what they did to be more productive. To weed out spurious explanations, a control group of average performers was asked the same questions; a number of obvious answers, such as superior cognitive skills or advanced technical knowledge, were quickly eliminated. Instead, researchers zeroed in on the striking differences in the two groups' descriptions of "taking initiative." To the stars, the phrase meant networking widely, pursuing tasks that went beyond stated job requirements, pretesting ideas, and seeking out constructive criticism. Middling performers put far more weight on self-promotion, glitzy presentations, and impression management. Using these insights, the Bell Labs team designed an innovative, hands-on training program, which the star performers then delivered to a subset of their peers. The results were immediate and impressive. Participants reported a quick 10 percent productivity improvement, rising to 25 percent a year later. There were equally striking gains in managers' evaluations of their ability to spot problems, conduct high-quality work, keep their bosses informed, work across organizational boundaries, and attend to customer and competitive needs.

At the group level, reviews often focus on complex, expensive capital projects.[44] Typically, the goal is to identify a few critical "rules of the road"—processes and procedures that keep quality high, schedules on track, and costs under control. Usually, the review process is ad hoc, conducted by participants themselves (as at Microsoft) or by a specially assigned group (as at Boeing). Occasionally, however, reviews are more structured, with standardized approaches and a dedicated, experienced team. For many years, British Petroleum had a small, five-person group, the Post-Project Appraisal unit (PPA), that collected information on major investment projects, wrote up case studies, and derived lessons for planners that were then incorporated in the annual revisions of the company's planning guidelines.[45] The group reviewed only six projects annually and presented their findings directly to the board, giving them high visibility as well as autonomy and clout. The bulk of their time was spent in the field, interviewing an average of forty individuals per project. All reviews covered the period from project conception, beginning before the submission of a formal proposal, through the first few years of operation. Members of the appraisal unit then synthesized the lessons in three separate booklets—one each for acquisitions, joint ventures, and project development and control—and distributed the findings to all project planners.

From the company's point of view, the value of this process is obvious. But why would individual managers or employees provide information for case studies that were certain to identify their flaws? Because the process was designed to be as objective and even-handed as possible. The appraisal unit was staffed with experienced, credible experts, without functional or divisional loyalties; case studies were sent to interviewees before submission to the board, ensuring that their comments and corrections were incorporated in final drafts; and individual cases, with their occasionally pointed critiques, were not circulated throughout the company but were abstracted and presented to a wider audience in the less threatening form of broad, generic recommendations. Today, the PPA no longer exists as an independent unit, but British Petroleum continues to conduct regular reviews at the project level.

Organizational reviews typically take one of two forms: studies of ongoing operations or assessments of change programs. The former normally focus on "best practices"—those structures, systems, and processes that have generated superior performance at one site or division and thus deserve rapid dissemination. There are often substantial opportunities for improvement. Even at well-managed companies, quality and productivity differences of 2:1 are commonly found when similar operations are compared.[46] Because these differences normally result from a bundle of mutually reinforcing practices, reviews should always be comprehensive and multifunctional. But they may involve different levels of management. In general, senior managers should be the focus when large-scale systems are involved, while middle- and lower-level managers should be the focus when daily operations are of interest.

Consider the contrasting approaches taken by Chrysler and Toyota. Chrysler's top executives asked outside experts to develop a case study featuring Diamond-Star Motors, its joint venture with Mitsubishi, and then to lead five hundred senior managers in small-group discussions of the implications for the company's current design, manufacturing, and purchasing systems. The highly successful LH cars were the result. Toyota, by contrast, rotated nearly three hundred middle- and lower-level managers and production coordinators, in groups of thirty to sixty, through three-month stints at New United Motors Manufacturing, Inc. (NUMMI), its joint venture with General Motors. Many went through multiple rotations: three months at the joint venture, observing production methods, charting quality performance, meeting with government officials, and developing an understanding of American employees; then three months back at Toyota City, reflecting on their experiences and developing lessons. Eventually, a large number of these employees transferred to Toyota's new plants in Kentucky and Ontario, where they were able to apply their new learnings firsthand.[47]

Reviews of change programs have a different focus. Rather than targeting best practices, they zero in on critical missteps and needed midcourse corrections. The goal is to "capture reality in flight," uncovering difficulties before they become sizable or entrenched.[48] Xerox, in an unusually thoughtful and well-designed process (called a Presidential Review because it was sponsored and led by Paul Allaire, the company's president and CEO), revisited its newly designed organization in 1993, one year after introduction. The process began with extensive interviews with more than thirty senior managers, who were asked to describe the transition from the old to the new organization, point out unexpected problems and difficulties, and highlight differences they had observed between Xerox's "design intent" (the stated goals of the redesign) and actual results. To ensure objectivity, all interviews were conducted by outside consultants, who then summarized their findings in a brief report. The consultants also developed a workbook to stimulate further reflection and sent it to all participants a month before the scheduled review meeting. The workbook included descriptions of Xerox's newly developed strategy, structure, processes, and culture, followed by diagnostic questions in each area designed to assess progress to date and evaluate the change management process. Among the questions: What has changed? What still needs to be done in this area? Where are the largest gaps between what is intended and what is currently true? If you were to outline the barriers that need to be dealt with, what comes to mind? What would you have done differently? What should we do now? Forty-five senior managers then assembled for a day-long meeting, where they pooled their reflections, identified major trouble spots, and developed recommendations and action plans.

All of these review processes are designed to avoid recurrent mis-

takes while reproducing successes. They are necessary because management, like many other professions, is more art than science. The right
choices are not always obvious in the heat of the moment. Sometimes,
plans are little more than inspired guesswork, and effective strategies and
practices can be identified only after the fact. As the philosopher
Kierkegaard put it: "Life is lived forward, but understood backward." To
move ahead, one must often first look behind.

## THE U.S. ARMY'S AFTER ACTION REVIEWS: SEIZING THE CHANCE TO LEARN

The U.S. Army is one of the few organizations to have institutionalized
these reflection and review processes, especially at the group level. After
Action Reviews (AARs) are now standard Army procedure.[49] They were
introduced in the mid-1970s and were originally designed to capture
lessons from the simulated battles of the National Training Centers. The
technique diffused slowly—according to the Army's chief of staff, it was
a decade before the process was fully accepted by line officers and
embedded in the culture—and only in recent years have AARs become
common practice. The turning point was the Gulf War. AARs sprang up
spontaneously as small groups of soldiers gathered together, in foxholes
or around vehicles in the middle of the desert, to review their most
recent missions and identify possible improvements. Haiti marked a
further step forward. There, for the first time, AARs were incorporated
into all phases of the operation and were used extensively to capture and
disseminate critical organizational knowledge.

The technique is relatively straightforward. It bears a striking resemblance to "chalk talks" in sports, where players and coaches gather
around a blackboard shortly after a game to discuss the team's performance. Both chalk talks and AARs are designed to make learning routine, to create, as one commander put it, "a state of mind where everybody is continuously assessing themselves, their units, and their
organizations and asking how they can improve." In practice, this means
that all participants meet immediately after an important activity or
event to review their assignments, identify successes and failures, and
look for ways to perform better the next time around. The process may

be formal or informal, may involve large or small groups, and may last for minutes, hours, or days. But discussion always revolves around the same four questions:

- What did we set out to do?
- What actually happened?
- Why did it happen?
- What are we going to do next time?

According to Army guidelines, roughly 25 percent of the time should be devoted to the first two questions, 25 percent to the third, and 50 percent to the fourth.

The first question is deceptively simple. Group members must agree on the purpose of their mission and the definition of success. Otherwise, there will be no basis for evaluating performance or comparing plans with results. In the Army, objectives are normally defined with great precision. They include three elements: "the key *tasks* involved, the *conditions* under which each task may need to be performed, and the acceptable *standards* for success. (For example, at a range of 2,000 yards, hit an enemy tank moving at 20 miles per hour over uneven terrain at night with an 80% success rate.)"[50] With objectives like these, there is little ambiguity, and it is easy to determine whether a job has been done well or poorly. Such clarity also avoids confused, inconclusive reviews. According to an experienced AAR facilitator:

> Unsuccessful AARs are often those where the boss has the attitude, "I don't know what I want, so I can't tell you exactly what to do. But I'll recognize it when I see it. So just go out there and do good things." That's not helpful. We insist that our leadership, from the very top officer to those in charge of three to five men, give soldiers clear guidance. They must have a standard.[51]

The second question requires that participants agree on what actually happened during a mission. This too is more difficult than it first appears. Facts can be slippery, especially when stress is high and events move rapidly. All too often, memories are flawed, leading to competing or inconsistent stories. Reality—what soldiers call "ground truth"—becomes difficult to pin down, resulting in gridlock and AARs that progress slowly if at all. But these problems can be overcome. At the National Training Centers, facts are verified by pooling information from three diverse, objective sources: observer-controllers, instrumentation, and taping.

Observer-controllers are skilled, experienced soldiers who shadow individual officers throughout their training exercises. They also provide on-the-spot coaching and lead AARs. (Not surprisingly, many later do a tour of duty at the Center for Army Lessons Learned [CALL], where they are assigned to the Lessons Learned Division.) A training exercise for three thousand to four thousand people normally involves approximately six hundred observer-controllers. Typically, their time in service makes them a bit senior to the officers they are observing, providing both credibility and clout. And because they have complete access to battle plans, are intimately familiar with the terrain, and are constantly present during maneuvers, they can effectively arbitrate debates when facts are in dispute.

Technology, in the form of instrumentation and taping, provides an additional source of objective information. The resulting record is extremely detailed and leaves little room for argument. Onboard microprocessors track the exact position and movement of vehicles over time, while sophisticated, laser-based technologies note when and where weapons were fired as well as the resulting hits and misses. Video cameras, mounted at critical locations throughout the training centers, record troop movements. These films provide vivid, compelling testimony, with extraordinary fidelity. As one officer put it: "If a picture is worth a thousand words, a motion picture must be worth a million." Audiotapes round out the story, conveying the exact timing and content of communications both within and across units.

Together, these tools and approaches ensure that facts are reconstructed with considerable accuracy. During AARs at the National Training Centers, soldiers have little problem answering the question, What actually happened? Unfortunately, they face many more difficulties in the field, where observer-controllers and recording technologies are not always available. Occasionally, CALL teams and combat video crews will be on hand to provide objective data. But in most cases, accurate reconstruction depends on pooling multiple perspectives in a process that resembles "majority rules." Then, immediacy is crucial to success, as is wide participation. To minimize memory losses, AARs must be conducted as soon after the event as practical—preferably, the very same day. They should include, whenever possible, all key participants, as well as unbiased, third-party observers, members of staff and supporting units, and even senior commanders. Participants should agree on some mechanism to resolve disagreements and ensure that discussion does not grind to a halt when differences emerge.

Once the facts are established, diagnosis can begin. Outside the Army, many groups start their reviews at this stage, assuming that prior steps can be omitted without problems. But agreement on both the standards to be met (question one) as well as actual performance (question two) is essential to avoiding endless debates. The Army's insistence that the first 25 percent of every AAR be devoted to these topics is a critical insight. And the benefits are hardly confined to the military. Companies can also gain by devoting time up front to clarifying goals and targets and setting unambiguous standards—expected levels of customer satisfaction, milestones for project completion, penetration rates for new products—and then comparing them with results during the review process. By deferring diagnosis, these two steps vastly improve the odds that ensuing discussions will be grounded and productive.

The third question begins the process of analysis by asking for an examination of cause and effect. At this stage, the goal is to tease out the underlying reasons for success or failure. A tank unit expected to reach a critical checkpoint at a certain hour but was twenty minutes late; what caused the discrepancy? A scout set out to inspect a position to the north but ended up five miles east; how did he become lost? A commander planned to coordinate artillery attacks with two other battalions but never communicated his intentions; what caused the breakdown? Answering these questions requires problem-solving skills, as well as a willingness to accept responsibility. Groups must brainstorm possible explanations and then find ways to choose among several plausible alternatives, often in the face of limited and conflicting data. They must also be ruthlessly honest. Individuals need to face up to their own deficiencies, avoiding the all-too-common tendency to turn a deaf ear when personal errors or weaknesses are uncovered. This is particularly true of leaders. As one commander observed: "If you're not willing to hear criticism, you probably shouldn't be doing an AAR."

At times, analysis is simple, and cause and effect are easy to untangle. Missed opportunities or roads not taken are usually obvious to both individuals and groups. In Haiti, a sergeant responsible for convoying soldiers to the beach returned several hours late because one of his trucks became stuck in the sand. The ensuing AAR was brief and to the point: he had failed to pack a tow bar. The first units entering Port-au-Prince were startled to discover that delivering babies was an important part of their mission. They quickly wrote an AAR to ensure that all medics received at least rudimentary obstetrics training.

On other occasions, challenges are more complex, and a series of AARs may be required to home in on the problem. Then, a process of progressive refinement is useful for teasing out explanations and developing possible solutions. Units assigned the task of clearing guns from suspected rebel strongholds in Haiti initially had little success. Their first AAR examined the current process, the resulting resistance, and how it might be overcome. Soldiers noted the absence of dogs in the area and the locals' frightened response to the German shepherds used by the military police. Perhaps, they suggested, the dogs should be more visible. In the next town, they were placed up front, and cooperation immediately improved. Soon after, during another AAR, soldiers noted that they had encountered no women in their sweeps through the towns. Perhaps they could be encouraged to assist in the collection effort if they had a woman soldier to identify with. In the next village, one unit assigned a female commander as leader and visibly acknowledged her authority. The result was further gains in cooperation. Finally, during a third AAR, soldiers noted that they faced far more resistance when confronting people in the streets than when they approached them in their homes. The unit shifted its modus operandi to house-to-house searches, and even more guns were secured.

This last example suggests that the final step in an AAR—deciding what to do next time—is often inseparable from diagnosis. Participants are usually eager to propose solutions, and many arise naturally once problems are well understood. It is particularly important that participants focus on things they can fix, rather than external forces outside their control. Otherwise, the process is likely to have little immediate impact. This stage has another goal as well: identifying areas where groups are performing well and should stay the course. In Army lingo, these are activities to be "sustained." Surprisingly, they are often difficult to identify. When standards are met, variation is limited and there are few obvious clues to the sources of superior performance. Failures are far easier to diagnose.[52] Yet if successes are to be repeated, the underlying causes must be clearly articulated.

Identifying activities to be sustained was one of the assignments of the first unit in Haiti. Because soldiers faced a host of unfamiliar challenges—keeping the peace, delivering food, overseeing elections, even collecting trash—they were asked to review virtually all of their missions and develop a set of standard operating procedures for follow-on units. AARs were the primary tool. As one participant recalled: "We AAR'd everything." Small squads conducted them daily, debriefing orally and informally; larger sections conducted them after every critical mission, presenting the results in formal reports; and platoon leaders conducted them weekly, submitting their findings to commanders for further distillation and review. Quick feedback led to quick implementation, sharply increasing the rate of learning.

Initially, soldiers found many areas for improvement and strove only to make each effort better than its predecessor. But with experience, there were fewer and fewer problems, and attention shifted to sustaining successes. Eventually, the unit developed a series of "cookbook recipes" that captured their own best practices, wrote them up, and submitted them for review. Frequently the practices were set in Army doctrine and used by both CALL and the National Training Centers to prepare follow-on units for their upcoming assignments.

Together, these examples show that AARs are a powerful, appealing tool. They have many advantages. The concept is easy to grasp and inexpensive to apply, amounting to little more than organized reflection. The four questions provide a simple roadmap, appropriate for any situation. The process demands few skills other than careful observation and systematic problem solving. Even so, success is not guaranteed. A number of conditions must first be met.

To begin, reviews must be framed as dialogues, not lectures or debates. Army experts suggest that participants speak as much as 75 percent of the time. The process must also be as egalitarian as possible: the broader and more even the participation, the better. Under no circumstances should leaders dominate discussions or seize control. They should also refrain from posing their own problems for analysis or lobbying for preferred solutions. Such actions undermine AARs by suggesting that they exist for the leader's benefit rather than the group's.

Skilled facilitation is essential. Facilitators guide the discussion from beginning to end, ensuring that participants stay on track. They introduce the topic, keep the group focused, establish and enforce ground rules, monitor and maintain the schedule, transition from one question to the next, and summarize the resulting action plans. Even more important, they personally set the tone. AARs require openness and candor, a willingness to set aside traditional lines of authority. There must be honest interchange between superiors and subordinates, a recognition, in the words of the Army's chief of staff, that "disagreement is not disrespect." Because this attitude seldom comes naturally to hierarchical organizations, it must be carefully and consciously cultivated. According to a facilitator at one of the National Training Centers:

> We preface our AARs by saying, "We're not judges, and we're not evaluators. We're not going to talk—you are. But to be successful, we have to have an information exchange between the lowest soldier in the ranks and the highest, because the highest ranking officer doesn't see everything that's going on. This is his opportunity to get feedback."

Of course, feedback will be forthcoming only if commanders are willing to publicly acknowledge their flaws. Such statements have enormous symbolic value, and skilled facilitators try to draw them out early in AARs. As one facilitator observed:

When leaders admit up front that they did some things right and some things wrong, it really opens up the whole group. They understand that this isn't a "Who shot John?" type of review. It's "Let's figure out what's best so that we can do better next time."

Straight talk must also be supported by the larger organization. Incentives and rewards must reinforce the openness required by AARs; otherwise, mistakes will never be discussed and the process will continue to be viewed with suspicion. Here, actions speak louder than words. According to a mid-level officer:

I think one of the reasons why we are able to talk so frankly in AARs is that our superiors have set the conditions that they want to know what is truly the problem and what you are really thinking— not just the answer they want to hear. If they find out that you are hiding a fact or are less than completely honest, recently that has been death to your career. People who have lacked integrity or candor are leaving the service because they are not getting promoted.

Yet even with the proper incentives, discussions can still derail. Candor comes in many forms, not all of them constructive. For this reason, the Army has developed ground rules for AARs that are enforced by facilitators. Tact and civility are required, and personal attacks are forbidden. There will be no searches for the guilty. As one facilitator put it: "We don't use the 'b' or the 'f' word. We don't place blame, and we don't find fault." Plain speaking, however, is essential, and facilitators normally suggest to participants that they enter AARs with "no thin skins." They are also told that "discussions will stay in house." There will be no report cards and no relaying of information to bosses. Mistakes admitted in an AAR cannot be held against soldiers later on. They are opportunities for learning, not blemishes on one's record, and are excluded from personnel evaluations. Reprisals—either during AARs or after the fact—are not allowed.

Some structure is necessary to ensure coherence and avoid random, rambling discussions. The best AARs therefore follow a well-defined path. They normally begin shortly after the activity was completed but not so soon that there is no opportunity to plan carefully or identify likely learning opportunities. To begin, facilitators usually write the topic of discussion on a flip chart in front of the group and suggest that speakers confine their comments to that topic. The group then marches through events in sequence, using the timeline of the mission to guide them. At each step, the facilitator pauses to ask participants the four basic questions. Occasionally, when tasks are complex, the group will break the chronology of events down further, using additional categories, such as intelligence and maneuver, drawn from the Army's Blueprint of the Battlefield, to organize discussion. Many facilitators anticipate factual disputes before they arise and have videotapes or other documentation on hand for resolving them. During wrap-ups, the entire group generates two lists, one of activities to be sustained and another of activities to be improved. To ensure that these learnings are not lost, one member is assigned the role of secretary and recorder.

As discussion unfolds, facilitators ask questions. This is a high art, for AARs must be tough and probing without causing defensiveness. Facilitators must therefore choose their words carefully, pressing for honest self-assessments without directing criticism at specific individuals. They must keep the spotlight on the group, asking, for example, how a platoon could have done better escorting a convoy, rather than questioning the platoon officer about his personal failings and lack of direction. At the same time, facilitators must remain attuned to differing points of view. They must ensure that disagreements surface and conflicts are ironed out; both are essential to learning. Not surprisingly, many facilitators have become experts at reading body language and drawing people into discussions at just the right moment, using subtle cues: "I see you shaking your head over there; do you see the situation differently?" Poor AARs can often be traced to facilitators who have misunderstood their roles and use the occasion to tell personal war stories and anecdotes.

Clearly, facilitators require a multitude of skills. They must be sensitive observers and artful discussion leaders. They must be knowledgeable about the subject at hand. And they must be respected by subordinates and peers. This combination is hard to find in one person, so the

Army draws on diverse sources. At the National Training Centers, all facilitators are observer-controllers. They are considered to be ideal for the task because they combine intimate, objective knowledge of operations with extensive experience leading discussions. But because they are seldom available in the field, line officers must at times lead their own AARs. This presents few problems for small, intimate groups like squads or sections, which have close working relationships. Difficulties increase, however, as units become larger. Then, one mid-level officer observed, "too often, the person in charge is intimidating." A few commanders still insist on leading their own AARs because they consider themselves capable of encouraging openness and debate. But most Army experts agree that the task is best left to individuals with less at stake, either staff members outside the chain of command or higher ranking officers with a broader perspective. Commanders, they believe, are more likely to benefit from AARs by listening attentively and contributing selectively, rather than assuming their customary positions of leadership.

AARs, then, have a number of strict requirements (see Table 4-1). Among the most critical are immediacy, broad participation, a structured process, the availability of objective data, skilled facilitation, attention to recording and dissemination, and a climate of openness and candor. Even more important, however, is simple repetition. Unless reviews are carried out routinely at all levels of the organization, they will never be viewed as more than an interesting diversion. Consistency breeds comfort and acceptance. It is for this reason that most Army training exercises now include daily AARs and that AARs were used so extensively in Haiti. It is also why General Gordon Sullivan, the Army's former chief of staff, did not exempt himself from the process. He too engaged in regular AARs. For example, early in his tenure, he and his staff reviewed responses to difficult questions from the House Appropriations Committee; later, they focused on major policy initiatives. Such practices ensure that AARs become second nature. Eventually, a new mind-set develops in the organization, a recognition that no activity is truly complete until participants have reflected on their experiences and understood the reasons for success or failure. Then, and only then, has learning been incorporated into daily work.

# TABLE 4-1

## CONDUCTING AFTER ACTION REVIEWS

| Do | Don't |
|---|---|
| Schedule AARs shortly after the completion of an activity. | Conduct AARs without planning. |
| Make reviews routine. | Conduct reviews infrequently or irregularly. |
| Collect objective data whenever possible. | Allow debates to bog down when establishing the facts. |
| Use trained facilitators. | Allow dominating leaders to run AARs. |
| Establish clear ground rules: encourage candor and openness; focus on things that can be fixed; keep all discussions confidential. | Base performance evaluations or promotions on mistakes admitted in AARs. |
| Proceed systematically: What did we set out to do? What actually happened? Why did it happen? What are we going to do next time? | Permit unstructured, meandering, disorganized discussions. |
| Involve all participants in discussions. | Allow senior managers or facilitators to dominate discussions. |
| Probe for underlying cause-and-effect relationships. | Criticize or fault individual behavior or performance. |
| Identify activities to be sustained as well as errors to be avoided. | Conclude without a list of learnings to be applied in the future. |

## EXPERIENTIAL LEARNING

For all their power, reflection and review processes have an important weakness: they take place after the fact. Because reviews are the final step in a long chain of events, learning occurs with a lag. Reflection, after all, does not begin until all tasks have been completed. Most errors are therefore discovered relatively late in the game. This presents few problems for repetitive activities like convoys and patrols, service calls, or tasks on an assembly line, where second chances come quickly. But when assignments are drawn out or challenges recur infrequently, the process is far less efficient. Immediate applications are often hard to find, and opportunities for practice are limited. In such settings, the lessons of experience are easily lost.

They can be found with the help of a well-designed educational process. The goal remains the same—to develop practical, applied knowledge by drawing on experience—but with an important twist. Reflection and action are now intimately intertwined. After-the-fact reviews are replaced by alternating periods of learning and doing. Work-related tasks remain the focus, since most studies suggest that adults absorb new ideas best when they are linked directly to everyday challenges.[53] But learning is more proactive than in the typical review process, combining three elements: an introduction to relevant concepts, theories, and tools; a carefully selected problem or simulation to test and apply new knowledge; and a process that includes pauses along the way to evaluate progress, share learnings, and make midcourse corrections. The approach goes by various names—action learning, experiential learning, problem-centered learning—but all can be traced to the writings of John Dewey and his insistence on the "intimate and necessary relation between the processes of actual experience and education."[54]

Today, most corporations seem to agree. Theories and abstract discussions are out; tangible, results-oriented programs are in. Their goal is to mimic or reproduce experience, while providing practice in essential skills. Management development executives for example, clearly prefer classes that are active, anchored, and applied. They cite workshops as the most popular—and by far the most effective—instructional approach.[55] Traditional methods, such as lectures, are still widely used, but primarily for conveying facts, principles, and basic techniques. Because they are one step removed from application, they are less likely to produce lasting change. As one educator archly observed: "All too often, information flows from the notes of the professor into the notebooks of students without passing through the minds of either."[56]

## A Focus on Problems

Experiential learning programs are completely different. They are built around problems and concrete challenges that ensure active participation. The problems may be real or simulated. Real problems have the advantage of immediacy and fidelity; simulated problems can be tailored to specific learning needs.

**Real Problems.** When real problems are used, they typically involve pressing, high-visibility projects, with measurable results that matter to important people in the organization. If solved, they are likely to produce substantial payoffs. The best projects are multifunctional; require face-to-face contact with customers, competitors, or suppliers; and lack obvious, easy solutions. Today, they often include an international component to increase global exposure. A group at GE was asked to develop a consumer-lighting strategy for western Europe; a team at Whirlpool was chartered with recovering overpaid duty on compressors that the company was importing from a Brazilian affiliate; and a group at Motorola was assigned the task of assessing the company's opportunities in the Latin American market.[57] In each case, the problem was nominated by top managers, with the assistance of training experts. At times, teams will select their own problems. When Xerox introduced quality training in the 1980s, all work groups were required to apply the new techniques to a problem of their choosing. The senior executive team, for example, tackled operations reviews, which were frustrating and time-consuming, and completely redesigned the process.[58]

Real problems clearly motivate learners by putting them on the firing line. With few boundaries between the classroom and the workplace, students focus on the "here and now," not the "there and then."[59] But there is a downside as well. Programs built around real problems have two limitations: failure is highly visible, and innovative ideas are hard to teach. Significant problems, almost by definition, command the interest and attention of senior managers. Proposed solutions are certain to receive careful scrutiny, especially if they challenge the status quo. At GE, all action-learning projects conclude with a presentation to division presidents or other business leaders. Tough, occasionally hostile, questions are the norm. This is by design. According to the former head of GE's executive training center: "The key to action learning . . . is . . . to create performance anxiety [with] the illusion of pretty high risk. . . . [If] you did a crummy report, you're not going to lose your job, but you're going to be professionally embarrassed."[60] While these conditions are certain to stimulate intensive work, they are less likely to encourage risk taking. New ideas and techniques are difficult to apply; participants are understandingly reluctant to experiment when the results will be displayed in an open forum. The exposure is too great, and a crucial ingredient is missing: psychological safety. The result, according to a leading cognitive scientist, is limited learning: "[W]hen people who have made mistakes or taken risks that didn't pan out receive public tongue-lashings from the boss . . . it's difficult to learn . . . rather than admitting an error and seeking help, employees prefer to cover it up and avoid public humiliation."[61] For these reasons, the use of real problems is likely to be most effective in settings where tough, trial-by-fire cultures are already in place or where critical feedback can be provided in ways that minimize public embarrassment.

Real problems have another disadvantage: they are seldom designed for learning. Top managers usually select problems for their importance and potential payoff, not their ability to illustrate critical concepts or techniques. The goal, of course, is to identify problems that are broad and representative, requiring the application of knowledge that will be useful in other settings. But they are difficult to find, and the resulting activities are often more valuable for the generic process skills they impart—teamwork and negotiation, for example—rather than the associated frameworks, principles, or tools.

**Simulated Problems.**  Simulated problems offer a solution. They are designed with specific skills in mind and come in many forms, ranging from simple to dauntingly complex. The associated learnings may be physical, social, or cognitive. A manufacturer training employees to pack boxes of biscuits has them practice with wooden cutouts so that they learn how different sizes and shapes fit together.[62] Flight crews fly complete trips in high-fidelity simulators, where they face instrument malfunctions, engine failures, and other unexpected emergencies "that *require* the coordinated actions of all crewmembers for success."[63] Wal-Mart trains new managers with its Always Store, a simulated version of a real store that includes in-basket exercises, customer service problems, and the strategic challenge of stealing market share from a tough local competitor.[64] Despite their differences, all of these programs share the same goal: providing the lessons of experience at a fraction of the cost.

The best simulations combine realism, variety, and low risk. Failure is acceptable because real catastrophes are avoided. Critical variables are easily manipulated, producing new wrinkles and variations. Conflict and difficulty are ever-present, ensuring that learners are drawn in and treat exercises seriously. Immersion is seldom a problem because participants identify closely with the challenges at hand. In fact, most simulations are tailored to the needs of specific groups. Pilots, for example, have long been selected for their technical proficiency and self-reliance—the elusive "right stuff." Yet over the past twenty years, air carrier accidents and incidents have consistently been traced "to inadequacies in leadership qualities, communication skills, crew coordination, or decision making."[65] Today's Line-Oriented Flight Training (LOFT) presents pilots and crews with complex, simulated problems that demand precisely these talents. LOFT also provides the opportunity to experience, in advance, such rare but important events as equipment failures. The result is a compression of actual experience and vastly accelerated learning.

Simulations must be as realistic as possible. If participants view them as a game or can easily anticipate outcomes, the lessons are unlikely to stick. Some element of surprise is usually essential. Typically, it takes one of two forms: an expected success fails to materialize or a sudden, emotional identification occurs. Unexpected failures lead to reflection and new approaches; emotional reactions produce deeply etched imprints on our minds.[66] BARNGA, an exercise designed to show the difficulties of cross-cultural communication, is representative. Groups sit at different tables and learn to play a simple card game. They believe that they are all playing the same game. But without their knowledge, each table has been given slightly different rules. After five minutes, participants are instructed to play silently and resolve any disagreements with gestures and hand signals. Then, two members of each group rotate to another table. Again, silence is enforced. Problems soon arise because participants are in fact playing by different rules. Newcomers to the table fail to relate to established players. Neither's moves make sense to the other. Yet because of the limits on communication, the resulting disagreements can seldom be resolved. During debriefing, the real-world parallels quickly become clear: people in different cultures work under different, often unspoken rules. Because participants have experienced the associated disagreements, this lesson is understood at a visceral rather than an academic level. As one participant observed: "The anger and confusion that BARNGA produces in 10 minutes is worth 10 hours of lecture from an anthropologist."[67]

Verisimilitude and fidelity are equally important to successful simulations. Role plays, for example, are often used to teach employees how to handle performance appraisals, negotiations, and other stressful situations.[68] Most exercises use interpersonal conflict and easily recognized characters to create involvement and identification. Bad Mouth Betty, Hysterical Harold, and other "customers from hell" are featured in the role plays used by Target Stores to teach new salesclerks the basics of customer service.[69] Here, the primary risks are poor casting and unconvincing acting. Without truly believable characters, participants will play along, but there will be little deep learning. Diamond Technology Partners, a strategy and technology consulting firm, found a creative solution. It asked a retired CEO, rather than an employee, to be the client in a simulated reengineering assignment. He played his part to perfection. When a trainee criticized his company's strategy and called him incompetent, he fired the team on the spot, even though the exercise was only partially completed. His decision, while not in the script, was perfectly in character. It also provided participants with a vivid, unforgettable lesson.[70]

Management games are even truer to life. They focus on competitive interactions, with outcomes that are difficult to predict in advance. Teams develop strategies, commit resources, and struggle for advantage as events unfold in real time. Because most games are built around a complete business or industry model, they are usually more comprehensive than simple exercises.[71] Polaroid's Graphic Imaging (PGI) division drew valuable lessons from a game that had participants competing to pitch their company's products at a fictitious industry trade show. Several teams were assigned the roles of competitors such as Kodak and Fuji, one played PGI, and another, the Wild Ducks, was instructed to come up with an unexpected technology that might blindside the market. All teams drew from the same two-hundred-page preparation book, which was filled with market data and competitive intelligence, including complete descriptions of competitors and their products. Teams then made presentations to a panel of judges, primarily peers but with a few real customers sprinkled in. The results were a much deeper understanding of the market and several quick changes in product positioning.[72]

## Program Design

These arguments suggest that well-chosen problems, whether real or simulated, share several characteristics, including complexity, scope, and unexpected surprises (see Table 4-2). Effective experiential programs share other traits as well. Concepts and tools are introduced only when needed. They are tightly coupled to problems, delivered "just-in-time" rather than days or weeks in advance. Most managers, after all, when faced with a new approach, will use it or lose it. The best tools are therefore accessible and easy to apply; they map neatly onto the task at hand. GE learned this lesson early in its Work-Out program. After introducing complex techniques with little success, trainers developed the RAMMPP Matrix. Named for the most common sources of unnecessary work—reports, approvals, meetings, measures, policies, and practices—it was immediately and enthusiastically embraced by employees, who saw it as a mirror of their own experiences. The result was quick acceptance and a steady stream of productivity improvements.[73]

Time is another ingredient in successful experiential programs. Skill builds slowly, and alternating periods of teaching, discussion, application, and reflection are usually needed for cementing critical lessons. Inaction is an obvious concern, but it can be overcome with the proper incentives. GTE's Quality: The Competitive Edge program was offered to teams of business-unit presidents and the managers reporting to them. Each president was allowed to bring as many people as desired, with no limits on the composition or size of teams. After assembling for the three-day

## TABLE 4-2
### PROBLEMS THAT STIMULATE LEARNING

1. They are significant (the issues matter to people in the organization).
2. They are complex (the solution is not obvious).
3. They are multifunctional (participants must work across boundaries).
4. They involve difficult people issues (the problems are organizational as well as technical).
5. They are action-oriented (the goal is to do something, not simply analyze a situation).
6. They are ill-structured (participants must frame and define problems as well as solve them).
7. They involve surprises (neither the data nor the results are completely predictable).

course, participants received a notebook of materials, together with a personalized covering letter from the sector head who oversaw their unit. The letter came as something of a shock: it explained that the team was expected to deliver a complete quality plan, based on the course concepts, within sixty days. Motivation was no longer an issue; now the problem was execution. Two-to-three-hour discussion periods were spread throughout the program so that teams could internalize lessons and begin working on their plans. Work continued when they returned to their units, and all plans were soon submitted to the relevant sector heads for evaluation. They were then reviewed, revised, and implemented with considerable success.

As this example suggests, senior managers are an essential part of experiential learning programs. They wear many hats. As sponsors, they bestow attention, resources, and rewards, keeping learning high on the agenda. As evaluators and clients, they help select projects and judge proposals, offering feedback and advice to participants. As role models, they provide examples to emulate, allowing others to benefit from their personal experiences. The action-learning programs at GE and GTE illustrate the first two roles; the China Accelerated Management Program (CAMP) at Motorola illustrates the third. CAMP was designed to rapidly develop local Chinese management talent and includes a six-week assignment in which participants live in another part of Asia and "shadow" a higher-level manager in order to gain experience.[74] Such senior management involvement is often critical to program success. At Motorola, training in quality tools and process skills had a negative return when there was no management support. But when the same training was actively reinforced by senior managers through sponsorship, evaluation, and conscious modeling, every dollar invested produced a $33 return.[75]

Teams also play a pivotal role in the learning process. They provide opportunities for pooling complementary skills, exploring new frameworks, and sharing tacit, experiential knowledge. Depending on the project, teams take one of three forms. *Natural teams,* like those at Xerox and GTE, already exist; typically, they consist of a boss and his or her direct reports, or a group of functional experts who work together frequently. Their primary advantage is the ease with which projects can be transported back to the workplace; their primary disadvantage is the persistence of existing stereotypes and roles.

*Peer teams,* like those at Motorola and GE, consist of individuals at roughly the same level who have been assembled, on a one-time basis, for a particular program. Normally, they lack any previous affiliation. The primary advantage of peer teams is freedom of thought and action; the primary disadvantage is the difficulty participants often have reforming their home organizations. The problem is particularly acute in traditional action-learning projects, which meet regularly in "sets," small groups of four to eight led by a facilitator.[76] Each individual works on a separate project that continues for months, and the group's role is to provide counseling, support, and room for reflection. The focus is on personal growth rather than new factual knowledge, and participants are often deeply changed by the experience. Their organizations, however, have seldom moved as far. Reentry is invariably a difficult process.

Alternatively, *diagonal-slice teams* consist of a cross-section of individuals drawn from a single organization. As the name implies, trainers form these teams by taking a deep, diagonal cut across levels and functions. Their primary advantage is the presence of a wide range of skills and perspectives; their primary disadvantages are a lack of shared experience and occasional difficulties overcoming hierarchical and functional barriers.

Experiential programs, then, involve a multitude of choices. Problems must be chosen with care; sessions must include a mix of concepts, applications, and pauses for reflection; incentives must encourage action;

senior managers must be assigned appropriate roles; and teams must contain the right set of participants. The process is time-consuming, but the payoff is worth the price. Experience is a wise teacher, with lessons that are often best discovered by combining learning with doing.

## GE'S CHANGE ACCELERATION PROCESS: MAKING CHANGE STICK

One of the most effective experiential learning programs is GE's Change Acceleration Process (CAP), taught at Crotonville, the company's education and training center.[77] Crotonville was founded in 1956 by Ralph Cordiner, the CEO, to develop a cadre of general managers to support GE's shift to decentralized business units. Initially, a single comprehensive advanced management program was offered. Later, Crotonville was used by subsequent CEOs to introduce a broad range of concepts and tools: strategic planning, which GE pioneered, as well as improved cash management and advanced accounting methods. Programs bore a striking resemblance to those at leading business schools. The goals were virtually identical—to convey the latest knowledge to up-and-coming managers—and most courses were straightforward and conventional, a combination of lectures, case studies, and in-depth technical discussions.

All this changed in 1981 when Jack Welch became CEO. Welch had a radically new vision of the company and saw Crotonville as one of his primary levers for change. GE, he believed, was slow, stodgy, and plagued by bad habits: "parochialism, turf battles, status, 'functionalitis,' and, most important, the biggest sin of a bureaucracy, the focus on itself and its inner workings."[78] Managers and employees were separated by a vast gulf; teamwork was poor to nonexistent; and applied problem-solving skills were lacking. Welch therefore gave Crotonville a new mandate: to open up dialogue, instill corporate values, and stimulate cultural change. As Steve Kerr, vice president of corporate leadership development and current head of Crotonville, observed, learning was redefined as "a change in behavior. If people don't act differently, we feel that

we've wasted the shareholder's money. So it was logical to connect learning and doing."

The resulting courses fall into three distinct categories. Management development programs, geared to critical career transitions such as
the shift into first-line management, business-unit leadership, and control of a global business, are offered on a regular schedule to help
managers gain the skills required for their new responsibilities. Focused
workshops, aimed at companywide initiatives such as cycle-time reduc-
tion and quality management, are offered on an ad hoc basis to introduce managers to best practices both within and outside GE. Broad-
based improvement programs, designed to produce fundamental
changes in work practices and behaviors, are offered continuously to
ensure that significant cultural changes occur simultaneously in all parts
of the organization. Work-Out, described in chapter 1, was Crotonville's
first large-scale improvement program; CAP was its successor.[79]

CAP grew from Welch's realization that the future was inherently
uncertain—and was likely to stay that way. Surprises were inevitable,
and it was impossible to anticipate upcoming events. But it was possible
to manage the change process more effectively. What was needed was a
set of concepts, tools, and techniques for making rapid adjustments and
adaptations—in Kerr's terms, "a generalized coping mechanism." Welch
assigned the task to four well-known consultants, asking them to review
the literature and develop a state-of-the-art model. Kerr, who was one of
the four, recalled:

> We studied and studied and studied and brought forth a mouse—a
> very pedestrian model of change. It was the old unfreezing, chang-
> ing, refreezing. Lewin had it in the 1940s, Schein had it in the
> 1970s, and Beckhardt had it in the 1980s. We were kind of embar-
> rassed.
>
> But this was a case where the client made the consultants feel
> good. Welch said to us: "The trouble with you academics is that
> you value creativity. If you've done something once, you don't like
> to do the same thing again. We don't have that hang up. I have only
> two questions for you: Is what you found true?" We said yeah. "And

are my people doing it now?" We said not consistently. So he said: "Stop apologizing and start teaching."

The resulting program, with its seven-step model of change, was launched in 1992. To ensure acceptance, Welch paid for all of the initial training; in return, he insisted that the top managers at GE, including every company president, corporate officer, and senior executive, commit to seven days of classes spread over a ninety-day period. Attendance was mandatory. A year later, nearly 750 managers had participated, and the program was firmly established.

All participants come to CAP in teams, and each team brings a problem of its own to solve. At Welch's insistence, the problems are "need to do, not nice to do"; they are competitive necessities. At GE Supply, the task was rolling out a quality improvement program to 120 geographically dispersed sites; at GE Plastics Japan, the task was turning around a business that had been unprofitable for five straight years; at GE Aircraft Engines, the task was reducing the cycle time from engine order to remittance; and at GE Lighting, the task was integrating separate technology groups into a single, global organization. Typically, problems are selected by business-unit presidents or leaders; if corporate services are involved, they are selected by department or function heads. As a further check on the process, in the early days Welch personally received lists of all current projects. This had the great advantage of ensuring that problems were of sufficient scale to warrant sustained commitment and attention. According to Jacquie Vierling, manager of Work-Out, Best Practices, and Change Acceleration:

People were always complaining, "I don't have time to go away to Crotonville and learn." So we said, "If it's a strategic issue and you have to do it anyway, then coming to Crotonville is not time away from your work. It's time away to work on your work."

Participants seem to agree. As one member of the GE Supply team put it:

The nice thing about CAP is that it's relevant. You can relate the
theory to something that's really practical, that's actually real. It has
a hell of a lot more meaning. We were working on our project in a
very structured fashion, but it didn't feel as though we were in a
class.

Projects must meet several tests. They must involve cultural and
organizational dilemmas, must require work beyond the few days devoted to CAP classes, and must have a significant payoff for both the
business and the corporation as a whole. The first requirement ensures
that CAP's tools and techniques are relevant and helpful, since they are
designed to tackle people problems rather than technical or financial
barriers to change. The second requirement ensures that participants do
not see the course as a bounded, one-time event, demanding only a few
days of class time, but as a learning experience that continues well
beyond Crotonville. It also highlights the program's twin goals: solving a
pressing problem and learning broader, more generic change management skills. The third requirement ensures that CAP's limited training
slots are allocated in ways that are likely to provide the greatest value.
Because classes are time consuming and expensive, projects must have
an acceptable return if the company's investment is to be recouped.

Each project is officially sponsored by a senior manager, who provides oversight and support. Sponsors must have the authority to act on
the recommendations of CAP teams, as well as overcome the political
barriers that so often derail change projects. As Kerr observed, these
roles are crucial to success:

We have had cases where the project was important, the team was
bright, and the content of the program was good, but all we did was
frustrate participants because they didn't have the high level entrée
and air cover that were needed to make the project work.

Sponsors serve several other important functions as well. They select
program participants, set goals and expectations, receive and review
progress reports, and hold groups accountable for meeting milestones
and results.

Because success normally requires a concerted, collective effort, CAP training is offered only to teams. Otherwise, critical mass is lacking, and little is accomplished. According to Kerr:

> The golden rule of organizational development is, "Never send a changed person back to an unchanged environment." Yet 99% of training breaks that rule. People go off to Harvard or Stanford or Michigan or Crotonville in ones and twos, and they're not united in any way. Even if they get excited, they come back to a full desk and a boss who doesn't understand their passion. Most of the time, no learning occurs, since we define learning as a change in behavior. But when people come in teams with a "need-to-do" project, it's much more successful.

Typically, teams consist of eight to twelve people, who represent a diagonal slice of the organization. But there is considerable flexibility, depending on the project and the sponsor's preferences. Peer teams, for example, are used when necessary, as they were on a project that assembled a large number of the company's environmental health and safety officers to tackle a common policy challenge. In all cases, selection is guided by the same two criteria: team members must have credibility within their organizations and must represent a variety of critical stakeholders. Both are considered essential because they increase the odds of effective implementation. Membership is also carefully tailored to the problem at hand. Successful CAP teams have included, when necessary, union members and factory workers as well as vice presidents. At GE Plastics Japan, where unquestioning acceptance of the status quo had produced a string of financial losses, participants were selected in large part for their independence and willingness to consider radically new directions.

All teams have their own coaches. Most have been through special training or have been involved in earlier projects as participants. Coaches are educators and facilitators, process experts who are knowledgeable about change and skilled in applying CAP concepts and tools. Their primary responsibility is to maintain the order and discipline of the change process. Because teams work under intense pressure, coaches also arbitrate disagreements and ensure that destructive conflict is avoided. Surprisingly, most have limited knowledge of the problem at hand. Teams are assumed to possess all necessary content knowledge; they own the problem and remain responsible for devising solutions.

Initially, all coaches were provided by Crotonville; today, they come from the divisions. There are now dozens in every GE business, working with teams before, during, and after CAP classes. Coaches are constantly present—at the home site, as teams frame their projects; at Crotonville, as teams learn and then apply unfamiliar concepts; and again at the home site, as teams carry their work to completion. They provide seamlessness and continuity, linking the various stages of the learning process. The best coaches are also objective and open-minded; they are able to serve as disinterested guides rather than impassioned advocates. According to Vierling:

> If the coach feels that he or she has the answer or wants to drive the team in a certain direction, they will not be successful. You need someone who doesn't have a vested interest in the project. In fact, we've had coaches say: "Take me off this team because I know what I want. I can't be objective. I can't pull the best ideas out of the team because I have my own ideas."

All CAP courses are organized around a common framework and set of tools. The framework is straightforward and easy to apply. It divides the change process into seven steps: leading change, creating a shared need, shaping a vision, mobilizing commitment, making change last, monitoring progress, and changing systems and structures (see Table 4-3). As Kerr observed, this framework has several appealing features. It is simple, "not rocket science but a parsimonious list that people can get their arms around." It is concrete, not "esoteric and metaphysical but puzzles and structural questions that people can deal with." It is credible, "probably 90% common sense." And it is complete, a comprehensive series of steps that managers use as a "pilot's checklist."

The pilot's checklist analogy came originally from Welch; it is now used in all CAP sessions. Checklists are employed by even the most

## TABLE 4-3
### THE CHANGE ACCELERATION PROCESS (CAP)

1. Leading Change
   Having a leader who owns and champions the change and commits his or her personal time and attention

2. Creating a Shared Need
   Ensuring that employees throughout the organization understand the reason for change

3. Shaping a Vision
   Ensuring that employees see the desired outcome of change in concrete behavioral terms

4. Mobilizing Commitment
   Understanding the interests of diverse stakeholders, identifying key constituents, and building a coalition of supporters

5. Making Change Last
   Taking the initial steps to get change started and developing longer-term plans to ensure that change persists

6. Monitoring Progress
   Creating and installing metrics to assess the success of change, including milestones and benchmarks to chart progress along the way

7. Changing Systems and Structures
   Altering staffing, training, appraisal, communication, and reward systems, as well as roles and reporting relationships, to ensure that they complement and reinforce change

experienced pilots. Yet they offer no new insights. Instead, they make existing knowledge more visible and accessible, ensuring that all essential steps are followed. Discipline, not discovery, is the goal of the checklist—just as with CAP, which teaches a familiar and widely recognized change process. According to Kerr: "It's basic stuff, but people don't do it every time. With CAP, they do it every time." Still, there are subtleties and refinements. For example, the process is not as linear as it first appears:

When we say these steps happen in sequence, there's a tendency for managers to respond, "Okay, I did number one. Let's go on to number two." They're great at starting stuff, but don't stay with it. They have the organizational equivalent of attention deficit disorder.

So to teach CAP, we use the metaphor of the circus act with the spinning plates. You start the first one. Then you start the second, then the third. By now, the first plate is wobbly, so you go back and spin it some more. In other words, you don't stop Shaping a Vision or Mobilizing Commitment to start Making Change Last. You have to keep them all going at once.

To help participants apply the framework, CAP includes a comprehensive set of tools and techniques. There are thirty-nine in all, although few teams use more than half a dozen. Most are staples of the change literature and have been culled from long-forgotten sources; a number are GE innovations. They are spread across the seven steps in the process and come in two varieties: tools for diagnosing an organization's readiness for change and tools for managing change more effectively.

Representative tools include the Calendar Test, the Elevator Speech, and Stakeholder Analysis. The Calendar Test, which is associated with the first step in the change process, Leading Change, is a simple audit of time spent. It teaches two powerful lessons: that leaders must invest time in their projects if they hope to succeed and that managers' stated priorities seldom match their actual commitments. Participants identify four to five important work or personal objectives and then review their calendars for the preceding thirty to sixty days to determine the percentage of time they actually devoted to these activities. The discrepancies are invariably stark—as one observer put it, "people are just weeping in the aisles because of the disconnect"—and team members then discuss how to ensure more efficient allocations as they move forward. To avoid slippage, many coaches repeat the test at regular intervals as the change process unfolds.

The Elevator Speech is associated with the third step in the process, Shaping a Vision. It is a response to an important dilemma facing all teams—how to communicate the essence of the desired change to colleagues back home but in a limited amount of time. Consider a typical scenario. A CAP team member has returned from training and has a

## FIGURE 4-2

### STAKEHOLDER ANALYSIS

| Names | −2<br>Strongly<br>Against | −1<br>Moderately<br>Against | 0<br>Neutral | +1<br>Moderately<br>Supportive | +2<br>Strongly<br>Supportive |
|---|---|---|---|---|---|
| Tony | | | X ———————— | | ➤ O |
| Sally | | X ———— ➤ O | | | |
| Harry | | | | X ———— ➤ O | |
| Joan | X ———————— | | | ➤ O | |

X = current position
O = required position

chance meeting with a senior vice president in an empty elevator. As the doors close, she turns and says: "I understand that you've just come back from Crotonville. What happened?" Her office is on the sixth floor, so the elevator ride will last less than ninety seconds. How should the team member respond? Participants work to craft a concise, compelling response during CAP classes; before departing, they rehearse until they have committed it to memory. Most speeches use the same four-part design: "Here's what our project is about . . . ; here's why it's important to do . . . ; here's what success will look like . . . ; and here's what we need from you. . . ." The result is a common, consistent message that is continually replayed by all members of the CAP team.

Stakeholder Analysis is helpful for assessing an organization's political landscape. It is used in the fourth step of the process, Mobilizing Commitment, and positions individuals according to their likely reactions to the proposed change. The resulting diagram (see Figure 4-2) has obvious implications for action. Kerr described the process:

We start by asking people, "For your change to be successful, who has to be involved?" They put down names. "There's Tony, there's Sally, there's Harry, there's Joan." Then we ask, "Where are they now? From minus two, 'strongly against,' to 'neutral,' which is zero, to plus two, 'strongly supportive.'" Then we say, "Where do they have to be?" Some people have to be positive. Some just have to be neutral. Then we say, "What are the strategies for getting people to where they have to be? Who interacts with whom? Who do you have who's positive and can affect so-and-so?" And they build action plans to communicate and market their ideas to these people.

Today, the entire CAP course, including the framework and all associated tools, is taught in an intensive, three-day session. Seven to ten teams, drawn from diverse GE businesses, are invited to attend. By the time they arrive at Crotonville, they have already done substantial work, identifying the problem to be solved, meeting with their sponsor and their coach to clarify expectations and develop working relationships, and profiling their business's past change efforts to see where they have been strong or weak. The latter is an especially important step. Teams not only become acquainted with the basic CAP model but often discover that they have systematic biases: they have omitted the same stages in the process in several failed projects. They therefore arrive at Crotonville with considerable motivation to improve. GE Supply, for example, found that a number of past change efforts had failed because headquarters staff had dictated new approaches to the field, rather than mobilizing the commitment of line managers. By the time they came to Crotonville, team members knew exactly where they needed help.

A typical day in the program begins with a two-hour "content burst" that introduces one or two steps in the CAP framework. All teams attend these large sessions. Formats are diverse and include lectures, discussions, sharing of best practices, and "buzz sessions" in which teams tackle a brief exercise and then share their conclusions with others. All sessions are "coproduced." Rather than rigidly following a uniform syllabus, courses vary according to the needs of participants. If, for example, groups feel that they need little help shaping a vision, instructors will move quickly to another, more demanding step in the process.

Teams then disperse to separate breakout rooms, where, with the assistance of coaches, they spend the rest of the day working on their projects. New concepts and tools are applied immediately; they do not remain as abstract concepts but are quickly married to the problem at hand. Content and breakout sessions continue to alternate as the course unfolds, creating a comfortable rhythm. According to one participant: "It was a little bit of learning, a little bit of doing, a little more learning, and a little more doing, until the whole model came out." Eventually, each team develops an action plan to guide its activities back home. As Vierling observed, this is a crucial step, for it provides continuity and momentum:

> To ensure that the project doesn't stop when they leave Crotonville, we ask teams to identify a set of action steps that they are going to follow, with names and dates. Some projects will take one or two years, and it's important to drive home the fact that they have to keep moving forward. At every meeting they need to ask: When do we get together next? What do we have to do before we meet? Who is responsible, and what are the key deliverables and dates? We want them to start developing these habits while they're at Crotonville.

Plans are often extraordinarily detailed. GE Supply, for example, identified nearly one hundred separate actions that had to be taken by team members in the eight weeks following training. The result, one participant recalled, was "a seamless and logical transition from the workshop to the workplace." The project continued with hardly a pause, and needed changes were introduced within a few months.

CAP is obviously thoughtfully and carefully designed. It represents the very best of experiential learning, a blend of practical problems, motivated participants, and easy-to-apply concepts and tools (see Table 4-4). But does it impact the bottom line? The answer, in most cases, is a resounding yes. At GE Supply, the payoff was $16 million in additional sales, due, in large part, to a rise in "promises kept" from 65 to 95 percent. At GE Plastics Japan, the turnaround was even more dramatic. From 1989 to 1993, there were was nothing but red ink; in 1993 alone, the loss was $26 million. Managers signed up for CAP training as a last resort, after a new president announced that the alternative was shutting the business down. Classes were held in 1994; by the end of the year,

---

### TABLE 4-4
#### EXPERIENTIAL LEARNING: LESSONS FROM CAP

---

*1. Link learning to practical problems.*

- Have business unit presidents or functional leaders select problems.
- Focus on problems that are strategically important and highly visible.
- Find problems that cannot be solved by current methods.
- Insist on projects that cannot be completed during training sessions and require further work at the home site.

*2. Secure high-level sponsorship.*

- Only accept sponsors with the power to act on recommendations.
- Require sponsors to select participants and provide ongoing oversight and support.

*3. Send participants in teams.*

- Select teams (natural, peer, or diagonal-slice) that best fit the problem at hand.
- Choose eight to twelve members for their knowledge, skills, credibility, and representativeness.
- Teach multiple teams simultaneously.

*4. Assign coaches.*

- Select coaches based on their process knowledge and facilitation skills and train them in advance.
- Choose coaches who are open-minded and do not have a point of view about the problem at hand.
- Assign coaches before training begins so that they can work with teams in advance of classes to scope out the problem and identify organizational challenges.
- Have coaches attend classes, facilitate discussions, and then return to their home sites to continue working with teams.

*5. Alternate classroom work with applications.*

- Schedule regular breakout sessions so that teams can apply lessons "just in time."
- Teach simple, generic approaches that can be tailored to individual problems.
- Support concepts and frameworks with easy-to-apply tools and techniques.
- Require fully developed action plans before teams leave training classes.

---

the business was breaking even. In 1995 net income was $18 million, and the company was on solid footing for the first time.

Programs like CAP represent the most active form of learning from experience. At times, these lessons arrive unconsciously as unintended by-products of repetitive activities. Learning and experience curves capture this effect. On other occasions, conscious reflection is involved, but only after the fact. Then, special forums or processes like AARs are needed to tease out important lessons. Experiential programs go a step further by actively coupling opportunities to learn with current, unfolding events. But in all three cases, learning deepens with increased familiarity, and skills improve with time. The old proverb is right after all. Practice does indeed make perfect.

# 5

## Experimentation

Most approaches to learning accept the world as given. They begin with data that already exist—in the field, in the minds of customers, in accumulated experience—and then draw inferences and conclusions. The resulting lessons are often invaluable, as the previous two chapters have shown. But they are limited in an important respect. Because critical variables are taken at face value, with their ranges defined by natural variation, managers seldom consider the full array of alternatives or possible explanations. This is rarely a problem when challenges are conventional or a large knowledge base exists. But when unfamiliar concepts or unproven theories are involved, the desired data may first have to be produced. For real innovation to occur, active approaches to learning are essential. As Charles Kettering, the inventor of the copper-cooled engine, put it: "I have never heard of anyone stumbling on something sitting down."[1]

Usually, this requires some form of experimentation. The word has several meanings:

*the action of trying anything, or putting it to proof . . . a tentative*
*procedure; a method, system of things, or course of action, adopted in*
*uncertainty . . . an action or operation undertaken to discover some-*
*thing unknown.*[2]

All of these definitions argue for a "try-it-and-see" approach. First, conditions are modified or changes are introduced; then, the results are observed and new conclusions are drawn. Often, multiple trials are required
to ensure success.

Scientists and engineers have long used this process to aid their
work. But it is far less common among managers. Experimentation is
surprisingly rare in most corporate settings—the obvious exceptions are
in R&D labs and marketing research departments—largely because they
require a change in mind-set and philosophy. For experiments to be
effective, the focus must shift from justification and commitment (where
the primary goal is making the case for one's preferred position) to skepticism and doubt (where the goal is keeping an open mind when faced with
competing views).[3] Managers must regard knowledge as provisional, and
conclusions as tentative. Otherwise, they will not subject prevailing views
to testing, and experiments will exist in name only.

Managers, in fact, routinely misuse the term, applying it in a blanket
fashion to any changes they have recently introduced.[4] But not all
changes are experiments. Only those activities carefully and consciously
designed to generate knowledge—normally through systematic trials and
comparisons—qualify. For example, eliminating a layer of the organization for effi- ciency reasons is not an experiment. But testing new reporting relationships for possible rollout to other sites usually is. Experiments, it should be clear, are as much matters of intent as matters of
proper design.

Inevitably, this approach involves a certain element of risk, since
conditions are changed with no assurance of a positive outcome. Failure
is always a possibility. Why, then, should managers experiment? Because
in certain circumstances, other approaches to learning offer little help.
They are simply incapable of generating the necessary data. When situations are novel, when experts disagree, or when multiple, difficult-to-
disentangle alternatives exist, experimentation is often the only option.[5]
Experience provides little guidance when "the state of knowledge is not
well understood and must be continuously discovered."[6] Intelligence

gathering normally produces ambiguous results when recognized experts disagree. And neither experience nor intelligence-gathering provides enough discriminating power when plausible alternatives coexist. In such settings, carefully constructed experiments are often the only way of distinguishing truth from fiction.

Unfortunately, it is easy to confuse experimentation with its close cousin observation. The latter is a largely passive act; it requires attentiveness and care but little change in the environment being studied. Astronomers and naturalists are the classic observers; they watch and wait as nature runs its course. Experimentation is a more intrusive activity; it involves the deliberate manipulation of conditions, often in a controlled environment. Chemists and physicists are devoted experimenters precisely because they can disentangle critical relationships only by subtly altering the status quo.

These same distinctions apply to business. Here, too, the "observer stands outside the course of events . . . and waits for nature to induce . . . changes . . . [while the] experimenter actively intervenes."[7] Both approaches are effective ways of gathering information but yield different insights. To learn more about customers, a department store manager might rely on observation, visiting competing stores in the hopes of picking up useful tips. Much would be learned about appealing floor layouts and customers' buying habits but little about unconventional displays or pricing practices not already in use. Alternatively, the manager might run a series of experiments, establishing pilot sites to explore novel selling approaches. Unfamiliar techniques could be tried and tweaked in real time. Banc One used this approach when it first developed Personal Investment Centers to package and cross-sell diverse financial services, while British Petroleum did the same with the first integrated food-and-fuel convenience sites it developed with Safeway.[8] In each case, a small number of pilot sites were created to test the original concept. Managers made changes as needed and collected additional data until the concept was deemed acceptable. Only then did full-scale rollout begin.

Corvel
w/ Voip — Accts Payable

## TYPES OF EXPERIMENTS

Experiments, of course, come in many varieties.[9] Two are of primary interest to managers: exploratory experiments and hypothesis-testing experiments. The former are designed for discovery, "to see what would happen if." Scientists use them to create a clearer map of an unknown territory, usually through determined but open-ended search. Researchers try a new technique or a new approach, then review results, and repeat the process with subtle variations. Sometimes, these steps are driven by preconceived ideas, but more often there is a large element of serendipity.

Such activity is hardly confined to scientists. Exploration is woven into the fabric of everyday life. It "is much of what an infant does when he explores the world around him, what an artist does when he juxtaposes colors to see what effect they make, and what a newcomer does when he wanders around a strange neighborhood."[10] The goal is to see what is out there, to collect impressions and develop a detailed picture of the surrounding world. These practices obviously extend to management. Most business examples involve a carefully constructed demonstration or test: an innovative product, process, or organization that stretches the boundaries of current practice and probes for reactions. GM created Saturn, a new division, to explore the benefits and risks of more cooperative labor relations, while Warner Cable and American Express established QUBE, a decade-long experiment in Columbus, Ohio, to explore customers' reactions to interactive television. Banc One and British Petroleum developed their pilot sites for similar reasons.

Hypothesis-testing experiments have different goals. They are designed to discriminate among alternative explanations and confirm (or discount) prevailing views. Here, proof is the desired end, not discovery. Two or more competing interpretations coexist; which one better fits the facts? Customers, for example, have stopped purchasing a popular product; is it because prices are too high, a competitor's offerings are superior, or a new advertising campaign is ineffective? A mixing process suddenly experiences a surge in defects; is it because of a bad batch of raw materials, inexperienced operators, or improper machine settings? Observation and exploration seldom provide complete answers; they normally produce descriptions and summary statistics that are consistent with diverse explanations.[11] Instead, a process of systematic elimination is usually required. Researchers alter one or more factors, while holding others constant; they record the results and rule out some explanations. The process is then repeated until only one possibility remains.[12]

Such efforts are designed to produce deep understanding, not superficial knowledge. At its simplest, the distinction is between knowing how things are done and knowing why they occur.[13] Knowing how is partial knowledge; it is rooted in norms of behavior, standards of practice, and settings of equipment. Knowing why is more fundamental; it captures underlying cause-and-effect relationships and accommodates exceptions, adaptations, and unforeseen events. The ability to control temperatures and pressures to align grains of silicon and form silicon steel is an example of knowing how; understanding the chemical and physical process that produces the alignment is knowing why.

Further refinements are possible. Scholars, in fact, have suggested that production and operating knowledge can be classified systematically into eight levels or stages of understanding (see Table 5-1).[14] At the lowest levels of knowledge, little is known other than the characteristics of a good product. Production remains an art, and there are few clearly articulated standards or rules. An example would be the construction of Stradivarius violins. Experts agree that they produce vastly superior sound, but no one can specify precisely how they were made because skilled artisans were involved. At intermediate levels of knowledge, understanding deepens, resulting in tighter specification and control. Recipes are developed, and well-defined processes ensure repeatable performance. An example would be a set of instructions for extruding plastic that includes both a complete list of raw materials and detailed machine settings. Finally, at the highest levels of manufacturing knowledge, all aspects of production are known and understood. All materials and processing variations are articulated and accounted for, with rules and procedures for every contingency. Here, an example would be a "lights out," fully automated factory that operates for many hours without any human intervention.

In this context, hypothesis-testing experiments foster learning by moving organizations up the hierarchy from lower to higher stages of knowledge. They lead to a more refined understanding of causal relationships, a more expansive list of critical variables, and a better appreciation of potential difficulties. Their cumulative impact can be enormous. In a few years, with limited capital investment but careful and systematic hypothesis testing, semiconductor companies are usually able to double their yields on new chip fabrication lines from below 40 percent to above 80 percent.[15]

## TABLE 5-1

### STAGES OF KNOWLEDGE

1. Recognizing prototypes (ability to determine what is a good product or service).

2. Recognizing attributes within prototypes (ability to define some conditions under which the process gives good output).

3. Discriminating among attributes (ability to distinguish those attributes that are important from those that are not).

4. Measuring attributes (ability to measure some key attributes using qualitative, quantitative, or relative metrics).

5. Controlling attributes locally (ability to achieve repeatable performance).

6. Recognizing and discriminating among contingencies (ability to mechanize process and monitor it manually).

7. Controlling contingencies (ability to automate the process).

8. Understanding procedures and controlling contingencies (ability to understand completely all aspects of the process).

Source: Adapted with permission from Ramchandran Jaikumar and Roger Bohn, "The Development of Intelligent Systems for Industrial Use: A Conceptual Framework," in Richard S. Rosenbloom, ed., Research on Technological Innovation, Management, and Policy, vol. 3 (Greenwich, CT: JAI Press, 1986), pp. 182–188.

## EXPLORATION

Exploration has long been associated with the frontier. It conveys a sense of promise and opportunity that, even today, retains a powerful hold on our collective imaginations.[16] The frontier marks the boundary between the civilized world and the wilderness that lies beyond it: a vast, largely unpopulated region filled with unknowns. Originally, this meant large expanses of open, unsettled land; today, it applies equally well to untapped markets, untested technologies, and untried forms of organization. In all of these settings, exploration is essential to success. Scouting and reconnaissance are critical activities because so little is known about the territory ahead. The landscape is largely uncharted, with few signposts or maps. The inhabitants are unlikely to be familiar, and much that is encountered will be new. Agendas will be difficult to frame because few, clear-cut categories exist. As historians have observed, these challenges have long plagued pioneers: "[They] were faced with a succession of unique problems where past precedents did not apply; only by devising new techniques and gadgets were they able to exploit the riches about them fully. So they were quick to experiment and scornful of traditional practice."[17]

In formal terms, frontier environments are characterized by ambiguity and great uncertainty, with problems that are poorly structured.[18] Most essential information is lacking. Potential solutions are therefore difficult to identify, and the relationship between means and ends is unclear. An airline wants to shift to electronic ticketing; how should it design the supporting processes? A retailer wants to offer its products over the Internet; how should it market the site? A manufacturer wants to introduce state-of-the-art machine tools; how should it configure the factory? These are all challenges that lack clear answers or even easy-to-define options. According to scholars: "This is not the decision making under *uncertainty* of the textbook, where alternatives are given even if their consequences are not, but decision making under *ambiguity*, where almost nothing is given or easily determined."[19]

When ambiguity is high, the usual sources of knowledge provide limited insight. Market research, in particular, is often incomplete and misleading because consumers lack a firm basis for describing their preferences or predicting future behavior. This is especially true for radical, discontinuous innovations: products, such as cellular telephones, xerography, and optical fibers, that break completely with established offerings and create wholly new markets. The usual tools of marketing research assume that "the target market is known, the product form is fairly well known, and the timing is understood." A recent study of discontinuous innovations found that none of these assumptions was met.[20] The result, not surprisingly, was a series of misinterpretations, misjudgments, and misunderstandings.

In the mid-1970s, for example, cellular telephones were in the early stages of development. It would be nearly ten years before the first fully licensed commercial systems were sold. To explore this market, Motorola sent a mail survey to several hundred thousand potential users. It then combined the survey results with evidence from focus groups and census data, applied sophisticated methods of conjoint analysis, and ranked the leading market segments. The thirty-first most important group was salespeople. Yet they soon proved to be devoted users, who led the adoption process and purchased the product in large numbers. Corning was similarly misled in the late 1960s when it interviewed current customers about the potential of optical fibers. Both AT&T and ITT, the dominant players in the market, firmly rejected the idea, arguing that it was unnecessary and at least 30 to 40 years ahead of its time.[21]

The experiences of Motorola and Corning are hardly unique. Radically new products and technologies frequently befuddle experts, who fail to see their true potential. The combination of their own focused experiences and conventional sources of information lead to serious errors. These problems have recurred throughout history and have involved some of the best minds of the time, as the following examples suggest:

- "Drill for oil? You mean drill into the ground to try and find oil? You're crazy." Drillers when asked by Edwin L. Drake to enlist in his project to drill for oil, 1859.

- "The telephone has too many shortcomings to be seriously considered as a means of communication. The device is inherently of no value to us." Western Union, internal memo, 1876.

- "The phonograph . . . is not of any commercial value." Thomas Alva Edison, inventor of the phonograph, 1880.

- "Who the hell wants to hear actors talk?" H. M. Warner, Warner Brothers, 1927.

- "I think there is a world market for about five computers." Thomas J. Watson, chairman of IBM, 1943.

- "There is no reason anyone would want a computer in their home." Kenneth Olson, president, chairman, and founder of Digital Equipment Corporation, 1977.[22]

Given this sorry record, how should managers respond when faced with unfamiliar innovations? How can they collect the information they need for sound decision making, while avoiding the errors of their predecessors? The answer is exploration, or what scholars have termed the "probe-and-learn" process. When faced with novel technologies or markets, it is often the only reliable source of knowledge. Both Motorola and Corning used this approach to overcome the limitations of their early market research. GE did the same with CAT scanners, as did Searle with NutraSweet. In each case, "these companies developed their products by probing potential markets with early versions of the pro~~duct~~ ~~l~~earning from the probes, and probing again. . . . Probing and learning is an iterative process . . . a process of successive approximation . . . each time striving to take a step closer to a winning combination.[23]

Often, early versions of the product were considerably off base. In fact, "in all four cases, the initial experience was mostly if not entirely negative."[24] Motorola's first cellular telephones were far too heavy and bulky, while GE's first CAT scanners had poor resolution and slow scanning times. None of the early versions fully met the needs of established customers or had the features necessary to appeal to untapped markets. But they were still invaluable because they provided feedback under real-world conditions. Each succeeding iteration was a step in the right direction, ensuring that the next version was that much more likely to hit the mark.

## The Probe-and-Learn Process

This approach to exploration has four critical elements: a starting point, one or more feedback loops, a process for rapid redesign, and a stopping rule. The starting point must be "good enough." It need not be perfect but must generate enough interest among potential users to induce them to try the product or service and provide reactions. Once the first trial is underway, feedback loops are needed to collect information and funnel it to those who are capable of putting it to good use. A rapid redesign process is then required to ensure that useful feedback is immediately incorporated into the next iteration of the product or service. Finally, a stopping rule is needed to avoid endless fine-tuning and the fruitless pursuit of dead ends. Eventually, a decision has to be made. Either the innovation is ready for launch—despite any lingering imperfections—or managers must pull the plug because the project lacks promise.

The probe-and-learn process is not limited to product and service design. It is equally useful for exploring other uncharted domains. In fact, much entrepreneurial activity proceeds in this fashion, with new ventures being used to establish a toehold in unfamiliar domains. Once established, these ventures present managers, in the language of finance, with "real options" for proceeding further, which would not otherwise be available.[25] New markets, new technologies, new operating systems, and new organizational forms can all be pursued using this approach. Consider the following examples:

- Serengeti Eyewear, a maker of high-end sunglasses, has used "test launches" to explore the potential of new markets. Before entering Europe on a large scale, the company chose to sell for the first year in Finland only, a country somewhat outside the European mainstream but regarded as representative enough to provide cultural and institutional learnings. A relatively small number of retail outlets were involved in the hopes that competitors would fail to take notice. After a successful test launch, distribution was broadened to include other parts of the Continent.[26]

- Boeing used a similar process to evaluate the potential of composites, a new technology, for airframe manufacturing. Composites are formed by combining two or more complementary materials. They have the advantage of offering both great strength and light weight. But in the 1960s and 1970s their performance was still unproven. To begin, Boeing's engineers conducted a number of laboratory tests using large, composite panels; eventually, they found a promising material, a mixture of graphite and Kevlar. To explore its properties in the "real-world airline environment," the engineers then worked with a small number of airlines to conduct limited, in-service tests. Boeing fabricated structural parts, such as wing control surfaces or spoiler panels, using composites; had them installed on a plane then in production; and monitored the material's performance as the plane underwent normal use. These tests soon indicated a problem with water absorption in environments of high heat and humidity, such as Brazil. Further analysis suggested that adding a layer of fiberglass to the composite panels would solve the problem; engineers made the changes and continued monitoring to ensure that problems did not recur. When they did not, the decision was made to use composites to construct a variety of parts for the 767.[27]

- In 1986 Motorola formed Team Bandit to design and develop a highly automated assembly line. By employing robots, fault-tolerant computers, and a sophisticated material control system, the line was expected to produce customized versions of the new Bravo pager, in lot sizes of one, with exceptionally short cycle times and few if any defects. The project schedule was built around four prototype cycles; in each case, prototypes were to be assembled on the line, even if the computer system was not up and running. In the initial two cycles, the full line was not yet ready, so assembly was completed by hand. But the goal remained constant: to explore the fit between product and process and resolve difficulties as they emerged. The entire project took 18 months, and the automated line was introduced with minimal problems. Its performance quickly exceeded expectations, achieving the highest quality record in Motorola's history.[28]

- IDEO, a leading product design firm, has long had a culture that encourages experimentation. Brainstorming is widespread, and physical prototypes are constantly generated, distributed, reviewed, and revised. David Kelley, the CEO, recently extended this approach to structural change. In 1995 and 1996, he introduced a number of organizational innovations, including work teams and a smaller "company within the company." Kelley urged employees to view these arrangements the same way that they treated physical prototypes: as "temporary and reversible experiments" that could be refined and altered as needed.[29]

These examples suggest that the probe-and-learn process can be used to generate knowledge in a variety of settings. Its advantages should be obvious: immediacy, relevance, and the involvement of users under real-world conditions. The process also appears to be simple and straightforward. But it is easily misused. In particular, probe-and-learn techniques are poorly suited to settings that require continuous, error-free operation. It is difficult, for example, to imagine them being used to redesign air traffic control procedures or streamline the manufacturing process for pharmaceuticals.

It is equally important to recognize that probe and learn is not the same as unguided trial and error. The former requires careful planning and distinctive habits of mind; the latter is largely an ad hoc affair, with enormous inefficiency and findings that are often difficult to interpret. Perhaps the primary design skill in effective probe-and-learn processes is the ability to create prototypes that are simultaneously inexpensive and representative. A delicate balancing act is required. On the one hand, prototypes must be easy to modify, since repeated iterations are inevitable. This suggests the use of "quick-and-dirty" mock-ups, streamlined processes, inexpensive methods of construction, and low-cost materials such as cardboard and clay. On the other hand, prototypes must meet the test of fidelity. They must be close enough approximations of the final version of the product or process—matching it in form, fit, function, and features—that they provide insights into real-world performance and use.[30] Otherwise, experiments will be of little value, for generalizations will be impossible. Here, the pressures are in the opposite direction, suggesting the need for more inclusive designs, sophisticated processes, careful construction, and enduring materials such as metal and glass.

How can this dilemma be resolved? One approach is to rely on "incomplete" models that lack essential features but still capture enough of reality to provide useful data. Aircraft manufacturers have long used this approach in wind tunnel tests. Their prototypes have no interior design details (seats, aisles, or cockpit configurations) but are still valuable because those details are largely irrelevant when assessing aerodynamic properties such as wind resistance.[31] A second approach is to use computer simulation, creating digital prototypes that mimic the properties and performance of a proposed product or process. Automobile manufacturers have used this technique to explore the crashworthiness of new designs. Compared to physical models, digital prototypes offer equal fidelity at much lower cost. A typical computer "crash" costs less than $5,000; when the same crash involves a physical prototype, the cost is more than $300,000.[32] Computer simulations can also be easily and endlessly repeated, with minor modifications, allowing a wider range of options to be explored.

A third approach is to rely on intensive interactions with users to compensate for overly simple prototypes. This technique, which goes by the name of "participatory" or "cooperative" design, has deep roots in Scandinavia, where it was used successfully in the early 1980s to help Swedish trade unions shift from manual to computerized typesetting.[33] Because budgets were limited, real computers could not be purchased, and inexpensive prototypes were used to design the new process. Initially, typesetters interacted with Styrofoam and plywood mock-ups to map out the steps in page makeup. Later, they used slide projectors to project images that mimicked the way that text and pictures might appear on computer screens and then manipulated them to explore alternative compositions and formats.

Probe-and-learn processes must also be designed with repetition in mind. Managers must recognize that in ambiguous environments it is seldom possible—or even desirable—to "get it right the first time."[34] It is usually far too expensive and time-consuming to produce a perfect prototype. Instead, experiments should be conducted early and often. They should be as comprehensive and complete as possible, given the facts at hand. They should focus on interactions at the systems level, not purely local impacts. And they should lead to a gradual convergence over time as designers eliminate extraneous features, enhance critical functions, and define goals with greater clarity and precision. These improvements will be made only if prototypes are viewed as learning opportunities, rather than as simple go/no go decisions. According to a recent study of product development:

> The most successful teams . . . frequently and regularly built a variety of prototypes; started creating prototypes of the entire system very early in the development process; and made each successive model more closely approach the desired final product in terms of form, content, and the customer experience it provoked . . . The most successful teams also built multiple copies of each prototype so that everyone involved in the development and eventual production, sale, use, and servicing of the product (including suppliers, prospective customers, and dealers) could rapidly evaluate it and offer feedback. . . .
>
> But the projects that exploited prototypes in this manner were the exception. Indeed, most of the projects studied . . . failed to create enough prototypes. And often the prototypes they did build (1) were not created early enough to solve problems that took more time and resources to solve later; (2) focused on only one of two components and not on the entire system; (3) were not used to test the manufacturing processes that would produce the final product; and (4) were not widely tested in the field, meaning that an opportunity to glean potentially invaluable reactions from customers was missed.[35]

It is also essential to involve diverse observers. Multiple lenses and complementary perspectives help reduce bias and overcome problems of interpretation. Most exploratory experiments involve a limited number of trials and extremely small samples; in such settings, "meaning is not self-evident . . . [and] many different interpretations are both supportable and refutable."[36] Causality is difficult to determine, and some degree of guesswork is normally required. But the interpretative process can be made more robust by including observers with conflicting interests and varied functional backgrounds. Their presence provides a set of checks and balances and counteracts the natural tendency to discount surprises. "Because different individuals and groups experience . . . events differently, they learn different lessons from the same experience . . . reduc[ing] the standard confirmatory bias of experience."[37]

A final design issue concerns data collection. Effective probe-and-learn processes require baseline data. Researchers must first understand prevailing conditions in order to properly evaluate experiments; otherwise, the observed impact is as likely to be a statistical artifact as the result of a planned intervention. All too often, performance improvements that are thought to result from innovative programs or policies actually reflect preestablished trends or natural processes of maturation and growth.[38] Successful exploration therefore demands "skillful application of the measurement package before the change is introduced, so that it will be in place to 'capture'" the impact of the interaction.[39] An innovative service delivery system can be evaluated properly only by comparing customer satisfaction levels before and after the system is introduced, just as the impact of self-managing work teams can be assessed only by drawing on climate surveys that include periods before and after teams were formed. For truly comprehensive evaluations, the data must be even more inclusive. The "ideal measurement package . . . should be longitudinal, usually covering several years"; should include "roughly comparable areas where . . . the change will not be introduced"; "should involve a broad range of economic and behavioral measures"; and should be administered by an objective third-party "not actively involved in the change process."[40]

Probe-and-learn processes, it should be clear, demand careful planning (see Table 5-2). But design alone does not guarantee success. The process also requires distinctive personal qualities and habits of mind.

---

## TABLE 5-2

### DESIGNING EFFECTIVE PROBE-AND-LEARN PROCESSES

---

*1. Create representative, inexpensive prototypes.*

- Design prototypes that are appealing enough to induce users to try the product or service.
- Ensure that designs are accurate enough to ensure valid feedback about users' needs.
- Use materials and configurations that are cheap enough to permit multiple revisions.

*2. Collect feedback directly from the market.*

- Connect designers with users, suppliers, distributors, and service personnel.
- Keep cycles short so that market information remains current and up to date.
- Add new features and design characteristics as required, then return immediately to the market for further testing.

*3. Expect to revise repeatedly.*

- Treat early designs as works in progress.
- Don't try to produce the perfect prototype.
- Don't be disappointed by repeated rejections, especially if users are finding some features to be of interest.
- Expect the initial market research to be misleading.
- Stay attuned to unanticipated requirements and emerging needs.

*4. Employ a comprehensive measurement package.*

- Agree on objective measures before beginning the experiment.
- Collect data over time (before, during, and after) to capture the initial impact of the experiment as well as subsequent changes in designs.
- Use comparative data (on similar products, services, or sites) to isolate experimental effects.

*5. Know when to stop.*

- Establish guidelines in advance for evaluating success and failure.
- Allow enough time for experiments to produce representative results.

---

Explorers are seekers and searchers; they must be open to the unexpected and sensitive to their own biases and preconceptions. As Thomas Huxley, the famed British biologist and writer, put it: "My business is to teach my aspirations to conform themselves to fact, not to try to make facts harmonize with my aspirations."[41] Explorers must be equally skilled at teasing out patterns from fragmentary, incomplete data. The primary challenge is homing in on a target that in the early stages is only dimly understood—"to see," in the words of an experienced engineering man-

ager, "what could be from what is." For this reason, and because reactions
to early prototypes are seldom definitive, probe-and-learn processes require that practitioners learn to think longitudinally and developmentally,
acquiring "a sense of how to cumulate questions, tests or experiments so
that they build on one another in sequence."[42]

Surprisingly, scholarly values are equally important to success. Exploration demands discipline as well as inquisitiveness. Sound conclusions
require a firm foundation; they cannot be based on speculation and
wishful thinking but must rest on clear logic, untainted evidence, and
techniques that are above reproach.[43] Otherwise, errors can quickly sneak
in. To avoid them, a certain integrity and honesty is required, a bending
over backwards to keep conclusions pure. Gordon Forward, the CEO of
Chaparral Steel, an innovative minimill renowned for its commitment to
exploratory learning, has provided an eloquent summary of the required
mind-set:

> [W]hen you're trying to go one step beyond in research, one of the
> things you learn fast is that you can't fool yourself. . . . You've got to
> be open in your questioning. You can't play games. And you can't
> succeed by pretending you know things you really don't. You have
> to go find them out. You have to try an experiment here, an experi-
> ment there, make your mistakes, ask your questions, and learn from
> it all.[44]

## Demonstration Projects

Exploration is especially difficult when large, complex systems are involved. Even when the individual pieces of such systems are well understood, their combined impact is almost impossible to predict. Parts and
components are often tightly coupled, forced into confined spaces with
multiple, shared connections. Because of the associated complexity, any
number of things can go wrong: "unfamiliar or unintended feedback
loops; many control parameters with potential interactions; indirect or
inferential information sources; and limited understanding."[45] The nuclear power accident at Three Mile Island provides a vivid example of
how complex systems can go awry in unexpected ways. Changing environments and diverse operating conditions only exacerbate the problem.

Particularly when human and technological systems are to be linked in novel ways, error-free operation requires an unusual degree of harmony and alignment of the underlying processes.

In these settings, the probe-and-learn process remains vital for effective exploration. But because experimenters must assess a much wider range of interactions than is usually the case with a new product or service, a distinctive approach is required. Prototyping is still necessary, but the focus shifts from marketing and design to operations and use. Now, the critical task is putting the system through its paces: seeing how it works under varied conditions, environments, and behaviors. Success, after all, requires components that work together smoothly, subsystems that are mutually supportive, technologies that are resistant to stress, and operators who are willing and able to follow procedures. All of these conditions must be demonstrated; they cannot be taken for granted or assumed to be true.

The associated experiments are best called demonstration projects. Most involve holistic, large-scale changes, introduced at a single site, that are undertaken with the goal of developing new organizational capabilities. Frequently, they are associated with breakthroughs in technology or fundamentally new operating philosophies. Because these projects represent a sharp break with the past, they are usually designed from scratch, using a "clean slate" approach. General Foods' Topeka plant, one of the first high-commitment work systems in this country, was a pioneering demonstration project initiated to introduce the idea of self-managing teams and high levels of worker autonomy. A more recent example, designed to explore environmentally sound operating methods and new approaches to energy conservation, is Wal-Mart's "green store."[46] The approach has also been used in the public sector. The 1978 Civil Service Reform Act gave the Office of Personnel Management the authority to conduct and supervise demonstration projects that explored innovative approaches to pay and job classification. Experiments were later conducted by groups as diverse as the U.S. Navy and the Department of Commerce, and successful approaches were incorporated in subsequent legislation.[47]

Demonstration projects normally take one of two forms: on-line experiments or large-scale simulations. The former involve fully functioning businesses, with real employees and customers, that present living examples of the system in action; the latter involve prototypical operations or systems, constructed of mock-ups or models, in which participants play out their roles over time so that designers can learn more about how their newly created processes and equipment are likely to work. Both approaches share a number of distinctive characteristics:

- They are usually the first projects to embody principles and approaches that the organization hopes to adopt later on a larger scale. For this reason, they are more transitional efforts than endpoints and involve considerable real-time readjustment and learning. Mid-course corrections are common.

- They implicitly establish policy guidelines and decision rules for later projects. Managers must therefore be sensitive to the precedents they are setting and must send strong signals if they hope to establish new norms.

- They often encounter severe tests of commitment from employees who wish to see whether the rules have, in fact, changed.

- They are normally developed by strong multifunctional teams reporting directly to senior management. (For projects targeting employee involvement or quality of work life, teams should be multilevel as well as multifunctional.)

- They tend to be developed by impassioned advocates who have difficulty communicating their vision to peers. Those peers may also be resentful of the attention that demonstration projects receive. For these reasons, projects tend to have only limited impact on the rest of the organization if they are not accompanied by explicit strategies for transferring learning.

All of these characteristics appeared in an on-line demonstration project launched by Copeland Corporation, a highly successful compressor manufacturer, in the mid-1970s.[48] Matt Diggs, then the new CEO, wanted to transform the company's approach to manufacturing. Previously, Copeland had machined and assembled all products in a single facility in Sidney, Ohio. Costs were high, and quality was marginal. The problem, Diggs felt, was too much complexity.

At the outset, Diggs assigned a small, multifunctional team the task of designing a "focused factory" dedicated to a narrow, newly developed product line. The team reported directly to Diggs and took three years to complete its work. Initially, the project budget was $10 million to $12 million; that figure was repeatedly revised as the team found, through experience and with Diggs' prodding, that it could achieve dramatic improvements. The final investment, a total of $30 million, yielded unanticipated breakthroughs in reliability testing, automatic tool adjustment, and programmable control. All were achieved through exploration and real-time learning.

The team set additional precedents during the plant's start-up and early operations. To dramatize the importance of quality, for example, the quality manager was appointed second-in-command, a significant move upward. The same reporting relationship was used at all subsequent plants. In addition, Diggs urged the newly hired plant manager to ramp up slowly to full production and resist all efforts to proliferate products. These instructions were unusual at Copeland, where the marketing department normally ruled. (They were especially surprising coming from Diggs, who had previously been the vice president of marketing.) Both directives were quickly tested; management held firm, and the implications were felt throughout the organization. Manufacturing's stature improved, and the company as a whole recognized its competitive contribution. One observer commented: "Marketing had always run the company, so they couldn't believe it. The change was visible at the highest levels, and it went down hard."

Once the initial focused factory was running smoothly—it seized 25 percent of the market in two years and held its edge in reliability for over a decade—Copeland built four more focused factories in quick succession. Diggs assigned members of the initial project to each factory's design team to ensure that early learnings were not lost; these people later rotated through operating assignments. Today, focused factories remain the cornerstone of Copeland's manufacturing strategy and a continuing source of its cost and quality advantages.

Perhaps the most important measure of success for projects like Copeland's is diffusion: the extent to which new policies, practices, and procedures spread to other parts of the organization. By this measure, focused factories fared extremely well. They quickly became part of daily operations. But all too often, new approaches run into massive resistance and are never accepted by the rest of the organization—even when they meet their initial targets. That was the fate of many of the early demonstration projects that involved innovative work systems such as self-managing teams. Their difficulties are instructive, for they suggest several potential problems.

Projects may receive too much favorable publicity, resulting in "star-envy" and resentment by peers. Projects may suffer a loss of credibility over time, regressing in performance after the great enthusiasm and intense dedication of early operation. Projects may be viewed as one-time commitments by senior management, making it difficult to find the time, money, and experienced talent necessary to develop second-generation sites. And projects may have been framed with ideological purity rather than practical business needs as the primary motivation, creating hesitancy about their likely contribution in the minds of less committed outsiders.[49]

These problems, while common, are not insurmountable. They can be overcome if demonstration projects are designed with diffusion clearly in mind. They are, after all, supposed to be copied by others. If learning is not shared, projects will not have served their intended purpose. Low public profiles, well-defined business objectives, personal incentives that predispose managers toward transfers, aggressive goals and milestones that carry projects beyond start-up, and the active transfer of resources (both dollars and personnel) to second-generation sites are helpful in meeting these larger goals.[50]

Demonstration projects that involve simulations bring different challenges. They are difficult to design because they face so many conflicting demands. Like all models, they must simplify reality without distorting it. They must be easy to construct, yet comprehensive enough to capture the complex links between systems design, human behavior, and operational and financial performance. They must be adaptable and robust, capable of accommodating different styles, approaches, and behaviors. And they must be engaging enough to encourage high levels of operator and user involvement. The best simulations, in short, are flexible, functional, and fun. The latter requirement is particularly important, because a spirit of playfulness is often essential for encouraging creativity and imagination. Frequently, the deepest learning occurs when a freewheeling, inquisitive approach is coupled with periods of reflection so that participants can periodically step back and draw lessons from their turns at the "game."[51]

## TIMKEN'S REDESIGN OF MANUFACTURING: EXPLORING THROUGH STORYBOARDING, CARDBOARD CITY, AND THE TRAINING MODULE

The Timken Company, America's leading manufacturer of tapered roller bearings, presents a dramatic example of exploration.[52] In 1988 Timken embarked on a bold project to revolutionize the production process for manufacturing customized bearings. Historically, its industrial customers had waited eight to ten months for Timken to fill their small, tailor-made orders; the new goal was to reduce the waiting period to weeks or days. To do so, Timken would have to develop leading-edge technology and pioneer radically new approaches to machining, hardening, gauging, and computer integration. Among the requirements were setup times less than ten minutes and equipment that made the first pieces of every production run without errors or defects. These requirements were difficult in themselves, but the problem was compounded by the extraordinarily tight tolerances required of bearings, which at times ran to the ten-thousandths of an inch. As Joe Toot, Jr., the company's president and CEO, observed: "We set out to do something that no one in manufacturing had done before, not simply in the bearing industry, but, to the best of our intelligence, no one in manufacturing." This challenge clearly demanded exploratory learning. According to Mike Arnold, the first plant manager: "There was no one to teach us. There were no classrooms to go to. There were no books to read. There were no manuals or models. So we had to learn as we went exactly what the right and wrong steps were."

Timken chose to tackle the problem in stages, breaking the task into smaller, more manageable parts. Complex, ambiguous problems are often far easier to solve once they have been parceled out, especially if tasks become progressively more concrete as the process unfolds. At Timken, four stages were involved; each was the responsibility of a different team (see Figure 5-1). The teams proceeded in

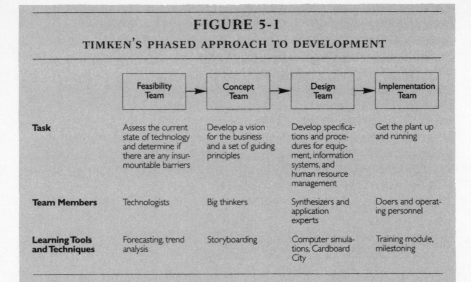

**FIGURE 5-1**

TIMKEN'S PHASED APPROACH TO DEVELOPMENT

|  | Feasibility Team | Concept Team | Design Team | Implementation Team |
|---|---|---|---|---|
| **Task** | Assess the current state of technology and determine if there are any insurmountable barriers | Develop a vision for the business and a set of guiding principles | Develop specifications and procedures for equipment, information systems, and human resource management | Get the plant up and running |
| **Team Members** | Technologists | Big thinkers | Synthesizers and application experts | Doers and operating personnel |
| **Learning Tools and Techniques** | Forecasting, trend analysis | Storyboarding | Computer simulations, Cardboard City | Training module, milestoning |

sequence, with some overlap in membership and tenure. Each team had a distinct, defined assignment. The Feasibility Team was asked to assess the current state of technology and determine if there were any insurmountable barriers to success. The Concept Team was asked to develop an overarching vision of the business as well as a set of guiding principles. The Design Team was asked to develop precise specifications for equipment, information systems, and human resource management. And the Implementation Team was asked to get the plant up and running; its tasks included training operators, programming equipment, and testing the various components of the system to ensure that they worked together. This four-phased approach, it should be clear, is directly analogous to the use of "successive approximations" in the probe-and-learn process.

The teams used simulations extensively to generate insights. In each case, they proceeded in stages and evolved from high-level abstractions to detailed, concrete representations. The Concept Team, for example, relied heavily on storyboarding to develop a vision of the business. This technique has a long history in filmmaking and television production, where it is used to develop an outline of the core elements of a show or story. It has recently migrated to corporate settings, where it is used as a primitive prototyping process.[53] Key words and phrases are written on large index cards that can be easily reshuffled. They are then arranged in order to map out process flows and sequences of required activities. At Timken, members of the Concept Team began with topic cards describing key portions of the production process; then, underneath them they developed supporting concepts and ideas. According to a participant:

> The storyboard technique allowed us to capture the picture of a particular portion of the business in a very confined space. And then to create another picture, for another portion of the business, on another storyboard. We then put those pieces on the wall together and could begin to visualize the linkages, which to some degree illustrated how the business would operate. We could begin to see whether we had the right priorities for each portion of the business. We could begin to see patterns and sort ideas. And we could take the storyboards away from our little conference room, working independently in small teams of two or three to refine the ideas and then bring them back and post them on the wall again.
>
> It was a very dynamic process. The storyboards enabled us to create a vision of the business we were trying to build in a way that was very flexible. They allowed us to come back from time to time and revisit that vision based on new information we had gathered or learned, or new ideas that had come to the table.

The Design Team made even more extensive use of simulations. They began with computer programs that mimicked the proposed product flow, equipment layout, and plant capacity. They then explored a large number of alternative designs and compared the results. A cellular approach, with machines arranged in a horseshoe fashion, proved to be superior. But it was difficult to pin down the exact layout because the data came with a serious limitation: all of the simulations were two-dimensional. Each layout appeared only within the confines of a flat computer screen. Engineers therefore had little sense of the proper spacing of equipment or the desired timing of adjacent operations. There were a number of unanswered questions: Would the plant's machine operators have enough room to load and unload? Would the aisles be wide enough for impromptu problem-solving sessions? Would operators bump into one another while carrying work-in-progress from station to station? Would employees have the necessary line of sight to communicate should problems arise?

Cost was an issue as well. If the plant was too large, millions of dollars would be wasted on unnecessary space; if machines were poorly positioned, thousands of dollars would be spent on relocation. The grinders presented a special challenge. To ensure precision, they had to be absolutely immobile, set in a foundation of six feet of concrete. As the director of engineering wryly observed: "Once you laid that machine down, it was not a trivial task to move it to a new location."

To resolve these questions, the Design Team created Cardboard City, a three-dimensional model of a manufacturing cell. It was built out of cardboard and two-by-fours and included full-scale mock-ups of each piece of equipment, placed on casters so that they could be moved easily. The location was an empty portion of the R&D building—essentially a warehouse—and the total cost was $2,000. The real innovation, however, was the associated learning process, which included elements of both competition and cooperation. It ensured that Cardboard City produced a wide range of possible layouts and simulated a wide variety of production flows.

Three teams were formed. Each contained ten to fifteen people, largely engineers and designers with a sprinkling of operating personnel. Each team was given approximately one hour to arrange the "equipment" in Cardboard City to its satisfaction. Their challenge was to create the best material flows and best interaction among operators while using the minimum amount of space. There were a few constraints—maximum allowable facility size, operating parameters, and performance targets—but otherwise teams were given free rein to create their own preferred layouts. Operators then simulated a production run for each layout, loading and unloading machines and carrying cardboard versions of partially completed bearings from station to station. The results were recorded on videotape for later review. All teams then met together to debrief, discuss the alternatives, and vote on their preferences. They could draw on any of the approaches, not only their own. At this point, the group came to an important realization: none of the proposed layouts was obviously superior. According to a participant: "We decided that each team had elements that were unique and creative. And we recognized that choosing any one of the three solutions might not be the best approach."

So, after a presentation to senior management, a fourth team was formed; it consisted of volunteers drawn from the three original teams. This group's task was to use the "best of the best" from prior simulations, rearranging Cardboard City a final time. Again, operators were asked to simulate the production process, and the results were videotaped. After another review, this last layout was approved. It resulted in a compact, tightly focused factory and well-positioned machines. According to engineers: "We saved a bundle of money. The building is quite a bit smaller than we thought it was going to be. . . . Today, every machine is right in the spot where the simulations put it. Nothing's been rearranged."

Cardboard City shows simulations at their best. The process was cleverly designed to produce the maximum amount of learning. It was, to use an earlier phrase, flexible, functional, and fun—and cheap, to boot. Inexpensive, movable mock-ups encouraged participants to try out alternative designs. Competing, multifunctional teams ensured diverse perspectives and high levels of interest and involvement. The use of experienced operators to simulate production contributed realism and credibility. Combining voting with an open, reflective debriefing process guaranteed that all voices would be heard, while improving the odds that the best possible solution would emerge. As one engineer summed up the process: "This was a multimillion dollar project. And I think that Cardboard City was the best $2,000 we ever spent."

Timken's simulations did not end with Cardboard City. The Implementation Team went a step further, creating a training module at R&D to test out unproven machinery and equipment. It had two purposes: teaching inexperienced operators how to run the new equipment and fine-tuning the technology and associated systems. By starting in a simulated environment, operators were able to move up the learning curve without facing the usual pressures of daily production. They were, in the language of chapter 2, working in an environment that was "psychologically safe," which encouraged risk taking and experimentation. Accord-

ing to an operator: "Nobody was afraid because this wasn't actual production; it was simulated production. Nobody was actually waiting for
the product. So if we messed up, we messed up."

Equally important was the ability to integrate the new equipment
and computer systems into a seamless whole—before the factory began
full-scale operation. If the process was to operate as planned, all of the
pieces had to fit. Again, Timken proceeded in stages, using the training
module as its laboratory. An engineer described the approach:

> This was something that we'd never done before. We knew we
> couldn't just jump in the middle and expect to be going down the
> road at a hundred miles an hour. So we started out slowly and then
> progressively upped the ante as we went through each phase.
>
> We used a concept called "milestoning." Each milestone had a
> specific objective: a product type, a level of systems integration, the
> number of machines that would be involved, and who would be
> running the machines. Each step was more difficult than the pre-
> vious one, and after each milestone we conducted an assessment.
> Did we make what we set out to make? Did we accomplish what
> we wanted on the information systems side?

Once again, the learning process was incremental and involved a
series of successive approximations. All milestones, in fact, were
grouped into three broad categories: "crawl, walk, run." Crawling involved the easiest tasks: the ability to make basic, unadorned products.
Here, the goal was to ensure that all elements of the operating system
were in place and worked together smoothly. Walking involved an expanded product range: the ability to produce complex shapes and respond to special orders. Here, the goal was to stretch the capabilities of
the operating system and ensure that it was both flexible and robust.
Running involved optimization and efficiency: the ability to execute orders rapidly and at maximum productivity. Here, the goal was to ensure
that operators and equipment were capable of achieving high through-
put rates. Each phase, in the words of the first plant manager, involved a
large number of exploratory experiments: a series of "test runs" that

"took the individual pieces of the project, put them together, and gave us a chance to try and run the business."

On September 30, 1994, Timken opened its 21st Century bearings business plant in Asheboro, North Carolina.[54] It came on line smoothly, with few problems, a highly unusual event for a factory with such state-of-the-art technology. The company's staged, iterative process and heavy investment in simulations paid enormous dividends. The Concept Team's business design and guiding principles remained intact, with little substantive change. The Design Team's placement of machinery and equipment proved to be unerring, with no need for reshuffling. And the Implementation Team's approach to training and development produced knowledge and skills that were easy to apply in the real-world operating environment. Exploration—the process of "going down alleys to see which ones are blind"—ensured that Timken made its way successfully through previously uncharted territory.[55]

## HYPOTHESIS TESTING

Hypothesis testing is quite different from exploration. It is deductive rather than inductive, disciplined rather than playful, targeted rather than open-ended. As noted earlier in this chapter, here the goal is proof, not discovery, and the approach is best used when there are competing views or explanations and less intrusive modes of learning are incapable of discriminating among them. Then, the only alternative is often to intervene actively in the environment, altering conditions until underlying cause-and-effect relationships become clear.

Such experiments are the bread-and-butter work of scientists. In any number of fields, they have played a vital role in generating data, validating theories, and ensuring that new ideas were accepted. Practicing scientists, in fact, are almost reverential in their regard for the process. According to a prize-winning researcher: "Ever since Bacon's day experimentation has been thought to be so deeply and so very necessarily a part of science that. . . . activities that are not experimental are often denied the right to be classified as sciences at all."[56] Yet for all its power, the approach is seldom seen outside the laboratory. There are a number of reasons why. Managers are not scientists; few have been trained in the associated methods and techniques, which can be dauntingly complex. The necessary conditions for success are often rigidly prescribed. Problems must be well structured; otherwise, experiments will be difficult to design. Understanding must be deep enough to generate diverse views; otherwise, there will be no basis for comparison. Environments must permit the manipulation of selected variables; otherwise, their contribution will be impossible to assess. Participants must have at least a nodding acquaintance with the processes of causal inference; otherwise, conclusions will lack broad application. Clearly, hypothesis testing, in its purest form, is not the simplest or easiest of tasks.

As if these challenges were not enough, there is an additional roadblock: the necessary mind-set is hard to come by. Hypothesis testing is of value only if one's preferred position remains open to scrutiny—whatever the outcome. Truth must be valued over advocacy, and considerable time must be devoted to testing (and possibly undermining) one's preferred explanation. The underlying philosophy has been well described by Richard Feynman, a Nobel Laureate in physics:

> It's a kind of scientific integrity, a principle of scientific thought that corresponds to a kind of utter honesty—a kind of leaning over backwards. . . . [I]f you're doing an experiment, you should report everything that you think might make it invalid—not only what you think is right about it: other causes that could explain your results; and things you thought of that you've eliminated by some other experiment, and how they worked—to make sure the other fellow can tell they have been eliminated. Details that could throw doubt on your interpretation must be given, if you know them.[57]

Managers often find these recommendations hard to swallow. They smack of ideological purity, while taking no account of organizational politics. For similar reasons, managers are frequently uncomfortable with the strict requirements that scientists insist are necessary for valid experiments. Two of the most obvious are control groups (comparable units that do not receive an experimental treatment) and random assignment (individuals or groups that, on a blind basis, are subjected to differing conditions).[58] Managers seldom employ these techniques when experimenting with new approaches because, in their eyes, they "fail to mesh with the realities of life in organizations."[59] Instead, the argument goes, considerations of equity should rule, with all customers or employees benefiting (or suffering) equally from a new policy or procedure. No one should be excluded simply to ensure a sound experimental design. And no new initiative should be delayed unnecessarily, especially if it promises substantial benefits. There are exceptions, of course—Dayton Hudson, the retail chain, developed REGARDS, a highly successful loyalty program, by first comparing the responses of a selected sample of frequent buyers with those of a carefully matched control group—but they are remarkably rare.[60]

## A Way of Thinking

Fortunately, a compromise exists. Many of the benefits of experimentation can be obtained without a full-blown scientific approach. The underlying logic and principles remain the same, but the methods are subtly altered to accommodate the realities of the workplace. Practices and techniques are no longer rigidly prescribed. Instead, the associated reasoning process becomes paramount and is highlighted as the key to success. This approach goes by various names—quasi-experimentation, adaptive experiments, field experiments, the modus operandi method; all, however, are designed to make hypothesis testing less burdensome, while preserving its insights and discriminating power.[61]

Experimentation, after all, is as much a mind-set and philosophy as a set of rigid rules. Whether one is a detective, chemist, anthropologist, engineering troubleshooter, or manager, the goal remains the same: to select one explanation, from many possibilities, by drawing on disciplined data collection. According to this view:

> [E]xperimentation is a process of observation, to be carried out in a situation especially brought about for that purpose. . . . [T]he functions of an experiment . . . are no more—and no less!—than to provide occasions for "controlled observation." . . . What experi-

ments can do is to minimize the errors of observation that are inseparable from casual encounters, or at any rate from unplanned ones.[62]

To minimize these errors, experiments must meet two conditions.[63]
First, they must demonstrate, with a high degree of confidence, that a
change in one variable actually causes a change in another. This is simply
a fancy way of saying that a good experiment firmly establishes the relationship between cause and effect. Findings must hold up to careful
scrutiny; they must not be statistical artifacts or traceable to unknown,
yet-to-be measured causes. Second, results must generalize beyond the
experimental setting. They must apply to a wider set of circumstances,
not only the narrow, idealized environment used for testing. This is simply another way of saying that experiments are of little use if they are true
only for a particular person, place, or time. To be of value, they must have
more universal application.

These concepts can be readily adapted to real-world settings. The
reasoning process remains the same, and the desired features continue to
include controlled observation, careful measurement, logical inference,
and reproducible results. This process is especially useful on the
shop floor, where problems arise continuously and hypothesis testing
is often needed to zero in on the desired corrective action. Consider
these scenarios:

- A company shifts to a new supplier of components. When they are
  first employed in production, they cause a host of difficulties—
  slower machine speeds, defective output, improper fits with other
  parts—even though the exact same specifications and tolerances
  have been used. What is the problem?

- A company finds that a critical machine tool works perfectly well on
  some days, but experiences massive quality problems on others. The
  problems do not have an obvious pattern and cannot be attributed to
  a particular operator, order, or equipment setting. What is the explanation?

- A company purchases the latest robotics technology and attempts to
  shift the assembly of diverse products from less advanced equipment. The results are highly variable. Some transfers work flawlessly,

others require constant changes in settings and speeds, while still others will not work at all. What accounts for the differences?

Each of these challenges can be solved only if variables are manipulated selectively and the results are carefully observed. Experiments are essential. They must be based on systematic planning and forethought, the active pursuit of alternative explanations, and techniques that uncover underlying relationships. But pristine laboratory conditions and textbook experimental designs are seldom needed. Distinctive habits of mind, however, remain crucial. The odds of success improve dramatically when managers follow a few simple guidelines.

## Conducting Experiments

These guidelines are not particularly complex (see Table 5-3). But they do require that the associated learning process be designed with care. The goal is to reduce or eliminate the most common errors in hypothesis testing—unfocused data collection, flawed reasoning, indeterminate findings—while improving discrimination and deepening understanding.

To begin, it is important to be clear about the purpose of the experiment. What exactly is the goal? What knowledge is being pursued? Which relationships are unclear? Unlike exploration, hypothesis testing is not an open-ended search (a "vacuum cleaner" approach to collecting data); rather, it is a focused inquiry that addresses tightly framed questions (more of a "directed telescope").[64] For this reason, it is essential to have one or more possible explanations in mind before starting out. These explanations, which scientists call *hypotheses,* guide the experimental process by dictating the information that must be collected. Typically, they take the form of "if . . . then" statements or predicted linkages that will be supported or undermined by the existence of certain evidence. Researchers thus know exactly what data to pursue. There is another, often unanticipated benefit of beginning with a hypothesis in mind. Observation is invariably more intelligent and insightful. Hypotheses offer focal points, evaluative frameworks that "help one see the significance of an object or event that would otherwise mean nothing." Such frameworks serve as guidance systems, leading the eye in certain directions. Surprisingly, benefits often accrue even when the initial explana-

## TABLE 5-3
### GUIDELINES FOR HYPOTHESIS-TESTING EXPERIMENTS

1. Be clear about the purpose of the experiment.
2. Begin with a hypothesis in mind.
3. Ensure that all needed measures (pretest and posttest) are in place.
4. Reproduce real-world conditions as closely as possible.
5. Manipulate a single variable at a time.
6. Use comparison groups or other natural controls.
7. Involve diverse, complementary observers.
8. Search for distinctive patterns.
9. Employ multiple, repeated trials.

tion is off the mark. Because they offer a way of structuring data, hypotheses can be helpful without being correct—as long as they are viewed as provisional and are not pursued beyond reason.[65]

The best hypotheses share several characteristics. They are clear and unambiguous, describe a relationship or connection among variables, and are capable of being disproved. The last requirement is especially important. If potential cause-and-effect relationships have been framed so generally that there is no way of pinning down their truth or falsity, even the best-designed experiments will fail. Here, precision is a virtue. Attributing defective products to "variability in incoming materials" is virtually useless as a guide for action; linking mixtures with excess acidity to "chemicals that arrive every other month with greater than 15 percent impurities" provides much more direction and focus.

But even with well-framed hypotheses, experiments will be of value only if appropriate measures are also in place. Quantification is part and parcel of effective hypothesis testing, for it provides the glue linking cause and effect. There are three associated requirements: First, there must be unambiguous measures of successful outcomes. Second, there must be refined measures of the variables being manipulated. And third, there must be comprehensive data on the direction that variables were moving before the experiment was initiated. The first requirement is needed for determining whether the desired results have in fact been produced; the second requirement is needed for establishing the precise link between the changes made and the desired ends; and the third requirement is needed for ruling out spurious effects due to preestablished trends or random variation. All too often, reductions (increases) in a variable of interest are falsely ascribed to actions or interventions when the results were already moving in the desired direction. The same outcomes would have occurred if the status quo were left undisturbed. Changes may also be statistical in nature, for extreme events tend to be followed, over time, by values that are closer to average scores.[66] Without historical data, it is impossible to rule out these alternatives.

Experiments must also be carefully designed. There are five critical elements: the choice of environment or setting, the process of manipulating variables, the inclusion of comparisons or controls, the selection of participants, and the confirmation of results. To begin, real-world conditions should be approximated as closely as possible; otherwise, findings are unlikely to be useful or representative. This means that if laboratory work is required, it should be combined with on-line experimentation to ensure that results remain equally true on the shop floor. To isolate presumed cause-and-effect relationships, only one or two variables should be manipulated at a time; otherwise, it is difficult to rule out alternative explanations.[67] Selectivity and forethought are essential. Before proceeding, experimenters should have some idea of the most likely patterns at work. They can then manipulate variables and search for expected patterns; if they do not appear, they can move quickly to another possible explanation. This is the process used by all good detectives, and it applies equally well to business.[68]

Several steps should be taken to avoid interpretative errors. Controls are essential; otherwise, it is easy to delude oneself about the true impact of an intervention or policy change. This does not mean that formal control groups are required. But it does suggest that experimenters should search actively for reference groups or points of comparison—departments with similar problems, factories with similar technologies, customers with similar needs—to contrast their behavior with that observed in the experimental setting. Often, the data is there for the taking. Few large, multinational corporations, for example, introduce new policies or programs at all sites around the world at exactly the same time. There are invariably leaders and laggards. Sites that are "late adopters" provide invaluable reference points, serving as implicit controls for evaluating the impact of a policy change.

To further reduce bias, multiple observers should be asked to review results. Whenever possible, they should represent different departments and competing points of view. Diversity provides checks and balances, creates divergent perspectives, and ensures that no single interpretation dominates. For example, shop-floor experiments should generally be reviewed by individuals from R&D, engineering, operations, and quality control. Each is likely to interpret the data in slightly different ways. Then, to validate the team's conclusions, multiple trials should be conducted. They ensure that critical findings hold up under diverse conditions—different operators, times of day, order sizes, and production sequences—and are not one-time events.

## ALLEGHENY LUDLUM STEEL'S SYSTEM FOR EXPERIMENTATION: HYPOTHESIS TESTING ON THE 91 LINE

All of the factors that lend to effective hypothesis testing can be seen at work at Allegheny Ludlum Steel, an extremely successful manufacturer of specialty steel that has a long history of experimentation.[69] At Allegheny, experiments are routine rather than rare, the rule rather than the exception. According to Richard Simmons, chairman and CEO of the parent company: "This isn't something that you do twice a year at a meeting. It is something that you do every day of every week of every month of every year. After a while, it becomes part of the culture."

Twenty experiments are typically underway at any given time, with over one hundred per year in the alloy product line alone. To manage this volume, Allegheny has developed a comprehensive approach, with four key elements: a detailed measurement system, which provides the impetus for experiments and permits before-and-after comparisons; an innovative incentive system, which encourages managers to pursue improvements and take risks; a formal proposal mechanism, which structures and coordinates the work by requiring affected departments to agree to common goals, approaches, and outcomes; and a disciplined experimental process, which ensures rapid turnaround and valid, verifiable results (see Table 5-4). All of these elements work in concert to produce an integrated, reinforcing system.

**Measurement.** Allegheny has an extraordinarily complete tracking system that compares, for every grade of steel and every grade of equipment, current operating results with the very best productivity, quality, and costs that the company has ever obtained. Work is actually tracked to the individual coil level. Literally millions of standards have been developed, and the database can be exploded in any way that engineers believe to be of value: by grade, by product, by customer, even by thickness of the material. The resulting reports, which focus on variances from both the current target and the company's best-ever performance (known as the "Olympic standard"), are available on-line and in real time. They serve as the basis for daily, weekly, and monthly meetings that pinpoint potential areas for improvement and suggest possible experiments. The associated historical data play two additional roles: they are an invaluable source of information on potential cause-and-effect relationships, and they provide an implicit set of controls that eliminate statistical artifacts and flawed attributions.

**Incentives.** Allegheny uses its accounting system to encourage experimentation. Because all plant personnel are held responsible for operating margins (and are penalized for excess costs), they would normally have little incentive to experiment with novel, untested approaches. But once experiments are approved, they are moved to a separate account. Operating managers are no longer charged for the associated material and production costs; instead, those costs are assigned to technical services, a separate department consisting largely of metallurgists and process experts. (For the few elaborate experiments that are designed to commercialize new products—usually, no more than two or three per year—entire 100-ton heats are written down to scrap value immediately, removing them completely from the cost accounting system.) These changes in scorecards have the predictable effect of eliminating resistance due to incompatible incentives. And because all managers commit themselves annually to aggressive improvement targets, which typically involve shared goals (e.g., "increase melt shop capacity by $x\%$"), they

# TABLE 5-4
## ALLEGHENY LUDLUM'S SYSTEM OF EXPERIMENTATION

| | Description | Purpose | Key Elements |
|---|---|---|---|
| **Measurement System** | Tracks productivity, quality, and costs at the level of individual coils and pieces of equipment | Identifies potential areas of improvement, suggests possible experiments, helps evaluate the impact of experimental changes | On-line, real-time reporting of variances, compared to current targets as well as best-ever performance |
| **Incentives** | Separates the costs of experiments from day-to-day operating expenses | Removes experiments from the scorecards used to evaluate operating managers, reducing their resistance | Separate budgets for small and large experiments |
| **Proposals and Work Plans** | Specifies the purpose, procedures, and personnel involved in experiments | Obtains approvals in advance, ensures interdepartmental coordination, and clearly specifies the nature of experiments and the desired results | Brief, two- to three-page documents that contain all critical information |
| **Experimental Process** | Generates plausible hypotheses and tests them systematically | Determines underlying cause-and-effect relationships | Manipulation of variables one at a time, alternating between the shop floor and laboratory as needed, drawing on the expertise of multifunctional teams |

have a positive interest in designing and executing successful experiments.

**Proposals and Work Plans.** At Allegheny, all operational experiments are documented using the same, simple format. Each experiment is given its own name and number and is described in a brief proposal. The initial document is two or three pages long, and includes seven sections: objective, background, procedure, evaluation, responsibility, prepared by, and approvals (see Table 5-5). This approach serves several ends. First, by requiring prework and preparation, it ensures that all experiments have been thought through. Spur-of-the-moment initiatives and poorly conceived flashes of inspiration seldom qualify. Second, by carefully laying out the experiment's rationale and goals, as well as the procedures and measures to be employed, it ensures that learning is disciplined and focused. Third, by explicitly assigning responsibility to and requiring sign-offs from all parties likely to be affected by experiments, it ensures that the process does not take place in a vacuum. As one metallurgist put it: "Everybody is on the same page." And because upstream and downstream impacts have been taken into account, unanticipated problems are rare.

The sign-offs are especially important. As Robert Miller, vice president of technical services, observed, the primary difference between laboratory and shop-floor experiments is that the former have much simpler logistics:

> When you go into the laboratory, everything you need is sitting there waiting for you. But when you go onto the manufacturing floor, that is generally not the case. You have to bring people, machines, and material together in the right place at the right time. You have to have good communication and coordination to make sure that the right things happen.

The documentation process ensures that the necessary coordination has occurred and that both operators and equipment are prepared for the proposed experiment.

---

## TABLE 5-5
### PLANNING FOR EXPERIMENTS AT ALLEGHENY LUDLUM

---

*Objective.* This section describes the purpose of the experiment—the operational problems it is designed to solve or the commercial ends it is designed to serve.

*Background.* This section describes the evolution of the experiment—how it came about, any relevant experience, and the critical operating issues that must be addressed.

*Procedure.* This section explains how the experiment will be conducted, paying special attention to the required activities on the shop floor and how they will differ from normal practice.

*Evaluation.* This section describes how the results of the experiment will be evaluated, including how success will be judged.

*Responsibility.* This section contains a list of the primary departments affected by the experiment and the individuals who have been assigned responsibility in each one.

*Prepared by.* This section names the person—typically, a metallurgist—who prepared the documentation for the experiment and orchestrated the experimental process.

*Approvals.* This section contains the names and signatures of those middle or senior managers who have approved the experiment. Four or five sign offs are normally required, typically from individuals one or two levels above those who have been assigned responsibility for actually conducting the experiment.

---

**The Experimental Process.** Allegheny applies a disciplined approach to the design, development, and deployment of experiments. The challenges may be diverse, but the process remains remarkably consistent in format and style. Typically, experiments begin with a review of historical data, shift to shop-floor activities that manipulate one or two variables at a time, migrate to the laboratory if deeper insights are required, and then return to the shop floor for final testing and confirmation. Each step is carefully designed to rule out measurement error or other spurious explanations. The steps are also carefully sequenced, so that early diagnostic activities are separated from later efforts to optimize performance. Throughout, managers are guided by a simple, golden rule: "First we make it right, then we make it cheaper." This process has obvious parallels to the guidelines for effective experimentation described earlier in the chapter. To see them in action, it is best to draw on a real-world example: a series of experiments that Allegheny conducted in 1996 to transfer a difficult-to-manufacture grade of steel from an older, slower annealing line to one using the latest, most up-to-date technology.

## THE PROCESS IN ACTION:
## ANNEALING 304DA ON THE 91 LINE

Annealing is a process that softens steel so that it can be fabricated and shaped more easily by customers. For many years, Allegheny relied on its number 45 line for annealing. The equipment was relatively old and slow but continued to yield high-quality output. One product long produced on the line was 304DA, used by customers to make expensive, highly polished pots and pans. This product differed from Allegheny's usual products in an important respect. Rather than involving coils or sheets of pure stainless steel, 304DA ("double armor") was a metal sandwich, composed of two outer layers of stainless steel and an inner layer of carbon steel.

This combination posed special challenges. After considerable experimentation, Allegheny had learned how to anneal 304DA on the 45 line to the softness required by a demanding customer. Then, in early 1996, the customer placed an unexpectedly large order. It came with very short lead times; worse yet, the 45 line was already fully scheduled and was without spare capacity. The only way that Allegheny could fill the order would be to anneal 304DA on its newer 91 line. But that line bore only a passing resemblance to its predecessor. It was four times longer, ran four times faster, and incorporated state-of-the-art heating and cooling technology. Moreover, the equipment had been in place for only a year, and its capabilities were still not fully understood. Managers therefore faced a difficult task. Could they make the required volume of 304DA on the 91 line—at double the usual production rate—while still meeting the customer's demanding standards?

To find out, they launched a series of experiments (see Figure 5-2). The process began with a review of past successful transfers from the 45 to the 91 line. All had involved pure stainless products, and all had required little more than a simple, one-to-one matching of temperatures and machine settings. The same approach was used for 304DA. The 91 line's furnace was set to the identical temperature used for the product

# FIGURE 5-2

## LEARNING TO ANNEAL 304DA ON THE 91 LINE

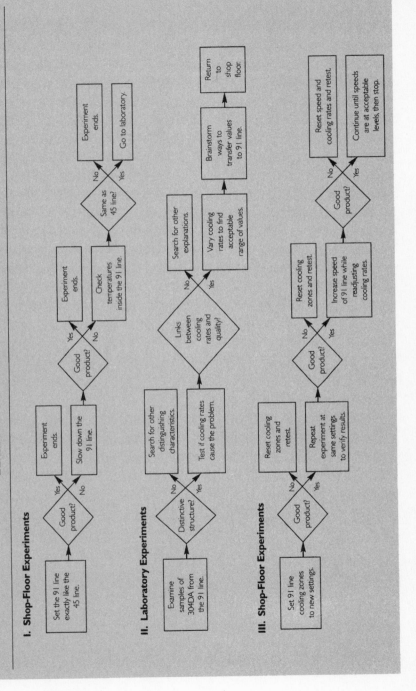

on the 45 line, and a small amount of material was annealed. The experiment could have ended right there if the steel came out soft enough. But the results were disappointing. As one participant recalled: "We got thrown a curve. The properties weren't close to those we were getting from the 45 line." The steel was far too hard. This time, a straightforward transfer of equipment settings had failed to produce the desired results. The question was, why?

Managers quickly launched a learning process that, within a few short weeks, produced the knowledge needed to successfully anneal 304DA on the 91 line. To begin, they tried to reproduce the old process *exactly*, slowing the 91 line down so that its speed was identical to that of the 45 line. This is an important step in real-world experiments: replicating, as closely as possible, the conditions that were previously successful in producing good product, but with new equipment, material, or operators. In essence, the goal is to mimic the old with the new—and, in the process, to isolate critical causal factors. Unfortunately, in this case the results were no better than before. The steel was still too hard.

So managers ran another experiment, taking the idea of replication a step further. Perhaps, they reasoned, the equipment's heating cycles—the time the lines took to heat up and hold a given temperature—were different despite the identical furnace settings. Their gauges and instruments might not be telling the whole story. Machine settings, after all, do not always capture actual operating conditions, nor do identical readings on different machines always reflect the same internal environments. To find out, managers would have to look inside the equipment. By opening up the "black box" of production, they would learn more about how the process really worked. They therefore attached a temperature probe directly to the unprocessed steel and ran it through the furnace, taking readings along the way. Unfortunately, here again there were few differences. The internal temperature of the 91 line was, in fact, 1,850 degrees—just like the 45 line. And the two lines' heating cycles were nearly identical.

Far from being solved, the mystery had only deepened. Managers were stumped. They could think of no other shop-floor experiments to conduct. At the same time, there were growing pressures to find a solution. Producing soft-enough 304DA was not a theoretical problem to be solved at leisure, but one with significant bottom-line implications. According to a participant: "The customer understood that we were going through a learning process. But their patience was becoming short. We needed to solve the problem immediately."

Further progress required even deeper analysis. At Allegheny, this meant shifting from the shop floor to the laboratory. A researcher was briefed about the early experiments. He then reviewed the accompanying data, requested samples of 304D from the 91 line, and examined them under a powerful microscope. He had definite ideas about where to look for clues: the carbon steel in the sandwich, since it was the primary factor distinguishing 304DA from the stainless products that had earlier been transferred without problems. On close examination, the carbon steel samples displayed a distinctive pattern (called a microstructure) that occurred only under certain conditions. According to the researcher:

> There are normally three critical variables that cause this kind of microstructure—how fast you heat the material, how long you hold it at that temperature, and how fast you cool it. They had already done experiments that showed the heating rate and the time at temperature had no effect on the material. So the only other thing that needed to be done was to determine if there was a third or a fourth variable that was not yet taken into account.

The researcher therefore focused his detective work still further. He conducted a series of experiments, heating and cooling small strips of 304DA on a tabletop version of a production line. It soon became clear that the cooling rate was the cause of the problems. But because it was difficult to meet a precise cooling target with large production equipment, the researcher broadened his experiments. Now his goal was to identify a "window" of opportunity—a range of cooling rates that would still produce acceptable softness. He used the cooling rate of the 45 line as a lower bound, since it was known to yield good results. By increasing the cooling rate in small increments until the steel finally became too hard, he came up with a range of values that would meet the customer's demands.

With these findings, the laboratory experiments came to an end. They were a resounding success but would have been far less effective—and far more time-consuming—without the initial work on the shop floor. Even though the early experiments did not solve the immediate problem, they helped rule out alternative explanations. They show that experimentation is a cumulative process in which even negative findings can be of value. As the laboratory researcher discovered, it is generally easier to "find the unknown . . . by . . . narrowing down the possibilities than by making direct but blind guesses."[70]

Yet even with the suggested cooling rates in hand, the problem was not fully solved. Managers still had to get the 91 line to act like the tiny, tabletop version used in the laboratory. Unfortunately, the translation from laboratory to shop floor is seldom straightforward. As a metallurgist observed:

> Lab work is done in a closed environment, where you can set parameters exactly as you like them. In a production facility, that isn't the case. You can approximate where you'd like to be, but there are some variables that cannot be set exactly. So the lab work gives you a direction, but it doesn't always give you the absolute values you need on the line.

At Allegheny, the problem was compounded by the fact that managers had no way of monitoring exactly what went on inside the 91 line's three cooling zones. For technical reasons, they could not attach a probe to the metal and send it through the equipment, as they had done with the furnace. The entire cooling section was sealed and impenetrable. All they could do was take the steel's temperature when it went in hot and again when it came out cool. The rest was guesswork—and experience.

Engineers and technical specialists therefore met as a group to discuss ways of meeting the cooling targets set in the laboratory. Thankfully, they had a range of values to shoot for rather than a single number and could adjust each of the cooling zones independently. As a first step, they decided to shut down the first zone, cut back the second, and leave the third on full. A few coils of 304DA were annealed using the new settings. Samples were rushed to quality control, where they were tested for softness. This time, the steel came out just right. But to confirm the results, managers ran several additional coils at exactly the same settings. When they too passed the tests for softness, the customer was informed. The new settings were then written up as standard operating procedure.

Surprisingly, the experimental process did not end there. Now the goal shifted to optimization: raising the speed of the 91 line without compromising the newly achieved softness. This is a time-honored practice at Allegheny. According to Simmons: "If we can experiment to make it better, then we should—and we do—experiment to make it more efficiently." Here, too, managers proceeded incrementally, running a series of experiments that steadily speeded up the line while simultaneously adjusting cooling rates. The critical variables were now well understood; the challenge was to keep them in balance. After considerable tinkering, the process was optimized. Today, Allegheny's 91 line produces three times more soft steel per day than it did at the start.

Nor was this the only benefit of the experiments. Because they produced deep, enduring knowledge about both product and process, there were several additional applications. Managers used their new knowledge to increase the 45 line's productivity when annealing 304DA and the 91 line's effectiveness when annealing other products. They were able to do so because they had moved, in the language of this chapter, from lower to higher stages of knowledge. They had progressed from "knowing how" to "knowing why."

As this story suggests, Allegheny has mastered the process of experimentation. A quick review of Table 5-3 shows that managers followed all of the guidelines for hypothesis-testing experiments. They began with clear goals, developed a definite set of hypotheses, drew on comprehensive measures, used diverse observers, and employed effective controls. They proceeded selectively, variable by variable, searching for patterns until the causes of the problem were well understood. They moved smoothly from the shop floor to the laboratory and then back to the shop floor, repeating experiments to ensure that their findings were valid. Throughout, they relied on a structure, format, and set of incentives that coordinated efforts and kept all parties aligned.

Equally important was the company's underlying philosophy. At Allegheny, experiments are valued for business reasons, not simply because they are fun to do. As Simmons observed:

> Experimentation is an investment, no different than an investment in a rolling mill, a melt furnace, or a refining vessel. It is an investment that you expect to get a return on. The fact that we don't solve every problem the first time is irrelevant. It is the learning process that creates a culture of continuous improvement, wanting to get better and outperforming your competition.

It should come as no surprise that the company has a sterling record of productivity improvement. In good years, the gains are as much as 7 to 8 percent—two or three times the national average and well ahead of peers. Experimentation deserves much of the credit.

# III

# THE LEADERSHIP CHALLENGE

99 institutionalization

Stages 143-144

Behavior - 12-13

definition 92 *

Supportive Environ. 34-43

13, 15, 17

# 6

## Leading Learning

Today managers and leaders are considered to be very different.[1] Managers are action-oriented; they spend their days doing, delegating, and deciding. Their eyes are on the present, and they measure success by skilled execution and effective implementation. Consistency and stability are the primary goals. Leaders, on the other hand, focus on the future; they spend their time setting targets, developing strategies, communicating vision, and aligning individuals and departments. Change is the primary objective, and the challenge is to get all parts of the organization moving in the desired direction at a rapid enough rate. Clearly, companies need both managers and leaders to succeed, for together they ensure attention to both short- and long-term goals.

Yet according to the preceding chapters, enduring success requires that both groups broaden their horizons. Both need to add a new goal, "improving organizational learning," to their already lengthy agendas. Managers, for example, need to master approaches like Allegheny Ludlum Steel's to ensure operational excellence, while leaders need to craft processes like Xerox 2000 to ensure that their organizations are targeting the right segments and strategies. Superior intelligence gathering, experiential learning, and experimentation are all required. Otherwise, atrophy and drift are inevitable. The challenge is great and becomes ever more pressing with time:

> When organizations and societies are young, they are flexible, fluid, not yet paralyzed by rigid specialization and willing to try anything once. As the organization or society ages, vitality diminishes, flexibility gives way to rigidity, creativity fades and there is a loss of capacity to meet challenges from future directions.[2]

It is for this reason that learning is the key to long-term survival and growth and that organizational effectiveness is so intimately linked to adaptability and flexibility.

Scholars have responded to the need for adaptable, flexible, learning organizations by suggesting that executives devote more of their time to teaching.[3] As one expert put it: "An organization cannot become a learning organization without first becoming a 'teaching' organization."[4] To that end, executives are urged to share their distinctive perspectives about their companies' strategies, purposes, and values. They are told to develop a "teachable point of view" that captivates and enlightens, communicating it to employees through stories and parables. They are instructed to lead management development sessions in which they share their own successes and failures and diffuse their favored approaches throughout the organization. Such prominent CEOs as Roger Enrico of PepsiCo, Jacques Nasser of Ford, and Andy Grove of Intel have taken up this challenge, spending weeks of their time in face-to-face meetings with direct reports and other high-potential managers. There, they tell war stories, describe their personal philosophies, and teach others to use their favorite tools and techniques.

This new role is vitally important. It provides a broad base of knowledge and understanding, gives purpose and meaning to organization members, and ensures commitment to common goals. But it remains incomplete—especially in environments that are changing rapidly and unpredictably. To succeed in those settings, the focus must broaden from teaching to leading learning. The difference is more than mere semantics; it reflects a fundamental shift in perspective and approach.[5]

## TEACHING AND LEARNING

Teaching puts the instructor front and center. Concepts and ideas flow from the top down or the center out, and the focus is on knowledge transfer. Teachers are the experts; their role is to deliver content, communicate clear messages, and instill better ways of working. Students are regarded as novices; their role is to absorb and accept. The effectiveness of the process is usually measured by the degree to which important information makes the trip from the first group to the second without distortion or loss. Unfortunately, all too often a completed trip results in little more than "inert ideas . . . that are merely received into the mind without being utilized, or tested, or thrown into fresh combinations."[6] Knowledge is repackaged and repositioned, but deeper learning is not achieved. As a noted business school professor observed over fifty years ago: "It can be said flatly that the mere act of listening to wise statements and sound advice does little for anyone....We cannot efficiently use the knowledge of others; it must be our own knowledge and insight that we use."[7]

A process designed to foster learning is quite different. New ways of thinking become the desired ends, not facts or frameworks. Discussion and debate replace ex cathedra pronouncements. Questions become as important as answers. And success, to use a currently popular phrase, is measured by the degree to which students "learn how to learn." Because the focus shifts from transferring knowledge to developing organizational skills and capabilities, executives' roles must change as well. They become shepherds of learning, responsible for creating supportive environments, probing for insights and deeper thinking, and constructing settings where employees can collect, interpret, and apply information. This, in turn, requires a significant shift in mind-set and attitudes. According to Charles Peirce, the pragmatist philosopher:

> In order that a man's whole heart may be in teaching he must be thoroughly imbued with the vital importance and absolute truth of what he has to teach; while in order that he may have any success in

learning he must be penetrated with a sense of the unsatisfactoriness of his present condition of knowledge.[8]

For these reasons, executives who are adept at communicating their own opinions and views are seldom equally skilled at shaping and participating in learning processes. To succeed at the latter task, most need to broaden their portfolio of skills. They need to develop a more comprehensive understanding of the elements and conditions that lead to effective intelligence gathering, experiential learning, and experimentation. They need to recognize that each mode of learning involves common activities—data collection, dialogue, and decision making—and that each provides an opportunity for interaction and the cultivation of cognitive and social skills. They need to become sensitive to the risks and barriers that impede learning. And, perhaps most important, they need to shift their attention from content to process.

Learning, after all, is simply another organizational process, not all that different from strategy formulation, product development, or order fulfillment. Like other processes, it unfolds over time, has inputs and outputs, involves diverse departments and levels, and consists of interconnected activities and steps.[9] And like other processes, it must be crafted and led. The concept of a "process owner" is as relevant to intelligence gathering, experiential learning, and experimentation as it is to better-known operational and business processes—and for many of the same reasons: lack of attention, diffused responsibility, fragmentation, and inefficiency. According to an expert on reengineering: "Why did we design inefficient processes? In a way, we didn't. Many of our procedures were not designed at all; they just happened."[10] It is no coincidence that the learning processes described in the preceding chapters all reflect planned, holistic approaches that were developed under the guidance of senior executives. They involve learning skills that were carefully cultivated, often in the face of formidable barriers.

There are three primary tasks. First, leaders and managers must create opportunities for learning by designing settings and events that prompt the necessary activities. Second, they must cultivate the proper tone, fostering desirable norms, behaviors, and rules of engagement. Third, they must personally lead the process of discussion, framing the debate, posing questions, listening attentively, and providing feedback and closure. Done properly, these three tasks go a long way toward building an organization's enduring capacity for learning.

## CREATING THE OPPORTUNITY

Today's managers and employees are inundated with work. They have far too much to do and far too little time to do it. Head counts are down, while workloads continue to rise. Products and services are proliferating, markets are globalizing, and technology is forcing radical changes. The pressure to produce is high and unrelenting. In such settings, the urgent frequently drives out the important, and learning, as chapter 1 observed, becomes an unnecessary frill. It is easily postponed in the face of more immediate demands.

### Learning Forums

To raise its visibility, executives need to create learning forums—assignments, activities, and events whose primary purpose is to foster learning. Think, by way of analogy, of the ancient Roman forum, a central gathering place where citizens discussed the great issues of the day. Organizations are equally in need of public and private settings where they can wrestle collectively with difficult questions. Several have already been discussed: Xerox 2000, which brought together senior managers to examine the company's changing competitive environment and desired product portfolio, technology, and market positioning; L.L. Bean's two-day gathering at Pinkham Notch, which brought together field testers, marketers, product designers, and suppliers to compare products and experiences and to develop a clearer picture of user needs; and the U.S. Army's After Action Reviews, which brought together soldiers and their commanders immediately after missions or training exercises to explore the reasons for success or failure. Each of these forums exposed participants to raw, unfiltered data and then offered time for reflection and interpretation, leading to improved understanding as well as concrete actions and plans.

Learning forums can take many other forms. They include systems audits, which review the health of large, cross-functional processes and delivery systems; internal benchmarking projects, which identify and compare best-in-class activities within an organization; and study missions, which dispatch employees to leading organizations around the world to better understand their performance and distinctive skills. All, it should be clear, involve a well-defined learning agenda and complete, compressed learning cycles. A small group of people is assembled and given a learning task; first-hand information is collected and alternative interpretations are explored; and implications are developed and quickly deployed.

All of these examples involve activities that are separate from daily work. They exist apart from employees' normal responsibilities, and learning is the primary, if not the sole, goal. But forums need not be one-of-a-kind events or assignments. Nor do they necessarily demand dedicated task forces. Even routine meetings and get-togethers—weekly telephone calls, monthly staff meetings, quarterly off-sites—can serve as learning forums, providing they are properly designed and led. The trick is to ensure that learning goals are well defined, decisions are deferred until ideas mature, and leaders steer participants toward insights as well as action. Improvements in collective understanding must be viewed as a prelude to bottom-line gains.

In more formal terms, executives must shift from a pure performance orientation—in which results are all that matter—to one that balances performance and learning goals. According to scholars, when people find themselves in settings such as the classroom or the workplace, they typically display one of two orientations.[11] Some focus primarily on performance; their goal is to gain favorable evaluations from superiors and perform well relative to peers. Others focus primarily on learning; their goal is to increase their competence and skills and develop increased mastery of the task at hand.

A performance orientation is desirable because it produces hard work. But it has a number of unfortunate side effects. When people evaluate themselves strictly on their current rankings and results, they are much more likely to shun difficult challenges, sacrifice potential learning opportunities, and avoid situations where there is a high risk of error. People with a learning orientation, on the other hand, tend to persist in the face of obstacles. They willingly assume challenges that broaden their portfolio of skills, even if errors are likely. Over time, they gain both competence and confidence, and their results improve. Put succinctly, a performance orientation ensures that people will work hard in order to look good; a learning orientation ensures that they will work smart in order to perform better.

While the two orientations are to some degree ingrained, they also reflect the surrounding environment. Psychologists have found that when teachers focus exclusively on results, respond negatively to errors, and praise students for their innate abilities, they tend to encourage a performance orientation. When they pay attention to personal development, use errors as opportunities for improvement, and praise students for their effort and hard work, they tend to encourage a learning orientation. The analogy to management should be obvious. Just as teachers are responsible for the environments of their classrooms, leaders are responsible for the climates of their organizations. For both short- and long-term success, they must attend to more than results alone. A performance orientation remains vital—otherwise, employees will engage in activity for activity's sake, with little direction or design—but its impact can be magnified when coupled with efforts to stimulate more of a learning orientation.

Chad Holliday, for example, the CEO of DuPont, works personally to improve his organization's skill at intelligence gathering. Every other week, he holds a telephone conference with twenty top managers from around the globe. The group is expected to stay on top of changes in customers, competitors, and local economies and politics by sharing the latest insights from the field. Sessions are highly interactive, with Holliday taking the lead. Not by giving answers, however, but by asking questions: "What's happening to our customers and their customers? To the political will of local leaders to deal with the downturn? To the changing competitive rules? What do we need to do now?" His goal is to help members of the group educate one another by learning more about critical issues in the marketplace. In his words: "By hearing the answers simultaneously from their peers, they broaden their perspective of the global landscape."[12]

Successful forums like Holliday's share several characteristics. They increase participants' exposure to information by introducing new, previously untapped sources of data. They encourage divergent thinking by cultivating a range of interpretations and views. They engage participants by assigning topics and themes that prompt open discussion without stirring up traditional functional and divisional loyalties. They counteract common learning disabilities by employing a variety of "debiasing" techniques.[13] And they stimulate exploratory thinking by injecting counterintuitive and unexpected perspectives into discussions. At heart, these are little more than clever techniques for overcoming the pressures and prejudices of daily work that so often short-circuit learning.

Planning meetings, for example, frequently operate on automatic pilot. They seldom encourage active engagement or new thinking. In many cases, senior managers arrive armed with the latest competitive or customer information and then report it to subordinates, who are expected to relay the same data to others with little or no embellishment. In other cases, participants arrive having read the same memo or report; they then compare notes and choose among prespecified alternatives, usually by giving a simple thumbs-up or thumbs-down. Discussion normally proceeds predictably, with few surprises and limited learning. Yet the process does not have to be so confining. More active, stimulating approaches are possible; typically, they involve pooling information from diverse sources and continually challenging, testing, and debating.

Chuck Knight, the CEO of Emerson Electric, has long embedded learning in his company's planning reviews. Division general managers submit their plans in advance, knowing that their presentations will be interrupted by difficult, often unsettling questions. All proposals are vetted, however carefully they have been constructed and designed. "The concept," according to a senior corporate officer, "is to disagree with the thesis being presented, irrespective of the thesis."[14] Why? Because Knight's primary goal is to establish the depth and quality of the supporting analysis, not simply approve proposals. He does so by probing each and every argument to uncover unfounded assumptions and logical flaws. This not only improves his understanding of the plans but also sharpens the thinking of division managers as well.

## Exploratory Assignments

Of course, meetings need not be contentious and argumentative to produce deep learning. Sometimes, the same results can be achieved simply by bringing together participants around a common challenge and setting aside enough time and space so that real thinking can occur. This is especially true when problems are ambiguous or poorly defined. Then, broad exploratory assignments, open-ended questions, and an atmosphere of give and take seem to work best. Jack Welch used this approach when he first introduced Work-Out at GE. He structured the two-day meetings of his Corporate Executive Council (CEC) as forums for sharing best practices and accelerating progress. The CEC is composed of the heads of GE's fourteen major businesses. For many months, Work-Out was virtually the only topic on its agenda. Moreover, the format and approach of CEC meetings were designed to foster collaboration and experiential learning. The setting was informal; meetings were run like workshops; all participants were expected to come with experiences to share, based on their successes and failures with Work-Out; formal presentations were not allowed; and sessions were highly interactive, with Welch guiding the discussion.[15]

John Fahey of Time Life used a similar approach to foster thinking by his senior team about multimedia products and the best use of the company's master file, editorial staff, and other shared assets. In 1992 he appointed a Corporate Strategy Committee, consisting of Time Life's three division heads as well as key functional leaders, to consider ways that the books, music, and video and television divisions might work together more productively. At the time, there was little interdivisional cooperation; the company, in Fahey's view, was little more than "a loosely confederated conglomerate." He therefore began by giving the group a wide-open assignment, designed to break down barriers and free up thinking rather than solve immediate problems. Members were asked to consider the meaning and possible extent of "strategic integration"; they met several times, away from the workplace and under the guidance of a trained facilitator, to brainstorm possible interpretations. A few weeks later, Fahey asked each member of the committee to prepare two brief documents: a vision of Time Life in the year 2002 and a description of what the corporate strategy statement should and should not be. These topics were also cleverly selected to encourage dialogue and discussion; they were chosen for their ability to stimulate thinking, not produce solutions or tangible outputs. Meetings continued for several months. By that time, the group had progressed to the point where they had developed a common vocabulary and shared understanding; then, and only then, did Fahey ask them to come up with a detailed agenda, including a small number of strategic goals and several significant organization changes. The final result was a tightly knit senior team, more efficient operations, an improved approach to multimedia products, and increased profitability.[16]

## Shared Experiences

At times, especially when radical changes are required, senior executives may find it necessary to put managers and employees through a learning process that mimics one they have personally experienced. Otherwise, they may fail to understand the rationale and need for new behaviors. Here, a common problem is surface agreement that cloaks deep uncertainties and doubts. Members of the organization may have heard the words but do not yet understand the music. Craig Weatherup, the president and CEO of Pepsi-Cola North America, overcame these barriers with a carefully crafted learning process. In September 1990, after several months of reviewing financial data, interviewing customers and employees, and visiting field operations, he launched a massive change process. Pepsi was facing pressure on several fronts because of shifting competitive requirements. According to Weatherup:

> In the late 1980s, we made a $4 billion bet, buying up many of our independent bottlers to gain control over distribution. Almost overnight, we went from a company with 600 customers—the franchised bottlers—to a company with 600,000 customers. And we moved aggressively into a wide range of alternative beverages, such as juices and teas, and added lots of new packaging. All of a sudden, we had an explosion of complexity in various shapes, forms, and sizes.
>
> At the same time, we were still a company with a "big event" marketing mentality. Our entire mindset was geared to superstar entertainers such as Michael Jackson and Ray Charles. However, we now had several hundred thousand customers, and we weren't spending enough time thinking about them. The complexity was a huge challenge and drove us to this compelling commitment: to devote as much time, energy, and passion to operations and service as we had historically devoted to marketing.[17]

To communicate these new priorities, Weatherup began with a four-day meeting of his direct reports, designed to introduce them to the new demands facing the company and win acceptance of the need for change. After considerable discussion, they accepted the challenge and began crafting a vision. But there were questions about how the rest of the organization would react. The business was still profitable and successful; Weatherup was anticipating problems, not responding to current difficulties. He and his team therefore designed a learning process to ensure that the new needs were better understood. Every three months they worked with a different group, starting with the 70 people who were on the rung below the senior team, moving to larger groups of 400 and 1,200, then to a huge meeting of 5,500 in Dallas, and finally to a one-day video presentation to all 20,000 frontline employees.

Each group followed the same format. After a three-day kickoff meeting, participants were given ninety days to complete assigned activities, which included interviewing customers, charting work processes, and designing and leading the three-day enrollment meeting for the next group of employees. As Weatherup observed, these ninety-day cycles were based on an explicit model of learning:

> We ended up calling it "head, heart, hands" because we believed that for change to occur, people had to do three things: develop a conceptual understanding of the rationale and proposed direction of change, internalize and commit emotionally to the new vision, and acquire new skills to ensure that the vision would be realized.[18]

In essence, Weatherup was requiring others in the organization to undergo a learning process similar to the one that he had personally experienced, but to do so in a vastly compressed period. Like Fahey, he was also triggering a process of "unlearning," dislodging long-established patterns of behavior by challenging ways of thinking that had worked successfully in the past.[19] It succeeded admirably, producing a new mind-set, improved service, more efficient operations, a new organization structure, and, over the course of eight years, a doubling of revenues and a tripling of operating income.[20]

Weatherup, Fahey, Welch, Knight, and Holliday were all able to devise processes that encouraged others in the organization to learn in new and different ways. All five executives designed or constructed settings that caused managers and employees to adopt, at least temporarily, more of a learning orientation. Participants shared information, pooled insights, explored innovative ideas, stretched their imaginations, and broadened their experiences to a degree that they would not have otherwise. In the process, they managed to keep traditional business concerns firmly in their sights. The results were both hard and soft gains: measurable improvements in bottom-line performance, as well as more knowledgeable, involved employees.

## SETTING THE TONE

All of these examples also show the importance of setting the proper tone. As chapter 2 observed, learning is a difficult and delicate process: it will flower only if the climate is right. Participants face considerable uncertainty and risk. Politics and gamesmanship often impede the smooth flow of information. Partisanship can easily derail discussions. Learning, after all, is seldom an unmixed blessing. There are normally competing interests at stake, and some parties will benefit at the expense of others. Executives must therefore work hard to encourage objective, open-minded inquiry. Otherwise, even the best-designed forums will produce only limited insight.

There are several requirements. The atmosphere must be one of challenge, skepticism, and doubt, so that easy, pat solutions are not accepted until they have been subjected to careful scrutiny. Participants must feel a sense of security, so that they can stretch themselves in new directions without fear of failure, and incentives must support experimentation and risk taking. A sense of fairness must prevail, with no group feeling that its ideas are getting short shrift. And the rules of engagement must encourage the sharing of knowledge, so that information is pooled and becomes common property. Cultivating such climates requires special sensitivities: extraordinary attention to context and tone, the ability to draw people out, and a deep familiarity with the forces that drive learning. In the words of Bob Galvin, the former CEO of Motorola, the focus shifts from deciding and directing "to creat[ing] and maintain[ing] an evocative situation, stimulating an atmosphere of objective participation,

keeping the goal in sight, recognizing valid consensus, inviting unequivocal recommendation, and finally vesting increasingly in others the privi-
lege to learn through their own decisions."[21]

## Challenge and Dissent

This does not mean that executives should strive to create "warm and
fuzzy" cultures that lack tension or pressure. Learning must be channeled
and directed; otherwise, "the result is likely to be a series of random
walks to personal enlightenment that do little for overall performance."[22]
Ensuring that employees deal with difficult business issues is a vital part
of the leader's role.[23] But challenges must be framed in ways that encourage inquiry and foster a learning orientation. Tough questions can be
raised, but they must be framed in ways that draw participants into the
problem. Neither stinging critiques nor fiery speeches are necessary. Instead, effective interventions typically take one of three forms: (1) tentative, partially developed proposals that stimulate discussion; (2) novel,
unexpected questions that prompt new thinking; or (3) changes in processes and procedures that introduce contrary, dissenting views.

Galvin used the first approach in 1983, when, at the company's bien-
nial meeting of top officers, he rose to deliver his usual summary speech
and instead made an unexpected request: that managers take a fresh look
at the structure of their organizations. He urged them to consider the
possibility of shifting to smaller, more focused business units, decreasing
the many layers of management while bringing executives closer to products and markets. He concluded with an invitation and a promise:

> I see a welling up of the evidence of need and today I think the
> window is open. So I decided to express my concern and my convic-
> tion to you, confident that you share my insights and that together
> we will find our way to an organized effort of change. When we
> come together in two years, we will report and share the changes
> made and the lessons learned.[24]

Galvin's remarks were unscripted and deliberately vague; they were
designed to surface an important concern, not resolve it. This was very
much in keeping with his concept of his own role—as one who stirs the

pot, raising important but overlooked issues, even though he lacks immediate answers. Galvin's brief, provocative speech prompted a multiyear
process of soul searching by Motorola's managers, as well as extensive
discussions of the current structure. In time, they led to several innovative experiments, a new program for organizational effectiveness, and
significant improvements in speed and responsiveness.[25]

Harvey Golub, the CEO of American Express, has long relied on the
second approach to set tone. He pushes hard on the reasoning process,
forcing managers to think creatively and in unexpected ways. Often, a
subordinate observed, he "comes at things from a different angle" to
ensure that conventional approaches are not accepted without first being
examined deeply. In Golub's words:

> I am far less interested in people having the right answer than in
> their thinking about issues the right way. What criteria do they use?
> Why do they think the way they do? What alternatives have they
> considered? What premises do they have? What rocks are they
> standing on?[26]

Such questions are not designed to lead to a particular answer but are
aimed at generating truly open-minded discussion. There is an important
difference between Golub's style of probing, which is designed to
broaden thinking, and a Socratic approach, in which the endpoint is
known and novices are led by the nose until they arrive at the desired
conclusion. Members of the senior team at American Express clearly
recognize the distinction:

> I can't remember Harvey ever telling anyone what to do. He pays
> more attention to *how* you think than anything else. He is always
> testing your thinking process. If he finds that you have thought
> about something really well, you get to do it. If not, you get coached.
>
> Harvey really has only two questions in business unit reviews:
> "How did you think about that? And how would it be different if you
> thought about it this way instead?"
>
> Harvey is the best counterintuitive thinker I have ever seen. If
> everyone agrees on something, he will ask, "Why?" For example,

when everyone agreed that we should lower credit card fees, he spent two days with us discussing his counterproposal—that maybe we should raise them. I don't think he meant it seriously, but he certainly taught us how to think about fees.[27]

Such interactions, it should be clear, produce in-depth discussions without the emotional fallout that so often accompanies barbed questions from the CEO. They also produce deep learning on multiple fronts— substantively, about the issue at hand, as well as cognitively, about how to approach problems better in the future.

President Kennedy used the third approach to create an atmosphere conducive to learning. After his disastrous experience with the Bay of Pigs, in which interdepartmental politics sharply restricted learning, he redesigned the national security decision-making process to ensure that dissenting views were encouraged and difficult issues were aired. Kennedy began by establishing new ground rules. Senior advisers were told that pure partisanship would no longer be acceptable. All assumptions would now be tested. Intelligence information would be regularly updated and shared, without filtering by intermediaries.

Then, Kennedy assigned new roles. Every participant was asked to function as a "skeptical generalist," assuming a broad integrated perspective rather than the narrow focus of his or her agency or department. Robert Kennedy and Theodore Sorensen, two of Kennedy's most trusted advisers, were asked to be "intellectual watchdogs," with the goal of "pursu[ing] relentlessly every bone of contention in order to prevent errors arising from too superficial analysis of the issues."

Finally, Kennedy tackled the process itself, reconfiguring it to open up debate. The usual rules of protocol were suspended so that respect for hierarchy no longer squelched discussion. New advisers were routinely brought into meetings to inject fresh views. Separate subcommittees were used to flesh out alternative positions. Kennedy deliberately absented himself from preliminary discussions to ensure that his personal views did not limit the alternatives generated by advisers. Together, these changes introduced far more challenge and breadth into the decision-making process. The new approach was quickly tested during the Cuban missile crisis, where it served the president to great effect.[28]

## Security and Support

Challenge alone, however, is not enough to guarantee learning. Individuals also need a sense of security if they are to throw off old ways of thinking and acting. As a noted educator observed: "Learning means leaving the known for the unknown—an exhilarating, but scary venture."[29] Fear of failure creates personal risk and vulnerability; both make it difficult to move forward. Some level of support is therefore required if the process is ever to get off the ground. Here, senior executives play a vital role, for they can personally shape the environment in ways that provide protection and support.

Linda Doyle, the president and CEO of Harvard Business School Publishing (HBSP), has long tried to create a secure, supportive environment—in her words, "a clearing where it is safe to talk about hard issues." In 1994 Doyle inherited a fragile organization that was still emerging from difficult, uncertain times. HBSP was only two years old, having been stitched together from several previously independent groups. Employees were struggling to find an identity and common goals. In addition, most members of the organization had a strong critical bent. HBSP was populated with editors and academics; bright people who by temperament and training had a critical cast of mind, enjoyed finding holes in arguments, and were skilled at explaining why new ideas would not work. The typical discussion, Doyle observed, often resembled a "skeet shoot. Someone would yell 'pull,' there would be a deafening blast, and the idea would be in pieces on the ground."

To create a more supportive setting, she took several reinforcing steps. (The goal, she later recalled, was to help people learn to "disagree without being disagreeable.") To begin, Doyle sent clear signals about the desired tone, intervening in meetings to halt overheated or nonproductive discussions. She sent the same messages privately during managers' performance reviews. Next, she set strict ground rules for strategy development, insisting that no one criticize ideas during the initial brainstorming process. Finally, she hired a consultant to introduce and train members of the organization in the use of Edward de Bono's "six thinking hats." De Bono is a leading expert on creativity; he developed the six thinking hats as a way of categorizing the types of comments that people make and the roles and positions they frequently take in discussions. A "white hat" comment is neutral or factual; a "red hat" comment is emotional or judgmental; a "yellow hat" comment is positive or constructive; a "black hat" comment is negative or critical; a "green hat" comment is creative or innovative; and a "blue hat" comment is process- or discussion-focused.[30] Doyle's goals in introducing this approach were to help people vary their own thinking styles and become more receptive to different types of thinking. She also wanted to open up and broaden discussion, giving people permission to express feelings or make negative comments while softening their effect. Over time, these interventions had a significant cumulative impact. They produced an environment that was more tolerant of dissent, more supportive of experimentation, and more committed to shared discussion and learning. They also led to sharp increases in growth and net contribution.[31]

An equally effective way of providing security is to give learners help when they first venture into the unknown. Like any high-wire act, learning is far less stressful when a safety net is near. Risks are greatly reduced when one works side by side with an experienced expert or can bounce ideas off a knowledgeable superior. Errors may still occur, but they are a lot less damaging. This principle has long been the mainstay of apprenticeship programs; it is easily adapted to other corporate settings. Managers at Chaparral Steel, for example, have developed a practice that they call "vice-ing." When a foreman or supervisor is absent, the most senior operator or craftsman is temporarily promoted to take his place. He becomes a "vice foreman," with expanded responsibilities. But his superiors ensure that he has help in the new role. A vice-foreman is always assisted by the foreman from the previous shift, who works extra hours at his usual pay level, but as second-in-command. He becomes a subordinate and a security blanket. This approach meets several goals simultaneously. It stretches and challenges employees, transfers expertise, avoids risky errors, and creates a supportive learning environment.[32]

Zaki Mustafa, vice president and general manager of Serengeti Eyewear, a division of Corning, used a similar approach to foster learning. Rather than delegating the task to others, he took personal responsibility for giving employees the needed sense of security. In part, he did so out of necessity, because there were few other resources available. In 1984, after years of weak sales and profits, Corning had decided to exit the sunglasses business; only a last-minute appeal from Mustafa, who was then operations manager, succeeded in keeping it afloat. After assuming the role of general manager, he began to create a new environment that would expand employees' knowledge and skills. His goals were developmental—to build the business by building the skills of the few remaining employees. The resulting process relied heavily on collaboration and hand-holding, as well as conscious efforts to reduce risk. As Mustafa described the process:

> People would come to me with a problem—say, expanding our distribution system. I would talk with them, and they would arrive at "a recommendation." I would say, "That's really your decision, so go do it." They wanted it to be my decision, but I wouldn't let it be. Gradually, a pattern evolved, with people coming to me to help them "think things through." Then, after awhile, they stopped coming to me for advice [either].
>
> My goal has been to get people to aspire to do more than they thought they could. Once they have experienced that, the sky's the limit. But they need to know that it's not exploitation for the sake of business. They have my support all the way, and if something goes wrong, I'll take the rap for it.

Using this approach, and with only limited additional investment, Mustafa succeeded in turning the business around and then growing it substantially. Serengeti's sales expanded more than tenfold between 1984 and 1992. By the end of the period, it was one of Corning's most profitable divisions.[33]

## Open Communication

A final element of tone is open access to information. Executives must send the signal that knowledge is to be shared, not hoarded, especially among peers. They are, after all, invaluable sources of insight, since they usually face similar problems and opportunities. As Ralph Waldo Emerson, the American essayist, noted over a hundred years ago: "I pay the schoolmaster, but 'tis the schoolboys that educate my son."[34] This is a concept that receives lip service at most corporations today but is surprisingly rare in practice. Why? Because knowledge is power, and shared knowledge usually means less power. To overcome the problem, leaders have three main options. They can alter incentives, rewarding individuals if they share knowledge with others. They can redesign work processes, legitimizing knowledge sharing as a form of behavior. And they can impose policies and directives that require managers to seek help from others in order to complete their assignments.

The first approach can be seen at Ernst & Young, which evaluates and compensates consultants on their contributions to companywide databases and other knowledge repositories.[35] The second approach can be seen at British Petroleum, which employs a knowledge-sharing process called Peer Assists. It brings together engineers, geologists, and other experts from around the globe to help divisions and departments solve difficult problems. Reciprocity becomes part of daily work, since as many as 3 to 5 percent of the people in a unit may be involved in assists at any given time.[36] The third approach can be seen at Rank Xerox, which recently asked a central group to compile a list of best practices in sales and marketing from all parts of Europe. Country managers were then told to choose four items from the list and adopt them without alteration. Because no single country was represented by more than one practice, most sales and marketing personnel found themselves serving as both teachers and learners, overcoming the one-way flow that so often impedes effective knowledge sharing.[37]

Finally, senior executives must remember to model personally the desired attitude and tone. The tenor and style of their communications matter a great deal. An open, inviting approach is essential; it is far more likely to be effective than one in which content is tightly controlled.[38] In fact, a well-tuned communication process is often the key to learning. According to social psychologists: "[T]he way the group 'utilizes' its resources and the procedures it employs for communicating essential information are as important, if not more important than 'knowledge' of the problem for determining its performance."[39] For example, routinely acknowledging that information has been received not only encourages greater information sharing but also leads to fewer errors. In addition, information can be solicited in many different ways, with widely varying impact. Some executives issue commands ("Ask the marketing department to collect information on customers"), others make observations ("I think we should ask the marketing department to collect information on customers"), and still others pose inquiries ("Why don't we ask the marketing department to collect information on customers?"). The resulting responses are not always the same, and the accompanying environments often differ dramatically in their levels of coordination and information exchange.[40]

## LEADING THE DISCUSSION

Once leaders have created the desired climate, learning can begin in earnest. Whether the focus is intelligence gathering, learning from experience, or experimentation, some discussion is usually involved. In fact, virtually every example in this book—Xerox 2000, L.L. Bean's use of field testers, the Center for Army Lessons Learned and After-Action Reviews, GE's Change Acceleration Process, Timken's Cardboard City, and Allegheny Ludlum's experiments with 304DA—involved intensive discussions at several points along the way. Findings were seldom self-evident. Meaning often had to be constructed, and participants usually found it necessary to engage actively with the material and with one another, debating alternatives until they reached a decision or conclusion.

Such discussions seldom proceed smoothly or of their own accord. They can easily derail, resulting in entrenched positions, superficial debate, finger-pointing, miscommunication, and an inability to move forward. For real progress to occur, considerable shaping and direction are required. Someone has to lead the process. Skilled executives recognize that this is one of their primary responsibilities. As Linda Doyle put it, describing her efforts to gain acceptance for centralized marketing from the heads of the largely autonomous units that been melded into Harvard Business School Publishing:

> Until people began to see the vision of what might be and could live it and breathe it, they were never going to give up control. If I had forced the issue, it would just have driven them underground. What

I had to do was lead the case discussion, so they would see the need for themselves.[41]

To succeed at this process, executives need skills in three broad areas: questioning, listening, and responding.[42] All are tools of effective discussion leaders. And all can be used equally effectively in corporate settings.

## *Questioning*

Questions, for example, are enormously powerful tools for leading learning. They are the motive and force that gives shape to inquiry. Unfortunately, managers often treat questions as second-class citizens and regard them as a badge of ignorance. They prefer bold assertions and strong statements because they convey a sense of mastery and control. Yet questions are vital for moving groups forward. Peter Drucker, in fact, has argued that "the most common source of mistakes in management decisions is the emphasis on finding the right answer rather than the right question."[43] Good questions get to the heart of a matter; they force deep thinking and reflection. They must therefore be formulated with care and applied with a deft, sensitive touch. Just as surgeons should not wield scalpels blindly or without proper training, managers should not use questions without first developing a clearer sense of their strengths, weaknesses, benefits, and risks.

To begin, it is important to recognize that not all questions are alike. They come in many forms and play diverse roles. There is no single best type of question; the preferred form depends on the situation and current needs. Questions can be used to:

- frame issues,
- offer instructions,
- solicit information,
- probe for analysis,
- draw connections,
- seek opinions, and
- ratify decisions.[44]

Framing, for example, is critical for defining and structuring problems properly. A manager's opening question often shapes the task for the group by setting boundaries and providing a context for discussion ("Why don't we consider this proposal in light of the likely responses of current and future competitors?"). At the same time, questions can be used to issue instructions. With a bit of imagination, leaders can use them to set the agenda and assign roles, while simultaneously focusing the group's attention ("Could we begin by having Larry discuss the most recent intelligence he collected on U.S. Industrial, since they seem to pose the greatest challenge going forward?"). Soliciting information and probing for analysis are two sides of the same coin; both are essential if leaders hope to deepen understanding and move the group beyond superficial arguments ("Do we have any evidence that supports this hypothesis? Are there other possible reasons why the 91 line might be producing steel that is too hard?"). Questions are equally effective at building bridges among participants and linking comments in constructive ways. They allow executives to create a sense of camaraderie and collaboration, while moving the debate forward ("Aren't Fred and Mary really saying the same thing—that we need to involve all operating units in our efforts to achieve an 85 percent learning curve?"). Finally, managers can use questions to test for agreement or disagreement and ultimately to bring discussions to a close ("Are we all in accord on this strategy? Does everyone understand their new assignments?").

Clearly, one implication of this list is that executives need to broaden the range of questions they employ. Excessive use of a single approach is unlikely to produce the greatest possible learning. But even after expanding their repertoires, most managers need to take additional steps to ensure that they are using questions most effectively. They need to adopt a few rules of thumb, since certain questioning styles are preferable if the aim is to encourage learning. For example, open questions, which allow for a variety of possible responses and do not point respondents in a particular, prespecified direction, are normally better than closed questions. Typically, they invite greater involvement and participation, and produce a wider range of options and alternatives. Designers at L.L. Bean, for example, are likely to learn a great deal more by asking field testers, "Why do you prefer this design?" than by asking them, "Do you prefer this parka because of its large pockets or drawstring hood?" The first question invites a range of possible answers; the second virtually dictates the response. According to a skilled practitioner:

> The open question is broad, the closed question narrow. The open question allows the interviewee full scope; the closed question limits him to a specific answer. The open question invites him to widen his perceptual field; the closed question curtails it. The open question solicits his views, opinions, thoughts, and feelings; the closed question usually demands cold facts only. The open question may widen and deepen the contact; the closed question may circumscribe it. In short, the former may widen the door to good rapport; the latter usually keeps it shut.[45]

In a similar fashion, questions should be designed to draw out assumptions and ensure that people are talking *to* one another rather than past each other. Discussions often founder needlessly because of unstated differences in meaning. Especially when groups span geographies or are composed of members with diverse backgrounds and experiences, even the simplest communication presents a challenge. Common problems include different uses of the same terms and different reference points. Lucent Technologies, for example, had considerable difficulty with a large software development project because programmers in New Jersey and Massachusetts used the word "test" so differently.[46] Lucent is hardly alone. Misinterpretation is distressingly common, as two classic studies of communication found:

> The one thing people tend to take for granted when talking to others is that they understand each other. It is rare, indeed, in a meeting to have someone hold up his own argument long enough to say, "I think you said . . . Did you?" or "Was I right in thinking you meant . . . ?" We found people ever so eager to parry what a man says without ever wondering whether *that* is what the man said.[47]
>
> People often think they disagree when actually they simply are not talking about the same experiences. In such cases they do not draw each other out far enough to realize that, although they are using the same *words*, they are thinking about different *experiences*.[48]

Such problems would disappear if discussion leaders, as well as participants, probed more actively for the roots of differing positions.

Questions are also powerful tools for overcoming the biases and learning disabilities described in chapter 2. By injecting contrary, divergent views into discussions, they broaden participants' field of view and counteract common errors. Groups are less likely to be blindsided by unforeseen events if they have tried to consider them in advance; individuals are less likely to be overconfident if they have faced humbling feedback or contradictory evidence.[49] Questions that produce such insights may take a variety of forms—counterfactuals, hypotheticals, even the illogical alternatives posed by Chuck Knight in his planning reviews. Here, a particularly useful questioning technique is the "pre-mortem," in which participants are asked to imagine, *before* a policy or practice is formally adopted, that time has elapsed, the approach has been introduced, and the results are extremely disappointing. They must then explain why. Researchers have found that this approach generates a longer list of potential weaknesses than traditional analysis, as well as more robust plans going forward. Looking back to the future—with what scholars call "prospective hindsight"—leads groups to imagine flaws more easily while generating richer, more concrete, often unanticipated insights.[50]

How, then, should executives develop these skills? Few managers are naturally talented at questioning; their training normally points them in other directions. To acquire the needed expertise, they have three main options: seeking instruction, learning through observation, and engaging in deliberate practice. Xerox used all three approaches in 1992. After a massive reorganization, members of the Corporate Office were having difficulty framing questions for the newly appointed business heads. They continued to delve into the same kinds of operational challenges as they had previously, even though they now needed to provide more strategic direction. To learn to ask the right questions, they requested that the director of strategy canvass the best strategic thinkers he could find—at leading consulting firms, as well as respected corporations—and ask them to identify the questions and frameworks they used when reviewing strategies, assessing markets, and evaluating competitors. Armed with these findings, they worked to develop an expanded vocabulary and better strategic insights. They then began to ask new and different questions of the business unit heads, leading to sharp improvements in their plans.[51]

## *Listening*

Of course, skilled questioning is not enough to ensure that discussions are productive. If real learning is to occur, there must also be active listening. The two go hand in hand, like the blades of a scissors. Questioning generates the needed raw material, while listening ensures that it is put to good use. As chapter 3 pointed out, listening is a demanding process that requires attentiveness; it is not "just the act of keeping still."[52] Since this will occur only if one is "genuinely interested in what matters to the other person," attitude is as important as skill.[53] But like questioning, listening can usually by improved by following a few, simple guidelines.

Perhaps the most important is practicing patience. All too often, managers interrupt before others have finished, short-circuiting the learning process. They jump to conclusions, assuming that they have understood someone's position before receiving a full briefing. Or they project so much of their own thinking into the conversation that the original message is lost. This problem is hardly confined to business. A study of seventy-four medical interviews found that over two-thirds of the patients were interrupted by their doctors within the first eighteen seconds of beginning to explain what was wrong with them. Only one got to finish. Most doctors assumed that the first complaint they heard was the most important and designed their treatment accordingly. Yet when patients were given the chance to say everything on their mind, their third complaint was actually the most troubling.[54] The analogy to managers, particularly when they interact with subordinates and peers, should be clear. They too must remember that it is difficult to hear words that are left unsaid.

In the same spirit, executives must learn to listen for "disconnects" during discussion. Effective communication requires a strong link between source and receiver. As the writer Henry David Thoreau put it: "It takes two to speak truth—one to speak and another to hear."[55] But these connections take work, as well as empathy and rapport. Members of a group must be willing to suspend their preconceptions long enough to internalize what others are actually saying. Here, a useful technique for leaders is to insist that participants repeat what they have just heard and then to ask the original speaker to verify that his or her point has been correctly stated. Only after participants have agreed that the message has been heard is debate allowed to begin.

It should be clear that effective discussions require leaders who are able to listen at multiple levels. They must learn to attend—simultaneously—to *what* is being said and *how* it is stated. They must listen for affect and tone—"the tremulous voice, the stereotyped role . . . the angry, belittling response"—as carefully as they listen to content.[56] They must be vigilant in rooting out personal attacks that so often accompany substantive disagreements. Otherwise, discussions will quickly lose their value, and inquiries will become inquisitions. Unfortunately, "many people seem not to realize that it is possible to quarrel on an issue without . . . doubting another's sincerity or casting aspersions on his integrity."[57] It is up to leaders to make sure that the line is not crossed.

For similar reasons, they must remain on the lookout for nonparticipants—voices not heard—and must find ways of bringing them into the dialogue. Silence is not always a sign of assent; it can just as easily signal apathy or disaffection. Here, it is wise to heed the advice of Bob Galvin, who defined his role, in part, as "look[ing] for the unattended, the void, the exception that my associates are too busy to see."[58] Listening to these voices provided him with a window into his company's most pressing problems.

## Responding

If leaders did no more than ask questions and listen for answers, many discussions would eventually bog down. Executives must also be able to respond—usually, on the spot and in real time. An issue is raised, an opinion is ventured, an argument breaks out, and all eyes turn to the most senior person in the room. How should she react if she hopes to stimulate learning? There are an almost infinite variety of choices, and many paths to success. But there are also a few practices that should be avoided at all costs because they are extremely damaging. Some create high levels of uncertainty and risk, others discourage dissenting or contradictory views, while still others condition speakers to clam up in the future. The results, in each case, are impediments to future participation.

Two of the most pernicious practices are "depreciation-of-the-learner" and "drowning-of-the-learner."[59] The former asserts an executive's superiority by dumping cold water on anyone else's comments; the latter asserts his expertise by responding to simple queries with prolonged, mind-numbing lectures. In both cases, further contributions are unlikely to be forthcoming. Dialogue disappears, and learning is severely hampered. This problem is not merely theoretical or confined to the classroom; it has been observed in a variety of real-world settings, with severe consequences. Studies of cockpit crews, for example, have found that insensitive, intimidating captains create a form of trained incapacity in their copilots and crew—an unwillingness to speak up even when faced with potentially dangerous situations. Several fatal crashes have been the result.[60]

To avoid these problems, executives need to broaden their repertoires. They need to approach responding as they approach questioning, with an arsenal of skills. No one technique is best, and each has its place. The possibilities can be arrayed on a spectrum, ranging from responses that are more reflective and speaker-centered to those that are more intrusive and interventionist (see Figure 6-1).[61] At one extreme are responses like silence, restatement, and clarification; they keep the focus on the speaker and encourage a more extended presentation. At the other end of the spectrum are responses like ridicule, denial, and threat; they involve the open use of power and invariably put distance between leaders and followers. Responses like encouragement and suggestion are somewhere in the middle; they remain upbeat and supportive in tone but inject a point of view. Also in the middle are responses like disagreement and criticism; they too inject a point of view but one that is opposed to the speaker's. The choice among these approaches is both situational and cultural; it reflects the issues at hand, as well as an organization's characteristic ways of acting and interacting. GE and Emerson Electric have flourished under leaders with a scrapping, combative style; Pepsi-Cola and Serengeti Eyewear have profited from leaders with a more supportive, accepting style. In general, however, when the goal is fostering

## FIGURE 6-1
### A SPECTRUM OF RESPONSES IN LEADING DISCUSSIONS

| Response | Characteristic | Position on Spectrum |
|---|---|---|
| • Silence<br>• Restatement<br>• Clarification | Keeps the focus on the speaker | Reflective, facilitative |
| • Encouragement<br>• Suggestion | Injects a supportive point of view | |
| • Disagreement<br>• Criticism | Injects a negative point of view | |
| • Ridicule<br>• Denial<br>• Threat | Involves the open use of power or authority | Intrusive, interventionist |

learning, executives should strive for more frequent use of responses at the reflective, facilitative end of the spectrum. Combative styles can be effective, but unless they are applied with great skill, they run the high risk of demoralizing employees.

Used properly, questioning, listening, and responding can generate discussions of real power. Learning blossoms in such settings, as the examples of Xerox, L.L. Bean, Allegheny Ludlum Steel, and the other organizations described earlier in this book suggest. In each case, group leaders strove to produce genuine thinking and debate, at the same time cultivating a collegial, collaborative atmosphere. The former kept ideas bubbling and in constant ferment, while the latter ensured that groups remained cohesive and were able to act decisively on their conclusions. As chapter 1 pointed out, both elements—reflection and action—are defining features of learning organizations. The combination is hard to find, for it requires discussions that are at once comfortable and contentious. David Hume, the Scottish philosopher, made much the same point over two hundred years ago, when he observed that "truth springs from arguments amongst friends."[62]

# FROM ORGANIZATIONAL TO INDIVIDUAL LEARNING

We are left with a paradox. The preceding chapters have focused primarily on organizations and the processes they use to cultivate learning. Most examples have featured groups and teams but have said little about individuals. Yet, without individuals who learn, there can be no learning organizations.[63] They are necessary for success.[64] Typically, those individuals—operators, technicians, customer service representatives, supervisors, and managers—look to their leaders for models to imitate, especially when it comes to learning, where attitude and tone are set at the top. If senior executives are committed to personal improvement and growth, their employees are likely to feel much the same way. But if they shun new ideas and stick with outdated views, employees are likely to be closed and unyielding. As with all attempts to shape behavior, leaders must walk the talk if meaningful changes are to occur.

Unfortunately, in all too many organizations, those at the top stopped learning long ago. They continue to travel the same well-trod path. As a leading organizational consultant put it, only partly in jest: "Too many senior executives who have been on the job thirty years don't necessarily have thirty years of experience—they have more like one year of experience, thirty times."[65] For these executives, the first step in building a learning organization is a personal one: they need to develop their own skills as learners. There are four main requirements: openness to new perspectives, an awareness of personal biases, immersion in unfiltered data, and a growing sense of humility.

## Openness to New Perspectives

Openness requires that leaders accept the provisional nature of knowledge. Even long established truths must eventually be revised and replaced. This principle has long been a staple of the sciences, and it applies equally well to business. In most cases, the best that we can expect from a theory—whether it is a cornerstone of biology or the foundation of a marketing strategy—"is that it should hold together long enough to lead us to a better one."[66] Such impermanence suggests the importance of repeatedly revisiting underlying assumptions. It also explains why executives need to be curious, open-minded learners. To remain current, they must continuously seek out competing concepts and evidence, wrestle with surprising and unfamiliar ideas, and consider new and unpopular points of view. Many executives think that they behave this way but fail to do so in practice. They suffer from a common problem: an excessively optimistic view of their own openness. As William James, the pragmatist philosopher, slyly observed: "A great many people think they are thinking when they are merely rearranging their prejudices."[67]

A good indicator of openness is one's attitude toward challenging questions. Do executives encourage subordinates to air dissenting views? Do they readily accept unsolicited suggestions? Do they carefully consider opposing positions? The presence of such dissonance is an important contributor to learning. But it should not be overdone. "Rates of disagreement and antagonism that are too high are sure indicators of trouble. Apparently, when ill feeling rises above some critical point, a 'chain reaction' or 'vicious circle' tends to set in."[68] Moderate levels of disagreement, which produce a manageable amount of debate, typically produce superior discussions. They are desirable for another reason as well. By increasing the amount of timely, diagnostic feedback, they contribute directly to improved performance. Leaders, however, must usually solicit that feedback, since it seldom arises spontaneously. In fact, a willingness to seek feedback from others is one of the hallmarks of experts in a variety of fields.[69]

A study of pilots found that those who were rated as outstanding "felt more strongly that first officers should be encouraged to question their decisions and that first officers should question decisions other than those that threaten the safety of flight. Pilots with below average performance held the opposite attitudes." In addition, superior pilots recognized that their decision-making abilities deteriorated in emergencies, increasing the likelihood that they would "become more receptive to inputs from others" when faced with stressful situations. Below average pilots were less receptive: they felt that there was no difference between their decision-making abilities in emergencies and routine conditions.[70] Again, the analogy to management should be clear. A genuine acceptance of differing views provides a lifeline in difficult times.

Another indicator of openness is the amount of exposure one has to unfamiliar, thought-provoking environments. Effective executives seek out these opportunities; they do not wait for challenging environments to come to them. As GE's businesses expanded globally, Jack Welch embarked on a series of around-the-world trips, where, for weeks at a time, he immersed himself in foreign cultures and climates. John McCoy of Banc One met personally with the heads of virtually all of the leading Internet portals before launching Wingspan, the company's foray into electronic banking. John Browne of British Petroleum joined the board of Intel to experience personally the ethos and decision-making style of Silicon Valley. Countless executives carry out benchmarking visits to see how other companies, often in radically different businesses and markets, conduct their work. Even participation in training programs, rotations, and special assignments can open managers' eyes if they stay long enough in challenging settings to question long-established routines.[71]

### Awareness of Personal Biases

A second requirement for effective learning is an awareness of one's personal biases. These biases may appear as distinctive cognitive styles or as pervasive learning disabilities. The former are unique to individuals, while the latter are common to all. Each of us, for example, has our own, idiosyncratic cognitive style. It is neither right nor wrong but predisposes us to think in particular ways. In business settings, a cognitive style is simply "the way in which an executive . . . defines his informational needs for purposes of making decisions. . . . [It] also refers to his preferred ways of acquiring information from those around him and making use of that information, and to his preferences regarding advisers and ways of using them in making decisions."[72]

Some of us, for example, are readers, who like to absorb material in written form; others are talkers, who flesh out ideas by discussing them. Readers tend to prefer memos, while talkers tend to prefer meetings.[73] Some of us enjoy being immersed in the details; others are more interested in the big picture. Detail-oriented people tend to prefer reports that dig into the nitty-gritty, while big-picture people tend to prefer broad, sweeping narratives. Some of us are comfortable juggling many topics simultaneously; others like to stay focused on a single subject. Jugglers tend to prefer rich, multifaceted agendas, while focused individuals tend to prefer narrower, targeted meetings.[74] None of these approaches is inherently superior. But each comes with predictable strengths and weaknesses. At a minimum, leaders need to be aware of their preferred styles and should try to ensure that they fit well with the tasks at hand. Otherwise, their learning is likely to be extremely inefficient.

Nor are these the only biases that affect learning. Leaders must also strive consciously to counteract the common disabilities discussed in chapter 2. All of us are flawed statisticians, who commit a wide range of interpretative errors. We have trouble separating signals from noise, do a poor job estimating probabilities, rely on misleading rules of thumb, and are overcertain of our own understanding and skills. To combat these errors and improve the accuracy and quality of learning, experts use a variety of techniques that could be easily adopted by managers. They keep running lists of their predictions to overcome hindsight bias. They solicit critical feedback to combat overconfidence. They review flawed choices to uncover hidden assumptions. They enlist the help of coaches and third-party observers to ensure that their words match their deeds. They compile extensive experience banks to enrich their repertoire of analogies and increase their skill at pattern recognition. They use formal decision aids to calibrate their judgments and improve consistency.[75] All of these techniques are designed to heighten awareness and develop a more refined understanding of how decisions are actually made. Harvey Golub of American Express has long pursued the same goal. In his words:

> When you make a decision, you explain how you made it. . . . You do
> not rely on unconscious competence. I do everything inductively, so
> I have to force myself to become deductive in order to explain
> things. The struggle is to tease out the reasoning process and make
> it clear.[76]

## Exposure to Unfiltered Data

A third requirement for leaders wishing to improve their learning is greater contact with raw, unfiltered data. Many executives are distressingly detached from the realities of their organizations. They rely on information that is prepackaged and highly compressed, making it difficult to interpret. According to a noted student of leadership:

As organizations (and societies) become larger and more complex, [those] at the top . . . depend less and less on first-hand experience, more and more on heavily "processed" data. Before reaching them, the raw data—what actually goes on "out there"—have been sampled, screened, condensed, compiled, coded, expressed in statistical form, spun into generalizations and crystallized into recommendations. . . .

But what does the information processing system filter out? It filters out all sensory impressions not readily expressed in words and numbers. It filters out emotion, feeling, sentiment, mood and . . . those intuitive judgments that are just below the level of consciousness. . . .

That is why every top executive . . . should periodically emerge from his world of abstractions and take a long unflinching look at unprocessed reality.[77]

Managers need to take charge of this process by finding ways of confronting, directly and experientially, the realities of organizational life: the stuff that goes on "out there." They need to tour factories, drop in on service centers, meet with disgruntled employees, and talk with customers. They need to "staple themselves to an order" or follow a product development process from beginning to end to see how the work really gets done.[78] They need to track, on a daily or weekly basis, bookings, billings, backlogs, receivables, inventory, and other real-time operational data, not simply aggregated financials.[79] Learning often improves markedly when executives return to the front lines and confront data in these tangible, concrete forms.

Why are these activities so important? Because, as Harvey Golub observed, "the first task of a leader is to define reality."[80] And leaders can do so only if they already possess a grounded, granular view of the challenges and opportunities facing their organizations. To develop that perspective, they often need to expose themselves to the same unwelcome story again and again. Repetition is a remarkably powerful technique for improving one's hearing.

It is for this reason that Zaki Mustafa, the vice president and general manager of Serengeti Eyewear, for many years spent about a third of his time on the road. Of that, 40 percent was spent visiting customers,

40 percent visiting suppliers, and the balance visiting Serengeti employees in the field. Other members of the senior team had similarly hectic travel schedules. In addition, every four to six weeks, sales staff invited different retailers to join them at Serengeti headquarters. All employees, from Mustafa on down, were invited as well. The purpose of these meetings was to learn as much as possible about customers' products, organization, people, and needs, while also uncovering Serengeti's weaknesses. Discussions were frank and covered a broad range of topics: What is your business? What does your company do? How do you do it? What does Serengeti do well? What does Serengeti need to improve on? Mustafa was quite clear on the reasons why it was necessary to expose himself, and others in the organization, to so much unfiltered data: "Our presumption is that if you're going to make a decision, you need to have first-hand information, because we want first-hand ownership and results."[81]

## A Sense of Humility

Finally, if they are to progress as learners, leaders need to develop a sense of humility.[82] They must recognize that they do not have all the answers. They must acknowledge that superior insights lie elsewhere—outside their offices, and at times outside their organizations. They must become skilled at defining the limits of their own knowledge. Learning, after all, is a profession of faith in the future, an admission that progress is possible. Senior managers at Xerox made this point explicitly when they observed, in the midst of a lengthy change process, that "we are no longer the organization we used to be and we are not yet the organization we intend to be." The same can be said of most companies—and most executives. Learning is the best way for both of them to bridge the gap.

# Notes

## Chapter 1: From Individual to Organizational Learning

1. See, for example, Erik H. Erikson, *Identity and the Life Cycle* (New York: W. W. Norton, 1980); Daniel J. Levenson et al., *The Seasons of a Man's Life* (New York: Ballantine Books, 1978); Morgan W. McCall, Jr., Michael M. Lombardo, and Ann M. Morrison, *The Lessons of Experience* (Lexington, MA: D. C. Heath, 1988); and Dennis O'Connor and Donald M. Wolfe, "From Crisis to Growth at Midlife: Changes in Personal Paradigm," *Journal of Organizational Behavior* 12 (1991): 323–340.

2. Allen Tough, *The Adult's Learning Projects*, 2d ed. (Toronto: The Ontario Institute for Studies in Education, 1979). Tough's samples were small but exceedingly broad, including professors, politicians, lower-level white-collar men, lower-level white-collar women, factory workers, teachers, and mothers. Such diversity suggests that learning projects are not confined to a single sector of the population. Subsequent studies have found somewhat lower numbers—three learning projects per year, each lasting fifty hours annually—but still support his basic finding of the pervasiveness of adult learning. See Ron Zemke and Susan Zemke, "Adult Learning: What Do We Know for Sure?" *Training* (June 1995): 31–40 for an update.

3. Edward Prewitt, "What Managers Should Know about How Adults Learn," *Management Update* 2 (January 1997): 5.

4. See, for example, Ronald Henkoff, "Companies That Train Best," *Fortune*, 22 March 1993, 62–75; Jeanne C. Meister, *Corporate Quality Universities* (Burr Ridge, IL: Richard D. Irwin, 1994); and Bruce A. Pasternack, Shelley S. Keller, and Albert J. Viscio,

"The Triumph of People Power and the New Economy," *Strategy & Business* 2d quarter (1997): 26–39.

5. Gordon R. Sullivan and Michael V. Harper, *Hope Is Not a Method* (New York: Times Business/Random House, 1996), 192.

6. Charles Handy, *The Age of Unreason* (Boston: Harvard Business School Press, 1989), 142.

7. Peter M. Senge, *The Fifth Discipline* (New York: Doubleday, 1990), 1.

8. Ikujiro Nonaka, "The Knowledge-Creating Company," *Harvard Business Review* 69 (November/December 1991): 97.

9. Aaron Wildavsky, "The Self-Evaluating Organization," *Public Administration Review* 32 (September/October 1972): 509, 513.

10. Ross Henderson, "A Management Program for Expedition and Control of Process Plant Startups," *Proceedings No. 52,* Institute of Electronic and Radio Engineers, December 1981, 127–145; Ross Henderson, "Prediction of Plant Startup Progress, Duration, and Lost Capacity," *International Journal of Operations and Production Management* 2 (1981): 14–28; and Ross Henderson, "Achieving Quality During Plant Startup," *Quality Progress* (May 1985): 36–40.

11. Gabriel Szulanski, "Intra-Firm Transfer of Best Practices Project: Executive Summary of the Findings," (Fontainebleau, France, and Houston, Texas: INSEAD and American Productivity & Quality Center, October 1994), photocopy; and Gabriel Szulanski, "Exploring Internal Stickiness: Impediments to the Transfer of Best Practice within the Firm," *Strategic Management Journal* 17 (Winter Special Issue, 1996): 27–43.

12. Craig S. Galbraith, "Transferring Core Manufacturing Technologies in High-Technology Firms," *California Management Review* (Summer 1990): 56–70.

13. Joseph Bower and Clayton M. Christensen, "Disruptive Technologies: Catching the Wave," *Harvard Business Review* 73 (January/February 1995): 43–53.

14. Michael Tushman and Charles A. O'Reilly III, "The Ambidextrous Organization," *California Management Review* 38 (Summer 1996): 1–3.

15. Andrew S. Grove, *Only the Paranoid Survive* (New York: Doubleday, 1996), 11–23.

16. This same point has been made, using different language, in James C. Collins and Jerry I. Porras, *Built to Last* (New York: HarperBusiness, 1994), especially ch. 4, 7.

17. Warren G. Bennis, "Toward a 'Truly' Scientific Management: The Concept of Organizational Health," *Industrial Management Review* (MIT) 4 (1962): 9.

18. Because of these diverse views, there is a long academic tradition of reviewing the literature on organizational learning. Well-known reviews include Chris Argyris and Donald A. Schön, *Organizational Learning: A Theory of Action Perspective* (Reading, MA: Addison-Wesley, 1978), 319–331; George P. Huber, "Organizational Learning: The Contributing Processes and the Literatures," *Organization Science* 2 (February 1991): 88–115; Barbara Levitt and James G. March, "Organizational Learning," *Annual Review of Sociology* 14 (1988): 319–340; Anne S. Miner and Stephen J. Mezias, "Ugly Duckling No More: Pasts and Futures of Organizational Learning Research," *Organization Science* 7 (1996): 88–99; and Paul Shrivastava, "A Typology of Organizational Learning Systems," *Journal of Management Studies* 20 (1983): 7–28.

19. Noel M. Tichy and Ram Charan, "Speed, Simplicity, and Self-Confidence: An Interview with Jack Welch," *Harvard Business Review* 67 (September/October 1989): 118.

For further details on Work-Out, see Noel M. Tichy and Stratford Sherman, *Control Your Own Destiny or Someone Else Will* (New York: HarperBusiness, 1994), 237–259.

20. Some of these litmus tests first appeared in P. Ranganath Nayak, David A. Garvin, Arun N. Maira, and Joan L. Brager, "Creating a Learning Organization," *Prism* 3d quarter (1996): 28–29.

21. David Nadler, "Even Failures Can Be Productive," *New York Times*, 23 April 1989, section 3, p. 3.

22. Myra M. Hart and Hugo Uyterhoeven, "Banc One–1993," Case 9–394-043 (Boston: Harvard Business School, 1993), 4.

## Chapter 2: The Learning Process

1. The concept of routines, also known as "standard operating procedures," has long been associated with the behavioral theory of the firm. See, for example, Richard M. Cyert and James G. March, *The Behavioral Theory of the Firm* (Englewood Cliffs, NJ: Prentice-Hall, 1963), 101–103; Barbara Levitt and James G. March, "Organizational Learning," *Annual Review of Sociology* 14 (1998): 319–340; and James G. March and Herbert A. Simon, *Organizations*, 2d ed. (Cambridge, MA: Blackwell, 1993), 160–161.

2. These frameworks go by various names, including perceptual filters, organizational frames of reference, and mental models. See, for example, William H. Starbuck and Frances J. Milliken, "Executives' Perceptual Filters: What They Notice and How They Make Sense," in Donald C. Hambrick, ed., *The Executive Effect* (Greenwich, CT: JAI Press, 1988), 35–65; Paul Shrivastava and Ian I. Mitroff, "Nonrationality in Organizational Actions," *International Studies of Management & Organization* 17 (1987): 90–109; and Peter M. Senge, *The Fifth Discipline* (New York: Doubleday, 1990), ch. 10.

3. The quotation is from Albert Szent-Gyorgyi, who won a Nobel Prize for studies showing that vitamin C prevents oxidation, and is cited in Robert Scott Root-Bernstein, *Discovering* (Cambridge: Harvard University Press, 1989), 186.

4. For example, scholars have described the learning process in the following terms: scanning, interpretation, and learning; hypothesizing, exposure, encoding, and integration; generating, integrating, interpreting, and acting; and observing, assessing, designing, and implementing. These examples are taken, respectively, from Richard L. Daft and Karl E. Weick, "Toward a Model of Organizations as Interpretation Systems," *Academy of Management Review* 9 (1984): 284–295; Stephen J. Hoch and John Deighton, "Managing What Consumers Learn from Experience," *Journal of Marketing* 53 (1989): 1–20; Nancy Dixon, *The Organizational Learning Cycle* (London: McGraw-Hill International, 1994), ch 4; and Daniel H. Kim, "The Link between Individual and Organizational Learning," *Sloan Management Review* (Fall 1993): 37–50. Other studies with similar descriptions of the learning process include David A. Kolb, *Experiential Learning* (Englewood Cliffs, NJ: Prentice-Hall, 1984), ch. 2; Arie de Geus, *The Living Company* (Boston: Harvard Business School Press, 1997), ch. 4; Stephan H. Haeckel and Richard L. Nolan, "Managing by Wire," *Harvard Business Review* 71 (September/October 1993): 122–132; and Charles Handy, *The Age of Unreason* (Boston: Harvard Business School Press, 1989), ch. 3.

5. For representative definitions, see Roberta Wohlstetter, *Pearl Harbor: Warning and Decision* (Stanford, CA: Stanford University Press, 1962), 1–3; Roger E. Bohn, "Learning by Experimentation in Manufacturing," working paper 88-001, Harvard Business

School, Boston, MA, 10; and Starbuck and Milliken, "Executives' Perceptual Filters," 40–46.

6. Wohlsetter, *Pearl Harbor,* 386–387.

7. Ibid., 387–388.

8. Diane Vaughan, "The Trickle-Down Effect: Policy Decisions, Risky Work, and the *Challenger* Tragedy," *California Management Review* 39 (Winter 1997): 86–87. For a more detailed discussion, see Diane Vaughan, *The Challenger Launch Decision* (Chicago: University of Chicago Press, 1996), especially ch. 7.

9. Roger E. Bohn, "Noise and Learning in Semiconductor Manufacturing," *Management Science* 41 (January 1995): 31, 38. See also Roger E. Bohn, "The Impact of Process Noise on VLSI Process Improvement," *IEEE Transactions on Semiconductor Manufacturing* 8 (August 1995): 228–238.

10. Starbuck and Milliken, "Executives' Perceptual Filters," 40.

11. For discussions of the role of hypotheses in information acquisition, see Berndt Brehmer, "In One Word: Not from Experience," *Acta Psychologica* 45 (1980): 223–241; Hoch and Deighton, "Managing What Consumers Learn from Experience," 3–6; and Judith E. Tschirgi, "Sensible Reasoning: A Hypothesis about Hypotheses," *Child Development* 51 (1980): 1–10.

12. Sara Kiesler and Lee Sproull, "Managerial Response to Changing Environments: Perspectives on Problem Sensing from Social Cognition," *Administrative Science Quarterly* 27 (1982): 559.

13. Rohit Deshpande and Gerald Zaltman, "Factors Affecting the Use of Market Research Information: A Path Analysis," *Journal of Marketing Research* 19 (February 1982): 14–31; Rohit Deshpande and Gerald Zaltman, "A Comparison of Factors Affecting Researcher and Manager Perceptions of Market Research Use," *Journal of Marketing Research* 21 (February 1984): 32–38; and George S. Day, "Continuous Learning about Markets," *California Management Review* 39 (Summer 1994): 9–31.

14. Karl E. Weick and Richard L. Daft, "The Effectiveness of Interpretation Systems," in K. S. Cameron and D. A. Whetten, eds., *Organizational Effectiveness* (New York: Academic Press, 1983), 74.

15. For introductions to schemas, scripts, and other interpretative frameworks, see Daft and Weick, "Toward a Model of Organizations as Interpretation Systems," 284–295; Dennis A. Gioia, "Symbols, Scripts, and Sensemaking," in Henry P. Sims Jr., Dennis A. Gioia, and associates, eds., *The Thinking Organization* (San Francisco: Jossey-Bass, 1986) 49–75; Kiesler and Sproull, "Managerial Responses to Changing Environments," 556–558; Starbuck and Milliken, "Executives' Perceptual Filters," 51–52; James P. Walsh, "Managerial and Organizational Cognition: Notes from a Trip Down Memory Lane," *Organization Science* 6 (May/June 1995): 280–321; and Weick and Daft, "The Effectiveness of Interpretation Systems," 84–85.

16. Peter F. Drucker, "The Theory of the Business," *Harvard Business Review* 72 (September/October 1994): 95–104.

17. Weick and Daft, "The Effectiveness of Interpretation Systems," 76.

18. Ibid., 82–87.

19. David A. Garvin, "How the Baldrige Award Really Works," *Harvard Business Review* 69 (November/December 1991): 93.

20. Grove, *Only the Paranoid Survive*, 20–21.

21. Lee S. Sproull and Kay Ramsay Hofmeister, "Thinking about Implementation," *Journal of Management* 12 (1986): 58.

22. Claudia H. Deutsch, "Competitors Can Teach You a Lot, but the Lessons Can Hurt," *New York Times*, 18 July 1999, sec. 2, p. 4.

23. Michael E. Porter, *Competitive Strategy* (New York: Free Press, 1980), 59.

24. Shaker A. Zahra and Sherry B. Chaples, "Blind Spots in Competitive Analysis," *Academy of Management Executive* 7 (1993): 9–12. For a discussion of other blind spots in competitive decision making, including capacity expansion and new business entry decisions, see Edward J. Zajac and Max H. Bazerman, "Blind Spots in Industry and Competitor Analysis: Implications of Interfirm (Mis)Perceptions for Strategic Decisions," *Academy of Management Review* 16 (1991): 37–56.

25. Scholars have named this phenomenon the "threat-rigidity effect." See Barry M. Staw, Lance E. Sandelands, and Jane E. Dutton, "Threat-Rigidity Effects in Organizational Behavior: A Multilevel Analysis," *Administrative Science Quarterly* 26 (1981): 501–524.

26. Hugo Uyterhoeven, "Phil Knight: Managing Nike's Transformation," Case 9–394-012 (Boston: Harvard Business School, 1993), 2.

27. Starbuck and Milliken, "Executives' Perceptual Filters," 40–46.

28. Charles G. Lord, Lee Ross, and Mark R. Lepper, "Biased Assimilation and Attitude Polarization: The Effects of Prior Theories on Subsequently Considered Evidence," *Journal of Personality and Social Psychology* 37 (1979): 2098–2109.

29. Karl E. Weick, "The Vulnerable System: An Analysis of the Tenerife Air Disaster," *Journal of Management* 16 (1990): 583–585.

30. Thomas H. Davenport, Robert G. Eccles, and Laurence Prusak, "Information Politics," *Sloan Management Review* 34 (Fall 1992): 53–65.

31. Jack L. Engledow and R. T. Lenz, "Whatever Happened to Environmental Analysis?" *Long Range Planning* 18 (April 1985): 98–99.

32. Levitt and March, "Organizational Learning," 323.

33. The problem is certainly not confined to managers. Clinical psychologists and doctors, for example, suffer from many of the same biases. Even statisticians are not immune. For a summary of the findings on the first two groups, see Lewis R. Goldberg, "Simple Models or Simple Processes? Some Research on Clinical Judgments," *American Psychologist* 23 (1968): 483–496. For a series of experiments involving statisticians, see Hillel J. Einhorn and Robin M. Hogarth, "Confidence in Judgment: Persistence of the Illusion of Validity," *Psychological Review* 85 (1978): 395–416.

34. On illusory correlation and illusory causation, see Kiesler and Sproull, "Managerial Responses to Changing Environments," 553–554; and David L. Hamilton and Terrence L. Rose, "Illusory Correlation and the Maintenance of Stereotypical Beliefs," *Journal of Personality and Social Psychology* 39 (1980): 832–845. On the illusion of validity, see Einhorn and Hogarth, "Confidence in Judgment," 395–416; and Goldberg, "Simple Models or Simple Processes?" 483–496. On framing effects, see Amos Tversky and Daniel Kahneman, "Rational Choice and the Framing of Decisions," *Journal of Business* 59 (1986), part 2, S254–S257. On categorical bias, see J. M. Feldman, "Beyond Attribution Theory: Cognitive Processes in Performance Appraisal," *Journal of Applied Psychology* 66 (1981): 127–148; and Hamilton and Rose, "Illusory Correlation

24226 NOTES

and the Maintenance of Stereotypical Beliefs," 832–845. On availability bias, see Amos Tversky and Daniel Kahneman, "Judgment under Uncertainty: Heuristics and Biases," *Science* 185 (1974): 1127–1128. On regression artifacts, see Donald T. Campbell, "Reforms as Experiments," *American Psychologist* 24 (1969): 409–429; and Thomas D. Cook and Donald T. Campbell, *Quasi-Experimentation* (Boston: Houghton Mifflin, 1979), 99–103. On hindsight bias, see Baruch Fischhoff, "Hindsight ≠ Foresight: The Effect of Outcome Knowledge on Judgment under Uncertainty," *Journal of Experimental Psychology: Human Perception and Performance* 1 (1975): 288–299; and Baruch Fischhoff and Ruth Beyth, "'I Knew It Would Happen': Remembered Probabilities of Once-Future Things," *Organizational Behavior and Human Performance* 13 (1975): 1–16.

35. S. Oskamp, "Overconfidence in Case-Study Judgments," *Journal of Consulting Psychology* 29 (1965): 264. Italics in original.

36. Ed Bukszar and Terry Connolly, "Hindsight Bias and Strategic Choice: Some Problems in Learning from Experience," *Academy of Management Journal* 31 (1988): 635, 637.

37. Fischhoff and Beyth, "'I Knew It Would Happen,'" 13.

38. "Jack Welch's Lessons for Success," *Fortune*, 25 January 1993, 88.

39. Chris Argyris and Donald Schön, *Theory in Practice* (San Francisco: Jossey-Bass, 1974), 7.

40. Frank Friedlander, "Patterns of Individual and Organizational Learning," in Suresh Srivastava and associates, *The Executive Mind* (San Francisco: Jossey-Bass, 1983), 192–220.

41. Janet Simpson, Lee Field, and David Garvin, "The Boeing 767: From Concept to Production (A)," Case 9–688–040 (Boston: Harvard Business School, 1988), 9.

42. Charles F. Knight, "Emerson Electric: Consistent Profits, Consistently," *Harvard Business Review* 70 (January/February 1992): 62.

43. Kathleen M. Eisenhardt, Jean L. Kahwajy, and L. J. Bourgeois III, "Conflict and Strategic Choice: How Top Management Teams Disagree," *California Management Review* 39 (Winter 1997): 42–62; and Kathleen M. Eisenhardt, Jean L. Kahwajy, and L. J. Bourgeois III, "How Top Management Teams Can Have a Good Fight," *Harvard Business Review* 75 (July/August 1997): 77–85.

44. For an introduction to these techniques, see David M. Schweiger, William R. Sandberg, and James W. Ragan, "Group Approaches for Improving Strategic Decision Making: A Comparative Analysis of Dialectical Inquiry, Devil's Advocacy, and Consensus," *Academy of Management Journal* 29 (1986): 51–71.

45. Irving Janis, *Victims of Groupthink* (Boston: Houghton Mifflin, 1972), 147–149.

46. Jack Feldman, "On the Difficulty of Learning from Experience," in Sims, Gioia, and associates, *The Thinking Organization*, 281.

47. Hart and Uyterhoeven, "Banc One–1993," 11.

48. These results were achieved between 1983 and 1992. In the mid-1990s, Banc One changed its approach, moving to a more centralized model to take advantage of the scale economies and consolidations that were reshaping the banking industry. For updates, see Saul Hansell, "Banc One Lives Up to Its Name," *New York Times*, 12 May 1995, D1, D4; Thomas N. Urban and James L. Heskett, "Banc One–1996," Case 9–396–315 (Boston: Harvard Business School 1996); and Matt Murray, "After Long

Overhaul, Banc One Now Faces Pressure to Perform," *Wall Street Journal,* 10 March 1998, A1, A10.

49. Dixon, *The Organizational Learning Cycle,* 96–97.

50. William Keenan Jr., "How GE Stays on Top of Its Markets," *Sales & Marketing Management* (August 1994): 61. Also see Richard J. Babyak, "Marketing with a Vision," *Appliance Manufacturer* (July 1995): GEA-8–GEA-10.

51. Gordon E. Forward, "Wide-Open Management at Chaparral Steel," *Harvard Business Review* 64 (May/June 1986): 96–102; Dorothy Leonard-Barton, "The Factory as a Learning Laboratory," *Sloan Management Review* 34 (fall 1992): 23–38; and "Chaparral Steel (Abridged)," Case 9-687-045 (Boston: Harvard Business School, 1987).

52. Joe McGowan, "How Disney Keeps Ideas Coming," *Fortune,* 1 April 1996, 131–134.

53. Robin Cooper and M. Lynne Markus, "Human Reengineering," *Sloan Management Review* 36 (Summer 1995): 46.

54. Edgar H. Schein, "How Can Organizations Learn Faster? The Challenge of Entering the Green Room," *Sloan Management Review* 34 (Winter 1993): 89. Also see Amy Edmondson, "Psychological Safety and Learning Behavior in Work Teams," *Administrative Science Quarterly* 44 (Summer 1999): 350–383.

55. Robert I. Sutton and Andrew Hargadon, "Brainstorming Groups in Context: Effectiveness in a Product Design Firm," *Administrative Science Quarterly* 41 (1996): 706.

56. Thomas A. Stewart, "3M Fights Back," *Fortune,* 5 February 1996, 94–99.

57. Feldman, "On the Difficulty of Learning from Experience," 283.

58. Lisa Belkin, "How Can We Save the Next Victim?" *New York Times Magazine,* 15 June 1997, 44. The quotation is from David Woods, a professor of cognitive systems engineering at Ohio State University.

59. Warren Bennis and Burt Nanus, *Leaders* (New York: Harper & Row, 1985), 76.

60. Amy C. Edmondson, "Learning from Mistakes Is Easier Said Than Done: Group and Organizational Influences on the Detection and Correction of Human Error," *Journal of Applied Behavioral Science* 32 (March 1996): 5–28.

61. Michal Tamuz, "The Impact of Computer Surveillance on Air Safety Reporting," *Columbia Journal of World Business* 22 (1987): 69–77; and Charles Perrow, *Normal Accidents* (New York: Basic Books, 1984), 168–169.

62. Atul Gawande, "When Doctors Make Mistakes," *The New Yorker,* 1 February 1999, 40–55.

63. Peter J. Frost, "Crossroads: Bridging Academia and Business: A Conversation with Steve Kerr," *Organization Science* 8 (May/June 1997): 335.

## Chapter 3: Intelligence

1. P. B. Medawar, *Advice to a Young Scientist* (New York: Harper Colophon, 1979), 18.

2. There are strong parallels between this progression and the distinction that scholars have made between "exploitation" and "exploration." Much of that discussion has appeared in comparisons of evolutionary and revolutionary change. See, for example, Michael L. Tushman and Charles A. O'Reilly III, *Winning through Innovation* (Boston: Harvard Business School Press, 1997).

3. Richard E. Combs and John D. Moorhead, *The Competitive Intelligence Handbook* (Metuchen, NJ: Scarecrow Press, 1992), 3. Combs and Moorhead focus primarily on collecting publicly held information but also discuss a number of other broader definitions.

4. For brief histories, see Allen Dulles, *The Craft of Intelligence* (New York: Harper & Row, 1963), ch. 2 and 3; and Richard Eels and Peter Nehemkis, *Corporate Intelligence and Espionage* (New York: Macmillan, 1984), ch. 2.

5. Herbert O. Yardley, *The American Black Chamber* (Indianapolis: Bobbs-Merrill, 1931).

6. Dulles, *The Craft of Intelligence*, 71, 75–76; and Eels and Nehemkis, *Corporate Intelligence and Espionage*, 30.

7. Shari Caudron, "I Spy, You Spy," *Industry Week*, 3 October 1994, 35–40; and "They Snoop to Conquer," *Business Week*, 28 October 1996, 172–176.

8. Larry Kahaner, *Competitive Intelligence* (New York: Simon & Schuster, 1996), 15.

9. Francis Joseph Aguilar, *Scanning the Business Environment* (New York: Macmillan, 1967), 19–20; Sumantra Ghoshal, "Environmental Scanning: An Individual and Organizational Level Analysis" (Ph. D. diss., Sloan School of Management, MIT, May 1985), 205–206; and Sumantra Ghoshal, "Environmental Scanning in Korean Firms: Organizational Isomorphism in Action," *Journal of International Business Studies* (Spring 1988): 72.

10. Aguilar, *Scanning the Business Environment*, ch. 4; John P. Kotter, *The General Managers* (New York: Free Press, 1982), ch. 4; and Henry Mintzberg, *The Nature of Managerial Work* (New York: Harper & Row, 1973), ch. 3.

11. For lists of potential sources, see Leonard M. Fuld, *Monitoring the Competition* (New York: John Wiley & Sons, 1988), ch. 2; and Kahaner, *Competitive Intelligence*, ch. 6.

12. On Coors, see Kahaner, *Competitive Intelligence*, 58–59. On the food-packaging company, see Richard S. Teitelbaum, "The New Race for Intelligence," *Fortune*, 2 November 1992, 106.

13. Herbert E. Meyer, *Real-World Intelligence* (New York: Grove Weidenfeld, 1987), 60–61.

14. Kahaner, *Competitive Intelligence*, 24; and Teitelbaum, "The New Race for Intelligence," 104–105.

15. Ghoshal, "Environmental Scanning in Korean Firms," 75–77.

16. Allen C. Bluedorn et al., "The Interface and Convergence of the Strategic Management and Organizational Environment Domains," *Journal of Management* 20 (1994): 211–219; Sumantra Ghoshal, "Environmental Scanning: An Individual and Organizational Level Analysis," 213–215; and Kathleen M. Sutcliffe, "What Executives Notice: Accurate Perceptions in Top Management Teams," *Academy of Management Journal* 37 (1994): 1360–1378.

17. "They Snoop to Conquer," 172. The estimate comes from David H. Harkerload, director of business intelligence for the Futures Group, Inc.

18. Aguilar, *Scanning the Business Environment*, 60.

19. Meryl Reis Louis and Robert I. Sutton, "Switching Cognitive Gears: From Habits of Mind to Active Thinking," *Human Relations* 44 (1991): 55–76.

20. Jack L. Engledow and R. T. Lenz, "Whatever Happened to Environmental Analysis?" *Long Range Planning* 18 (1985): 99. For additional evidence, see Subhash C. Jain,

"Environmental Scanning in U.S. Corporations," *Long Range Planning* 17 (1984): 126–127.

21. The Xerox story is drawn primarily from personal interviews conducted in 1992 and 1993 with Xerox's senior managers and internal company documents. I am especially grateful to William Buehler, senior vice president, for arranging and coordinating my visits and providing essential background information (11 May 1992 and 16 June 1992), and to Roger Levien, Xerox's vice president of corporate strategy during the 1980s and 1990s, for interviews (16 June 1992, 4 August 1992, and 29 April 1997) and access to unpublished material. The few public accounts focus on Xerox '92 and Xerox '95. They include Carol Kennedy, "Xerox Charts a New Strategic Direction," *Long Range Planning* 22 (1989): 10–17; Roger E. Levien, "Making Strategic Concepts Work," in Kenneth C. Laudon and Jon A. Turner, eds., *Information Technology and Management Strategy* (Englewood Cliffs, NJ: Prentice Hall, 1989), ch. 4; and David A. Nadler, *Champions of Change* (San Francisco: Jossey-Bass, 1998), ch. 8.

22. Because the studies were forward-looking, they were named for the year at the end of the decade ahead, not the year in which the study was conducted. Thus, Xerox '92 was conducted in 1982, Xerox '95 was conducted in 1985, etc.

23. The conceptual model involved two equations:

*Aggregate market size = economics + demographics ± social forces + technology*

and

*Xerox revenues and share of market = aggregate market size ± government policy – competition*

Plus signs indicated a positive influence on market size or revenues, minus signs indicated a negative influence, and plus/minus signs indicated that the influence might go in either direction, depending on the particular forces or policies at work. The entire analysis was conducted by products and regions, showing expected growth and revenues in a more segmented fashion.

24. There are two competing descriptions of the BMW option. Both are from insiders. The one included here follows Levien; it is drawn from my interview notes plus a brief discussion in Kennedy, "Xerox Charts a New Strategic Direction," 16. A second version appears in Nadler, *Champions of Change,* 167–168; it focuses more on technological superiority. From these accounts, it is impossible to tell which version is correct.

25. This problem appears in many settings. For example, a leading political scientist has observed of foreign policy disputes that "participants in these policy debates may not be fully aware of the fact that their specific disagreement over a policy rests fundamentally on different images of the opponent. When this is the case, participants in the policy discussion may fail to come to grips with the root issue." See Alexander L. George, *Presidential Decisionmaking in Foreign Policy* (Boulder, CO: Westview Press, 1980), 71.

26. Scholars have drawn similar conclusions. Students of strategic planning, for example, have argued that "most strategy differences are caused by differences in fundamental assumptions about the nature of the problem—not facts about the viability of a particular solution." See James R. Emshoff and Ian I. Mitroff, "Improving the Effectiveness of Corporate Planning," *Business Horizons* (October 1978): 55.

27. Irving L. Janis, *Crucial Decisions* (New York: Free Press, 1989), ch. 2.

28. T. Wonnacott and R. Wonnacott, *Introductory Statistics for Business and Economics,* 3d ed. (New York: John Wiley, 1984), 4.

29. Jeffrey Durgee, "New Product Ideas from Focus Groups," *Journal of Consumer Marketing* 4 (Fall 1987), 58.

30. Jeffrey A. Trachtenberg, "Listening, the Old-Fashioned Way," *Forbes*, 5 October 1987, 204.

31. For discussions of research designs and alternative approaches to data collection, see David A. Aaker and George S. Day, *Marketing Research*, 2d ed. (New York: John Wiley & Sons, 1983); and Gilbert A. Churchill Jr., *Marketing Research: Methodological Foundations*, 5th ed. (Chicago: Dryden Press, 1991).

32. For an example of a poorly worded questionnaire that includes many of these problems, see Philip Kotler, *Principles of Marketing*, 3d ed. (Englewood Cliffs, NJ: Prentice-Hall, 1986), 106–107.

33. These terms are drawn from marketing research. Both approaches are discussed at length in Aaker and Day, *Marketing Research*, 49–51; and Churchill, *Marketing Research: Methodological Foundations*, 128–130. Note that both texts also list a third approach, causal research, which is used to determine cause-and-effect relationships. It is discussed at length in chapter 5 of this book, when experimental methods are introduced.

34. John Koten, "You Aren't Paranoid If You Feel Someone Eyes You Constantly," *Wall Street Journal*, 29 March 1985, 1, 22.

35. Durgee, "New Product Ideas from Focus Groups," 57–59.

36. Howard Gardner, *Leading Minds* (New York: Basic Books, 1995), ch. 1–3; Roger Schank, *Virtual Learning* (New York: McGraw-Hill, 1997), 20–22, 32–33; and Helen B. Schwartzmann, *Ethnography in Organizations* (Newbury Park, CA: SAGE, 1993), 60–63.

37. Schwartzmann, *Ethnography in Organizations*, 54–63.

38. Mason Haire, "Projective Techniques in Marketing Research," *Journal of Marketing* 14 (April 1950): 650.

39. Ibid., 649–656.

40. Herman B. Leonard, "With Open Ears: Listening and the Art of Discussion Leading," in C. Roland Christensen, David A. Garvin, and Ann Sweet, eds., *Education for Judgment* (Boston: Harvard Business School Press, 1991), 139.

41. Norman R. Augustine, *Augustine's Laws* (New York: Penguin, 1987), 465.

42. The L.L. Bean story is drawn primarily from interviews conducted with nearly a dozen researchers, marketers, and product developers in February and March 1997, as well as unpublished company documents. Several discussion groups and work sessions were observed and filmed during the same period. Excerpts from that footage appear in the videotape *Working Smarter: Redesigning Product/Service Development* (Boston: Harvard Business School Video, 1997).

43. Eric von Hippel, "Lead Users: A Source of Novel Product Ideas," *Management Science* 32 (June 1986), 796.

44. Scholars use the term "triangulation" to describe the combining of research techniques when studying the same phenomenon. See Todd D. Jick, "Mixing Qualitative and Quantitative Methods: Triangulation in Action," *Administrative Science Quarterly* 24 (1979): 602–611.

45. The technique was originally described by Gary Burchill in his MIT doctoral disserta-

tion and draws heavily on earlier work in total quality management by Professors Noriaki Kano, Jiro Kawakita, and Shoji Shiba of Japan. Today, the term is a trademark of the Center for Quality of Management (CQM). Burchill worked for CQM and served as a consultant to L.L. Bean during the company's first experiences with concept engineering; design teams at Bean have subsequently refined and modified the approach. See Gary M. Burchill, "Concept Engineering: An Investigation of TIME vs. MARKET Orientation in Product Concept Development," (Ph.D. diss., Sloan School of Management, MIT, June 1993); and Center for Quality of Management, *Concept Engineering* (Cambridge, MA: Center for Quality of Management, 1995).

46. Clifford Geertz, *The Interpretation of Cultures* (New York: Basic Books, 1973), 28.

47. Technically, the team is constructing an "affinity diagram." For a complete description of the approach, including the silent clustering of ideas, see Michael Brassard, *The Memory Jogger Plus+*™ (Methuen, MA: GOAL/QPC, 1989), ch. 1.

48. Dorothy Leonard and Jeffrey F. Rayport, "Spark Innovation through Empathic Design," *Harvard Business Review* 75 (November/December 1997): 105–107.

49. Michael Polanyi, *The Tacit Dimension* (New York: Anchor Books, 1966), 4.

50. John Seely Brown, "Research That Reinvents the Corporation," *Harvard Business Review* 69 (January/February 1991): 108.

51. Paul Cornell and Pam Brenner, "Field Test Learning . . . Creating Knowledge," <http://www.steelcase.com>.

52. Brigitte Jordan, "Notes on Methods for the Study of Work Practices" Palo Alto, CA (Institute for Research on Learning and Xerox Palo Alto Research Center, undated, photocopy); Louise H. Kidder and Charles M. Judd, with Eliot R. Smith, *Research Methods in Social Relations,* 5th ed. (New York: Holt, Rinehart & Winston, 1986), ch. 8; Maurice Punch, *The Politics and Ethics of Field Work* (Beverly Hills, CA: SAGE, 1986), ch. 1 and 2; Leonard Schatzman and Anselm L. Strauss, *Field Research* (Englewood Cliffs, NJ: Prentice-Hall, 1973); James P. Spradley, *Participant Observation* (New York: Holt, Rinehart & Winston, 1980); and William Foote Whyte, *Street Corner Society,* 3d ed. (Chicago: University of Chicago Press, 1981), appendix A.

53. Schatzman and Strauss, *Field Research,* 22. Italics in original.

54. Yogi Berra, *The Yogi Book* (New York: Workman, 1998), 95. Berra was a baseball player renowned for his humorous, inconsistent, and often redundant sayings.

55. W. I. B. Beveridge, *The Art of Scientific Investigation* (New York: Vintage Books, 1957), 132.

56. Ibid., 69.

57. Schatzman and Strauss, *Field Research,* 54.

58. Ibid., 54.

59. Whyte, *Street Corner Society,* 303.

60. Kidder and Judd, *Research Methods in Social Relations,* 171–173; Schatzman and Strauss, *Field Research,* 58–63; and Spradley, *Participant Observation,* 58–62.

61. Lance Ealey and Leif G. Soderberg, "How Honda Cures 'Design Amnesia,'" *McKinsey Quarterly* (Spring 1990), 7.

62. Koten, "You Aren't Paranoid If You Feel Someone Eyes You Constantly," 22.

63. Karen Holtzblatt and Sandra Jones, "Contextual Inquiry: A Participatory Technique for System Design," in Douglas Schuler and Aki Namioka, eds., *Participatory Design* (Hillsdale, NJ: Lawrence Erlbaum, 1993), ch. 9.

64. Jonathan West and David A. Garvin, "Serengeti Eyewear: Entrepreneurship within Corning Inc.," Case 9–394-033 (Boston: Harvard Business School, 1993), 6.

65. Punch, *The Politics and Ethics of Field Work*, 17.

66. The CALL story is drawn primarily from interviews conducted with Colonel Orin A. Nagel, director, Center for Army Lessons Learned, in November 1994 and December 1995, and U.S. Army, "A Guide to the Services of CALL," 29 February 1996 <http://call.army.mil/call/handbook/96-2/calltoc.htm>. Portions of the second Nagel interview, plus footage from CALL's activities in Haiti and Bosnia, appear in the videotape *Putting the Learning Organization to Work: Learning After Doing* (Boston: Harvard Business School Video, 1996). Other sources include Lloyd Baird, John C. Henderson, and Stephanie Watts, "Learning from Action: An Analysis of the Center for Army Lessons Learned (CALL)," *Human Resource Management* 36 (1997): 385–395; John C. Henderson and Stephanie A. Watts, "Creating and Exploiting Knowledge for Fast-Cycle Response: An Analysis of the Center for Army Lessons Learned," (Boston, MA, Boston University, undated, photocopy); Thomas E. Ricks, "Army Devises System to Decide What Does and Does Not Work," *Wall Street Journal*, 23 May 1997, A1, A10; and Gordon R. Sullivan and Michael V. Harper, *Hope Is Not a Method* (New York: Times Business/Random House, 1996), 204–210.

## Chapter 4: Experience

1. Bertrand Russell, *The Problems of Philosophy* (London: Oxford University Press, 1912), 73–74.

2. John Dewey, *Experience and Education* (New York: Collier, 1938), 25.

3. John Dewey, *Democracy and Education* (New York: Free Press, 1916), 154.

4. Reginald W. Revans, *The Origins and Growth of Action Learning* (Lund, Sweden: Studentlitteratur, 1982).

5. Gordon H. Bower and Ernest R. Hilgard, *Theories of Learning*, 5th ed. (Englewood Cliffs, NJ: Prentice-Hall, 1981), 9–11.

6. John Seely Brown, Allen Collins, and Paul Duguid, "Situated Cognition and the Culture of Learning," *Educational Researcher* (January/February 1989): 32–42; Robert Glaser, "Education and Thinking: The Role of Knowledge," *American Psychologist* 39 (1984): 93–104; and J. Willems, "Problem-Based (Group) Teaching: A Cognitive Science Approach to Using Available Knowledge," *Instructional Science* 10 (1981): 5–21.

7. Lauren B. Resnick, *Education and Learning to Think* (Washington, DC: National Academy Press, 1987), 18.

8. Wesley M. Cohen and Daniel A. Levinthal, "Absorptive Capacity: A New Perspective on Learning and Innovation," *Administrative Science Quarterly* 35 (1990): 128–152.

9. K. Anders Ericsson and Neil Charness, "Expert Performance: Its Structure and Acquisition," *American Psychologist* 49 (1994): 725–747; and K. Anders Ericsson and Robert J. Crutcher, "The Nature of Exceptional Performance," in Paul B. Baltes, David L. Featherman, and Richard M. Lerner, eds., *Life-Span Development and Behavior*, vol. 10 (Hillsdale, NJ: Lawrence Erlbaum, 1990), 187–217.

10. The ten year rule was originally discovered among chess players but has since been observed in other settings as well. See Herbert A. Simon and William G. Chase, "Skill in Chess," *American Scientist* 61 (1973): 394–403.

11. Morgan W. McCall Jr., *High Flyers* (Boston: Harvard Business School Press, 1998), 65–79; and Morgan W. McCall, Jr., Michael M. Lombardo, and Ann M. Morrison, *The Lessons of Experience* (Lexington, MA: D. C. Heath, 1988).

12. McCall, *High Flyers*, 64, 76. Italics in original.

13. Neil A. Hayes and Donald E. Broadbent, "Two Modes of Learning for Interactive Tasks," *Cognition*, 28 (1988): 249–276; Arthur S. Reber, "Implicit Learning and Tacit Knowledge," *Journal of Experimental Psychology: General* 118 (1989): 219–235; and Richard M. Shiffrin and Susan T. Dumais, "The Development of Automatism," in John R. Anderson, ed., *Cognitive Skills and Their Acquisition* (Hillsdale, NJ: Lawrence Erlbaum, 1981), 111–140.

14. In their early writings, engineers and economists distinguished "learning curves" from "progress functions." Technically, learning curves focus on direct labor learning and measure the relationship between experience and direct labor costs, while progress functions include both direct and indirect labor learning and measure the relationship between experience and all manufacturing costs. For simplicity, the former term will be used here to describe both relationships.

15. The relationship was discovered by the engineer Theodore P. Wright in the 1920s and 1930s and was first reported in his article "Factors Affecting the Cost of Airplanes," *Journal of Aeronautical Science*, 3 (1936): 122–128. The same discovery was made independently by the commander of Wright-Patterson Air Force Base at roughly the same time. The seminal theoretical treatment within economics is Kenneth J. Arrow, "The Economic Implications of Learning by Doing," *Review of Economic Studies* 29 (1962): 155–173.

16. John M. Dutton, Annie Thomas, and John E. Butler, "The History of Progress Functions as a Managerial Technology," *Business History Review* 86 (1984): 204–233: and Louis E. Yelle, "The Learning Curve: Historical Review and Comprehensive Survey," *Decision Sciences* 10 (1979): 302–328.

17. William J. Abernathy and Kenneth Wayne, "Limits of the Learning Curve," *Harvard Business Review* 52 (September/October 1974): 110–111.

18. Nathan Rosenberg, *Inside the Black Box: Technology and Economics* (Cambridge: Cambridge University Press, 1982), ch. 6.

19. The Boston Consulting Group, *Perspectives on Experience* (Boston: The Boston Consulting Group, 1970).

20. Pankaj Ghemewat, "Building Strategy on the Experience Curve," *Harvard Business Review* 63 (March/April 1985): 146.

21. Winfred B. Hirschmann, "Profit from the Learning Curve," *Harvard Business Review* 42 (January/February 1964): 125–139. Also see David L. Bodde, "Riding the Experience Curve," *Technology Review* (March/April 1976): 53–57.

22. Armen Alchian, "Reliability of Progress Curves in Airframe Production," *Econometrica* 31 (1963): 679–693.

23. Marvin B. Lieberman, "The Learning Curve and Pricing in the Chemical Processing Industries," *Rand Journal of Economics* 15 (1984): 221–222.

24. Linda Argote, Sara L. Beckman, and Dennis Epple, "The Persistence and Transfer of Learning in Industrial Settings," *Management Science* 36 (1990): 150–151.

25. Bodde, "Riding the Experience Curve," 54.

26. Argote, Beckman, and Epple, "The Persistence and Transfer of Learning in Industrial Settings," 144–146; and Dennis Epple, Linda Argote, and Rukimini Devadas, "Organizational Learning Curves: A Method for Investigating Intra-Plant Transfer of Knowledge Acquired through Learning by Doing," *Organization Science* 2 (1991): 68–69.

27. Ghemewat, "Building Strategy on the Experience Curve," 147–149.

28. Matthew Hayward, "Acquiror Learning from Acquisition Experience: Evidence from 1985–1995" (London Business School, undated, photocopy), 22. Forthcoming in 1999, Academy of Management, Business Policy and Strategy Division, *Best Paper Proceedings*.

29. Jerayr Haleblian and Sydney Finkelstein, "The Influence of Organizational Acquisition Experience on Acquisition Performance: A Behavioral Learning Perspective," *Administrative Science Quarterly* 44 (1999): 29–56.

30. Ghemewat, "Building Strategy on the Experience Curve," 149.

31. Hirschmann, "Profit from the Learning Curve," 137.

32. Gerald B. Allan and John S. Hammond, "Note on the Use of Experience Curves in Competitive Decision Making," Case 9-175-174 (Boston: Harvard Business School, 1975), 4.

33. J. M. Juran, *Juran on Leadership for Quality* (New York: Free Press, 1989), 136–141.

34. Tracy Kidder, *The Soul of a New Machine* (Boston: Atlantic-Little Brown, 1981), 217.

35. James G. March, Lee S. Sproull, and Machal Tamuz, "Learning from Samples of One or Fewer," *Organization Science* 2 (1991): 1–13.

36. Sim B. Sitkin, "Learning through Failure: The Strategy of Small Losses," in B. M. Staw and L. L. Cummings, eds., *Research in Organizational Behavior,* vol. 14 (Greenwich, CT: JAI Press, 1992), 231–266.

37. Modesto A. Maidique and Billie Jo Zirger, "The New Product Learning Cycle," *Research Policy* 14 (1985): 299, 306, 309.

38. For a methodology describing how to develop and write "learning histories," see Art Kleiner and George Roth, "How to Make Experience Your Company's Best Teacher," *Harvard Business Review* 75 (September/October 1997): 172–177.

39. Michael A. Cusumano and Richard W. Selby, *Microsoft Secrets* (New York: Free Press, 1995), 331–339; and Julie Bick, *All I Really Need to Know in Business I Learned at Microsoft* (New York: Pocket Books, 1997): 9–10.

40. The quotation is from Fred Moody's book *I Sing the Body Electronic* and is cited in David Stauffer, "What You Can Learn about Managing from Microsoft," *Harvard Management Update* (September 1997): 3.

41. Janet Simpson, Lee Field, and David Garvin, "The Boeing 767: From Concept to Production (A)," Case 9-688-040 (Boston: Harvard Business School, 1988), 5–6.

42. These patterns are sometimes called "life themes." See Len Schlesinger, "How to Hire by Wire," *Fast Company,* November 1993, 86–91.

43. Robert Kelley and Janet Caplan, "How Bell Labs Creates Star Performers," *Harvard*

*Business Review* 71 (July/August 1993): 128–139; and Robert E. Kelley, *How to Be a Star at Work* (New York: Times Business, 1998).

44. Robert W. Johnson, "Theory and Policy of Post Audit," in Frank G. J. Derkinderen and Roy L. Crum, eds., *Readings in Strategy for Corporate Investment* (Boston: Pitman, 1981), 135–145.

45. Frank R. Gulliver, "Post-Project Appraisals Pay," *Harvard Business Review* 65 (March/April 1987): 128–132.

46. Gabriel Szulanski, "Intra-Firm Transfer of Best Practices Project: Executive Summary of the Findings," (Fontainebleau, France, and Houston, Texas: INSEAD and American Productivity & Quality Center, October 1994), photocopy, 4.

47. John Krafcik, "Learning from NUMMI," International Motor Vehicle working paper, MIT, Cambridge, MA, 15 September 1986, photocopy, 14–16.

48. Andrew M. Pettigrew, "Longitudinal Field Research: Theory and Practice," *Organization Science* 1 (1990): 270.

49. The AAR story is based primarily on interviews conducted in December 1995 and January 1996 with General Gordon R. Sullivan, chief of staff of the U.S. Army; Colonel Orin A. Nagel, director, Center for Army Lessons Learned; and various commanders and officers who had recently returned from Haiti and were participating in exercises and AARs at the National Training Center at Fort Polk, Louisiana (Lieutenant Colonel Michael Trahan, Colonel Ray Fitzgerald, Colonel Sharp, Major Patrick MacGowan, Captain Favio Lopez, Sergeant Dawson, and Lieutenant Fogg). Portions of these interviews, as well as excerpts from the AARs at the National Training Center, appear in the videotape *Putting the Learning Organization to Work: Learning After Doing* (Boston: Harvard Business School Video, 1996). Other sources include an interview with Captain Andrew D. Clarke, a former observer-controller at the National Training Center, in September 1998; and Baird, Henderson, and Watts, "Learning from Action," 385–395; William Blankmeyer and Terry Blakely, "Leaders Conducting After-Action Reviews Often Deliver Substandard Feedback," *ARMOR* (November/December 1998): 15–18; Henderson and Watts, "Creating and Exploiting Knowledge for Fast-Cycle Response"; Richard Pascale, "Fight, Learn, L\*E\*A\*D," *Fast Company* (August/September 1996): 65–69; Richard Pascale, Mark Millemann, and Linda Gioja, "Changing the Way We Change," *Harvard Business Review* 75 (November/December 1997): 127–139; Thomas E. Ricks, "Army Devises System to Decide What Does and Does Not Work," *Wall Street Journal*, 23 May 1997, A1, A10; Gordon R. Sullivan and Michael V. Harper, *Hope Is Not a Method* (New York: Times Business/Random House, 1996), 189–203; and U.S. Army, "A Leader's Guide to After-Action Reviews," Training Circular 25-20, 30 September 1993, photocopy.

50. Pascale, Millemann, and Gioja, "Changing the Way We Change," 137. Italics in original.

51. This principle has long been recognized by the quality movement. See, for example, John Guaspari, *I Know It When I See It* (New York: AMACOM, 1985).

52. Roger Schank, *Virtual Learning* (New York: McGraw-Hill, 1997), ch. 3.

53. Ron Zemke and Susan Zemke, "Adult Learning: What Do We Know for Sure?" *Training* (June 1995): 31–40.

54. Dewey, *Experience and Education*, 20.

55. Gina M. Walter, *Corporate Practices in Management Development* (New York: The Conference Board, 1996), 16.

56. K. Patricia Cross, "A Proposal to Improve Teaching or What 'Taking Teaching Seriously' Should Mean," *American Association for Higher Education* (September 1986).

57. On GE, see James L. Noel and Ram Charan, "GE Brings Global Thinking to Light," *Training & Development* (July 1992): 32–33. On Whirlpool, see Paul Froiland, "Action Learning: Taming Problems in Real Time," *Training* (January 1994): 32. On Motorola, see Timothy T. Baldwin, Camden Danielson, and William Wiggenhorn, "The Evolution of Learning Strategies in Organizations: From Employee Development to Business Redefinition," *Academy of Management Executive* (November 1997): 47–58.

58. David T. Kearns and David A. Nadler, *Prophets in the Dark* (New York: HarperBusiness, 1992), 214–215.

59. Charles J. Margerison, "Action Learning and Excellence in Management Development," *Journal of Management Development* 7 (1988): 44.

60. Froiland, "Action Learning: Taming Problems in Real Time," 29.

61. Schank, *Virtual Learning*, 35.

62. Eric O. Wheatcroft, *Simulators for Skill* (London: McGraw-Hill, 1973), 26.

63. H. Clayton Foushee, "Dyand and Triads at 35,000 Feet," *American Psychologist* (August 1984): 891–892. Italics in original.

64. Jeanne C. Meister, *Corporate Quality Universities* (Burr, IL: Richard D. Irwin, 1994), 115–117.

65. Roy E. Butler, "LOFT: Full-Mission Simulation as Crew Resource Management Training," in Earl L. Wiener, Barbara G. Kanki, and Robert L. Helmreich, eds., *Cockpit Resource Management* (San Diego: Academic Press, 1993), 235.

66. Schank, *Virtual Learning*, 30–33, 41–42.

67. Rick Becker, "Taking the Misery Out of Experiential Training," *Training* (February 1998): 80. For a complete description of BARNGA, see Sivasailam Thiagarajan, *Simulation Games by Thiagi*, 6th ed. (Bloomington, IN: Workshops by Thiagi, 1997).

68. Charles E. Watson, *Management Development through Training* (Reading, MA: Addison-Wesley, 1979), 178–186.

69. Ronald Henkoff, "Companies that Train Best," *Fortune*, 22 March 1993, 73.

70. Schank, *Virtual Learning*, 87–88.

71. Watson, *Management Development through Training*, 186–195.

72. Jane C. Lindner, "War Games: How Polaroid Links Knowledge to Innovation," in *The Knowledge Advantage: A Summary of the 1994 Colloquium on Organizational Knowledge* (Boston: Ernst & Young Center for Business Innovation, 26–27 September 1994), 79–86.

73. Peter J. Frost, "Crossroads: Bridging Academia and Business: A Conversation with Steve Kerr," *Organization Science* 8 (May/June 1997): 340.

74. Walter, *Corporate Practices in Management Development*, 21–22.

75. William Wiggenhorn, "Motorola U: When Training Becomes an Education," *Harvard Business Review* 68 (July/August 1990), 75.

76. Nancy Foy, "Action Learning Comes to Industry," *Harvard Business Review* 55 (September/October 1977): 158–168; Joseph A. Raelin, "Action Learning and Action Sci

ence: Are They Different?" *Organizational Dynamics* (Summer 1997): 21–33; and Revans, *The Origins and Growth of Action Learning*, 629–630.

77. The CAP story is based primarily on interviews conducted in January and February 1996 with Steve Kerr, vice president, corporate leadership development; Jacquie Vierling, manager, Work-Out, Best Practices, and Change Acceleration; and selected members of CAP teams from GE Supply (Frank Billone and Paul Slattery) and GE Plastics Japan (Nani Beccalli, Greg Adams, Masao Fukuda, and Mr. Kimura). Portions of these interviews, as well as excerpts from CAP sessions at GE's Crotonville training facility, appear in the videotape *Putting the Learning Organization to Work: Learning While Doing* (Boston: Harvard Business School Video, 1996). Other sources include John A. Byrne, "Jack: A Close-Up Look at How America's #1 Manager Runs GE," *Business Week*, 8 June 1998, 90–111; Frost, "Bridging Academia and Business," 332–347; Richard M. Hodgetts, "A Conversation with Steve Kerr," *Organizational Dynamics* (Spring 1996): 68–79; Noel M. Tichy, "GE's Crotonville: A Staging Ground for Corporate Revolution," *Academy of Management Executive* 3 (1989): 99–106; Noel M. Tichy and Ram Charan, "Speed, Simplicity, and Self-Confidence: An Interview with Jack Welch," *Harvard Business Review* 67 (September/October 1989): 112–120; Noel M. Tichy and Stratford Sherman, *Control Your Destiny or Someone Else Will* (New York: Harper Business, 1994), and Dave Ulrich, "A New Mandate for Human Resources," *Harvard Business Review* 76 (January/February 1998) 124–134.

78. Joseph L. Bower and Jay Dial, "Jack Welch: General Electric's Revolutionary," Case 9-394-065 (Boston: Harvard Business School, 1993), 8.

79. The latest of GE's broad-based improvement program is Six Sigma, designed to sharply improve quality levels. It was introduced in the mid-1990s, a few years after CAP.

### Chapter 5: Experimentation

1. Robert Scott Root-Bernstein, *Discovering* (Cambridge: Harvard University Press, 1989), 409.

2. *Oxford English Dictionary*, 2d ed. (Oxford: Oxford University Press, 1991), 550.

3. Martin Landau, "On the Concept of a Self-Correcting Organization," *Public Administration Review* 33 (1973): 533–542; and Aaron Wildavsky, "The Self-Evaluating Organization," *Public Administration Review* 32 (1972): 509–520.

4. Malcolm Warner, *Organizations and Experiments* (Chichester: Wiley, 1984), 8.

5. William R. Dill, Wallace B. S. Crowston, and Edwin J. Elton, "Strategies for Self-Education," *Harvard Business Review* 43 (November/December 1965): 124.

6. Sim B. Sitkin, Kathleen M. Sutcliffe, and Roger G. Schroeder, "Distinguishing Control from Learning in Total Quality Management: A Contingency Perspective," *Academy of Management Review* 19 (1994): 553.

7. Ron Harré, *Great Scientific Experiments* (Oxford: Oxford University Press, 1981), 21–22.

8. On Banc One, see Myra Hart and Hugo Uyterhoeven, "Banc One–1993," Case 9-394-043 (Boston: Harvard Business School, 1993), 15. On British Petroleum, see Steven E. Prokesch, "Unleashing the Power of Learning: An Interview with British Petroleum's John Browne," *Harvard Business Review* 75 (September/October 1997): 160.

9. For discussions of the many different types of experiments, see Roger E. Bohn, "Learning by Experimentation in Manufacturing," working paper 88-001, Harvard Business School, Boston, MA, June 1987; photocopy; Abraham Kaplan, *The Conduct of Inquiry* (San Francisco: Chandler, 1964), ch. 4; P. B. Medawar, *Advice to a Young Scientist* (New York: Harper & Row, 1979), ch. 9; and Donald A. Schön, *The Reflective Practitioner* (New York: Basic Books, 1983), 141–156.

10. Schön, *The Reflective Practitioner,* 145.

11. There are exceptions to this rule. Occasionally, "natural experiments" arise that include enough variation to draw firm conclusions even without manipulating critical variables. American Airlines, for example, took advantage of already existing differences in the time it took cabin crews to open an airplane's doors after gate arrival. It measured these times and then followed up with telephone surveys to assess passengers' perceptions of on-time performance. Managers found that perceptions improved dramatically if the doors were opened less than 25 seconds after gate arrival. See George S. Day, "Continuous Learning about Markets," *California Management Review* 36 (Summer 1994): 15.

12. W. I. B. Beveridge, *The Art of Scientific Investigation* (New York: Vintage Books, 1957), 21.

13. Raghu Garud, "On the Distinction Between Know-How, Know-Why, and Know-What," in James P. Walsh and Ann Huff, eds., *Advances in Strategic Management,* vol. 14 (Greenwich, CT: JAI Press, 1997), 81–101.

14. Roger E. Bohn, "Measuring and Managing Technological Knowledge," *Sloan Management Review* 36 (Fall 1994): 61–73, and Ramchandran Jaikumar and Roger Bohn, "The Development of Intelligent Systems for Industrial Use: A Conceptual Framework," in Richard S. Rosenbloom, ed., *Research on Technological Innovation, Management, and Policy,* vol. 3 (Greenwich, CT: JAI Press, 1986), 182–188.

15. Bohn, "Measuring and Managing Technological Knowledge," 61.

16. Frederick Jackson Turner, *The Frontier in American History* (New York: Henry Holt, 1920).

17. Ray Allen Billington and Martin Ridge, *Westward Expansion,* 5th ed. (New York: Macmillan, 1982), 689.

18. Sven Ove Hansson, "Decision Making under Great Uncertainty," *Philosophy of the Social Sciences* 26 (1996): 369–386; and Eric Von Hippel and Marcie Tyre, "How Learning by Doing Is Done: Problem Identification in Novel Process Equipment," *Research Policy* 24 (1995): 1–12.

19. Henry Mintzberg, Duru Raisinghanii, and André Théorêt, "The Structure of 'Unstructured' Decision Processes," *Administrative Science Quarterly* 21 (1976): 251. Italics in original.

20. Gary S. Lynn, Joseph G. Morone, and Albert Paulson, "Emerging Technologies in Emerging Markets: Challenges for New Product Professionals," *Engineering Management Journal* 8 (1996): 23.

21. Gary S. Lynn, Joseph G. Morone, and Albert S. Paulson, "Marketing and Discontinuous Innovation: The Probe and Learn Process," *California Management Review* 38 (1996): 13–14.

22. Christopher Cerf and Victor Navasky, *The Experts Speak* (New York: Pantheon Books, 1984).

23. Lynn, Morone, and Paulson, "Marketing and Discontinuous Innovation: The Probe and Learn Process," 15, 19.

24. Ibid., 18.

25. Timothy P. Luehrman, "Strategy as a Portfolio of Real Options," *Harvard Business Review* 76 (September/October 1998): 89–99; and Rita Gunther McGrath, "Falling Forward: Real Options Reasoning and Entrepreneurial Failure," *Academy of Management Review* 24 (1999): 13–30. Others have argued that this process occurs more by happenstance than by design, with lower-level managers taking actions that over time are then recognized by senior-level managers and articulated as a new strategic direction. See Robert A. Burgelman, "Strategy Making as a Social Learning Process: The Case of Internal Corporate Venturing," *Interfaces* 18 (1988): 74–85, and Henry Mintzberg, Bruce Ahlstrand, and Joseph Lampel, *Strategy Safari* (New York: Free Press, 1998), ch. 7.

26. Jonathan West and David A. Garvin, "Serengeti Eyewear: Entrepreneurship within Corning Inc.," Case 9-394-033 (Boston: Harvard Business School, 1993), 5.

27. Janet Simpson, Lee Field, and David Garvin, "The Boeing 767: From Concept to Production (A)," Case 9-688-040 (Boston: Harvard Business School, 1988), 8.

28. Geoffrey K. Gill and Steven C. Wheelwright, *Motorola, Inc.: Bandit Pager Project,* Case 9–690-043 (Boston: Harvard Business School, 1990), 4–5.

29. Robert I. Sutton and Andrew Hargadon, "Brainstorming Groups in Context: Effectiveness in a Product Design Firm," *Administrative Science Quarterly* 41 (1996): 704.

30. Bohn, "Learning by Experimentation in Manufacturing," 10–11, 30–34.

31. Stefan H. Thomke, "Managing Experimentation in the Design of New Products," *Management Science* 44 (1998): 745.

32. Stefan H. Thomke, "Simulation, Learning and R&D Performance: Evidence from Automotive Development," *Research Policy* 27 (1998): 66.

33. Susanne Bodker, Kaj Gronbaek, and Morten Kyng, "Cooperative Design: Techniques and Experiences from the Scandinavian Scene," in Douglas Schuler and Aki Namioka, eds., *Participatory Design: Principles and Practices* (Hillsdale, NJ: Lawrence Erlbaum, 1993), 157–175; Pelle Ehn and Morten Kyng, "Cardboard Computers: Mocking-it-up or Hands-on the Future," in Joan Greenbaum and Morten Kyng, eds., *Design at Work: Cooperative Design of Computer Systems* (Hillsdale, NJ: Lawrence Erlbaum, 1991), 169–195; and Robert Howard, "UTOPIA: Where Workers Craft New Technology," *Technology Review* 88 (April 1985): 42–49.

34. Thomke, "Managing Experimentation in the Design of New Products," 743–762; and Von Hippel and Tyre, "How Learning by Doing Is Done," 1–12.

35. Dorothy Leonard-Barton et al., "How to Integrate Work *and* Deepen Expertise," *Harvard Business Review* 72 (September/October 1994): 124.

36. James G. March, Lee S. Sproull, and Machal Tamuz, "Learning from Samples of One or Fewer," *Organization Science* 2 (1991): 6.

37. Ibid., 3, 8.

38. Donald T. Campbell, "Reforms as Experiments," *American Psychologist* 24 (1969): 409–429.

39. Edward E. Lawler III, "Adaptive Experiments: An Approach to Organizational Behavior Research," *Academy of Management Review* 2 (1977): 579.

40. Ibid., 579.

41. Quoted in Beveridge, *The Art of Scientific Investigation,* 68.

42. Dill, Crowston, and Elton, "Strategies for Self-Education," 126.

43. J. Richard Hackman, "Doing Research That Makes a Difference," in Edward E. Lawler III et al., *Doing Research That Is Useful for Theory and Practice* (San Francisco: Jossey-Bass, 1985), 148.

44. Gordon E. Forward, "Wide-Open Management at Chaparrel Steel," *Harvard Business Review* 64 (May/June 1986): 101.

45. Charles Perrow, *Normal Accidents* (New York: Basic Books, 1984), 85–86.

46. On General Foods, see David A. Whitsett and Lyle Yorks, "Looking Back at Topeka: General Foods and the Quality-of-Work-Life Experiment," *California Management Review* 25 (1983): 93–109. On Wal-Mart, see David M. Stipanuk and Jack D. Ninemeier, "Environmental Examples," *Cornell Hotel and Restaurant Administration Quarterly* (December 1996): 79–80.

47. David Hornestay, "Noble Experiments," *Government Executive* (October 1996): 56–59.

48. Artemis March and David A. Garvin, "Copeland Corporation: Evolution of a Manufacturing Strategy, 1975–1982 (A), (B), (C), and (D)," Cases 9–686-088, 9–686-089, 9–686-090, and 9–686-091 (Boston: Harvard Business School 1986).

49. Richard E. Walton, "The Diffusion of New Work Structures: Explaining Why Success Didn't Take," *Organizational Dynamics* (Winter 1975): 3–22.

50. Richard E. Walton, "Successful Strategies for Diffusing Work Innovations," *Journal of Contemporary Business* 6 (Spring 1977): 1–22.

51. William L. Anderson and William T. Crocca, "Engineering Practice and Codevelopment of Product Prototypes," *Communications of the ACM* 36 (1993): 49–56; Eran Carmer, Randall D. Whitaker, and Joey F. George, "PD and Joint Application Design: A Transatlantic Comparison," *Communications of the ACM* 36 (1993): 40–48; and Michael J. Muller, Daniel M. Wildman, and Ellen A. White, "Taxonomy of PD Practices: A Brief Practitioner's Guide," *Communications of the ACM* 36 (1993): 26–27.

52. The Timken story is based on internal documents and interviews conducted in August 1991, January 1992, August 1992, December 1995, and January 1996 with over a dozen members of the organization, including senior managers, representatives of the Feasibility Team, Concept Team, Design Team, and Implementation Team, operators, and project engineers. I am especially grateful to Joe Toot, Jr. (president and CEO), Peter Ashton (president of the bearings business), Jon Elsasser (head of the Design Team), and Mike Arnold (head of the Implementation Team, as well as the first plant manager) for their cooperation and support. Portions of the 1995 and 1996 interviews, as well as scenes from Cardboard City and the training module, appear in the videotape *Putting the Learning Organization to Work: Learning Before Doing* (Boston: Harvard Business School Video, 1996).

53. For an introduction to storyboarding, see Harry Forsha, *Show Me: The Complete Guide to Storyboarding and Problem Solving* (Milwaukee: ASQC Quality Press, 1995).

54. Six years may seem like an unusually long design period. At Timken, the reasons in part were economic. Because the market nose-dived unexpectedly in the middle of

the planning process, managers temporarily put the project on hold. Only after demand rose did planning resume. At least a year (and possibly more) was lost as a result.

55. The quotation is from Professor C. Roland Christensen of the Harvard Business School. He actually used it to define research, but it seems equally appropriate as a description of exploration.

56. Medawar, *Advice to a Young Scientist*, 69.

57. Richard P. Feynman, *Surely You're Joking, Mr. Feynman* (New York: Bantam Books, 1985), 311.

58. For a detailed discussion of these (and other) methodological requirements, see Thomas D. Cook and Donald T. Campbell, *Quasi-Experimentation* (Boston: Houghton Mifflin, 1979), ch. 1.

59. Lawler, "Adaptive Experiments," 577.

60. The Dayton-Hudson program is described at length in the videotape *Customer Loyalty: Measuring, Managing, Making Money* (Boston: Harvard Business School Video, 1995).

61. See, respectively, Cook and Campbell, *Quasi-Experimentation;* Lawler, "Adaptive Experiments"; Stanley E. Seashore, "Field Experiments in Formal Organizations," in William M. Evan, ed., *Organizational Experiments: Laboratory and Field Research* (New York: Harper & Row, 1971), 147–153; and Michael Scriven, "Maximizing the Power of Causal Investigations: The Modus Operandi Method," in G. V. Glass, ed., *Evaluation Studies*, vol. 1 ( Beverly Hills, CA: Sage, 1976), 101–118.

62. Kaplan, *The Conduct of Inquiry,* 144, 147.

63. For detailed discussions of these conditions, which scientists call *internal* and *external validity,* see Campbell, "Reforms as Experiments," 410–412, and Barry M. Staw, "The Experimenting Organization: Problems and Prospects," in Barry M. Staw, ed., *Psychological Foundations of Organizational Behavior,* 2d ed. (Glenview, IL: Scott, Foresman, 1983), 421–437.

64. The distinction between a "vacuum cleaner" and "directed telescope" approach to collecting data was originally used to describe the approach of the Center for Army Lessons Learned. See John C. Henderson and Stephanie A. Watts, "Creating and Exploiting Knowledge for Fast-Cycle Response: An Analysis of the Center for Army Lessons Learned" (Boston, MA, Boston University, undated, photocopy), 5–6.

65. Beveridge, *The Art of Scientific Investigation,* 63.

66. This phenomenon is called "regression toward the mean." For further discussion, see Campbell, "Reforms as Experiments," 413–414, and Max Bazerman, *Judgment in Managerial Decision Making,* 4th ed. (New York: Wiley, 1998), 23–26.

67. Occasionally, experiments can be crafted so that several variables can be altered simultaneously while still isolating their impacts. This technique, called "design of experiments," requires considerable statistical sophistication but can yield impressive benefits. Ford, for example, was able to cut test-development time for a new heat-treatment process by 63 percent using this approach. See Jill F. Minner, "DOE Slashes Test-Development Time by 63%," *Quality* (December 1996): 61.

68. Scriven, "Maximizing the Power of Causal Investigations," 103–108.

69. The Allegheny Ludlum story is based primarily on internal documents and interviews

conducted in March and April 1997 with Richard Simmons, chairman and chief executive officer, Allegheny Teladyne; Robert Miller, vice president, technical; Thomas DeLuca, director, process metallurgy; James Liput, manager, process metallurgy; Roy Andrews, manager, product metallurgy; Thomas Nese, senior product metallurgist; Roger Walburn, metallurgist; T. L. Swigart, superintendent, annealing & pickling, normalizing & plate finishing; Frank Spiecha, manager, hot working; and Thomas Parayil, research associate. Portions of these interviews, as well as scenes recreating the experimental process and showing the two annealing lines in action, appear in the videotape *Redoubling Shop Floor Productivity* (Boston: Harvard Business School Video, 1997). Additional information can be found in Artemis March and David A. Garvin, "Allegheny Ludlum Steel Corporation," Case 9–686-087 (Boston: Harvard Business School, 1985).

70. Beveridge, *The Art of Scientific Investigation,* 21.

## Chapter 6: Leading Learning

1. On management, see Colin P. Hales, "What Do Managers Do? A Critical Review of the Evidence," *Journal of Management Studies* 23 (1986): 88–115; F. Luthans, R. M. Hodgetts, and S. A. Rosenkrantz, *Real Managers* (Cambridge: Ballinger, 1988); Henry Mintzberg, *The Nature of Managerial Work* (New York: Harper & Row, 1973); and Henry Mintzberg, "The Manager's Job: Folklore and Fact," *Harvard Business Review* 53 (July/August 1975): 49–61. On leadership, and especially its differences from management, see Warren Bennis and Bert Nanus, *Leaders* (New York: Harper & Row, 1985); John P. Kotter, *The Leadership Factor* (New York: Free Press, 1988); John P. Kotter, *A Force for Change* (New York: Free Press, 1990); Abraham Zaleznik, "Managers and Leaders: Are They Different?" *Harvard Business Review* 55 (May/June 1977): 67–80; and Abraham Zaleznik, *The Managerial Mystique* (New York: Harper & Row, 1989).

2. John Gardner, *Self-Renewal* (New York: Harper & Row, 1964), 3.

3. Eli Cohen and Noel Tichy, "How Leaders Develop Leaders," *Training & Development* (May 1997): 58–73; Noel M. Tichy, with Eli Cohen, *The Leadership Engine* (New York: HarperBusiness, 1997); and Howard Gardner, *Leading Minds* (New York: Basic Books, 1995).

4. James Kelley, "Learning Is Not Enough," *Transformation* (Autumn 1998): 46.

5. Carl Rogers, *Freedom to Learn for the 80's* (Columbus, OH: Charles E. Merrill, 1983); and Christensen, Garvin, and Sweet, *Education for Judgment.*

6. Alfred North Whitehead, *The Aims of Education* (New York: Free Press, 1929), 1.

7. Charles Gragg, "Because Wisdom Can't Be Told," *Harvard Alumni Bulletin,* 19 October 1940.

8. Charles Hartshorne and Paul Weiss, eds., *Collected Papers of Charles Sanders Peirce,* vol. 5 (Cambridge: Harvard University Press, 1934), 405.

9. David A. Garvin, "The Processes of Organization and Management," *Sloan Management Review* (Summer 1998): 33–50.

10. Michael Hammer, "Reengineering Work: Don't Automate, Obliterate," *Harvard Business Review* 68 (July/August 1990), 110.

11. This distinction was first reported by social psychologists, drawing on studies of elementary school, junior high school, and high school students. See Carole Ames

and Jennifer Archer, "Achievement Goals in the Classroom: Students' Learning Strategies and Motivation Processes," *Journal of Educational Psychology* 80 (1988): 260–267; Carole S. Dweck and Ellen L. Leggett, "A Social-Cognitive Approach to Motivation and Personality," *Psychological Review* 95 (1988): 256–273; and Claudia M. Mueller and Carole S. Dweck, "Praise for Intelligence Can Undermine Children's Motivation and Performance," *Journal of Personality and Social Psychology* 75 (1998): 33–52. The findings were later expanded to business settings. See Harish Sujan, Barton A. Weitz, and Nirmalya Kumar, "Learning Orientation, Working Smart, and Effective Selling," *Journal of Marketing* 58 (1994): 39–52; and Ajay K. Kohli, Tasadduq A. Shervani, and Goutam N. Challagalla, "Learning and Performance Orientation of Salespeople: The Role of Supervisors," *Journal of Marketing Research* 35 (1998): 263–274.

12. Ram Charan, "Managing Through the Chaos," *Fortune*, 23 November 1998, 284.

13. Max Bazerman, *Judgment in Managerial Decision Making*, 4th ed. (New York: John Wiley, 1998), 168–170; and Alexander L. George, *Presidential Decisionmaking in Foreign Policy* (Boulder, CO: Westview Press, 1980), 58.

14. Seth Lubove, "It Ain't Broke, But Fix It Anyway," *Forbes*, 1 August 1994, 59.

15. Noel M. Tichy and Stratford Sherman, *Control Your Destiny or Someone Else Will* (New York: Harper Business, 1994), 190–194, 424–425.

16. Jonathan West and David A. Garvin, "Time Life Inc. (A)," Case 9-395-012 (Boston: Harvard Business School, 1994), 3–7.

17. David A. Garvin, "Leveraging Processes for Strategic Advantage," *Harvard Business Review* 73 (September/October 1995): 79.

18. Garvin, "Leveraging Processes for Strategic Advantage," 84.

19. Bo Hedberg, "How Organizations Learn and Unlearn," in Paul C. Nystrom and William H. Starbuck, eds., *Handbook of Organizational Design*, vol. 1 (Oxford: Oxford University Press, 1981), 3–27.

20. Don Sull and David A. Garvin, "Pepsi's Regeneration, 1990–1993," Case 9-395-048 (Boston: Harvard Business School, 1994); and Nikhil Deogun, "Pepsi's Mr. Nice Guy Vows Not to Finish Last," *Wall Street Journal*, 19 March 1997, B1, B5.

21. Mary Gentile and Todd D. Jick, "Bob Galvin and Motorola, Inc. (A)," Case 9-487-062 (Boston: Harvard Business School, 1987), 11.

22. Kelley, "Learning Is Not Enough," 46.

23. This is the essence of Heifetz's model of "adaptive leadership." See Ronald A. Heifetz, *Leadership Without Easy Answers* (Cambridge, MA: Harvard University Press, 1994); and Ronald A. Heifetz and Donald L. Laurie, "The Work of Leadership," *Harvard Business Review* 75 (January/February 1997): 124–134.

24. Gentile and Jick, "Bob Galvin and Motorola, Inc. (A)," 6.

25. Mary Gentile and Todd D. Jick, "Bob Galvin and Motorola, Inc. (B)," Case 9-487-063 (Boston: Harvard Business School, 1987); and Mary Gentile and Todd D. Jick, "Bob Galvin and Motorola, Inc. (C)," Case 9-487-064 (Boston: Harvard Business School, 1987).

26. Artemis March and David A. Garvin, "Harvey Golub: Recharging American Express," Case 9-396-212 (Boston: Harvard Business School, 1996), 6.

27. March and Garvin, "Harvey Golub," 5. Italics in original.

28. Irving Janis, *Victims of Groupthink* (Boston: Houghton Mifflin, 1972), 147–148; J. Richard Hackman and Richard E. Walton, "Leading Groups in Organizations," in Paul S. Goodman, ed., *Designing Effective Work Groups* (San Francisco: Jossey-Bass, 1986), 72–119; and Richard T. Johnson, *Managing the White House* (New York: Harper & Row, 1974), 136–147.

29. C. Roland Christensen, "Premises and Practices of Discussion Teaching," in C. Roland Christensen, David A. Garvin, and Ann Sweet, eds., *Education for Judgment* (Boston: Harvard Business School Press, 1991), 22.

30. Edward De Bono, *Six Thinking Hats* (Boston: Little, Brown and Company, 1985).

31. Artemis March and David A. Garvin, "Harvard Business School Publishing," Case 9-397-028 (Boston: Harvard Business School, 1996).

32. Dorothy Leonard-Barton, "The Factory as a Learning Laboratory," *Sloan Management Review* (Fall 1992): 33.

33. Jonathan West and David A. Garvin, "Serengeti Eyewear: Entrepreneurship within Corning Inc." Case 9-394-033 (Boston: Harvard Business School, 1993), and David A. Garvin, *Serengeti Eyewear: An Interview with Zaki Mustafa* (Boston: Harvard Business School Video, 1997). Despite Serengeti's success, Corning sold the division in February 1997 as part of a refocusing effort aimed at shedding all businesses not connected to telecommunications or computers. See Timothy Aeppel, "Corning's Makeover: From Casseroles to Fiber Optics," *Wall Street Journal,* 16 July 1999, B4.

34. Quoted in James Freedman, *Idealism and Liberal Education* (Ann Arbor, MI: University of Michigan Press, 1996), 63.

35. Artemis March and David A. Garvin, "A Note on Knowledge Management," Case 9-398-031 (Boston: Harvard Business School, 1997), 14.

36. Andris Berzins, Joel Podolny, and John Roberts, "British Petroleum (B): Focus on Learning," Case S-IB-16B (Palo Alto, CA: Stanford Business School, 1998); Nancy Dixon and Jonathan Ungerleider, "Lessons Learned," January 1998 <http://www.businessinnovation.ey.com/mko/index.html>; and Steven E. Prokesch, "Unleashing the Power of Learning: An Interview with British Petroleum's John Browne," *Harvard Business Review* 75 (September/October 1997): 146–168.

37. Gary Deutsch and Gabriel Szulanski, "Rank Xerox–Team C," Case 1997-001-1 (Philadelphia, PA: Wharton Business School, 1997).

38. Alexander L. George, *Presidential Decisionmaking in Foreign Policy* (Boulder, CO: Westview Press, 1980), 101–103.

39. J. T. Lanzetta and T. B. Roby, "The Relationship Between Certain Group Process Variables and Group Problem-Solving Efficiency," *Organizational Behavior and Human Performance* 11 (1960): 146.

40. H. Clayton Foushee, "Dyads and Triads at 35,000 Feet," *American Psychologist* (August 1984): 890.

41. March and Garvin, "Harvard Business School Publishing," 14.

42. These three skills were, to my knowledge, first spoken of collectively by Professor C. Roland Christensen, who used them as part of his seminar on case method teaching at the Harvard Business School. For further discussion, see Louis B. Barnes, C. Roland Christensen, and Abby J. Hansen, *Teaching and the Case Method,* 3d ed. (Boston: Harvard Business School Press, 1994), 62–63; and Christensen's essays in Christensen, Garvin, and Sweet, eds., *Education for Judgment,* ch. 2, 6, and 9.

43. Peter F. Drucker, *The Practice of Management* (New York: Harper & Row, 1954), 351.

44. For discussions of questions and the various roles they play, see Barnes, Christensen, and Hansen, *Teaching and the Case Method*, 62–63; James Austin, with Ann Sweet and Catherine Overholt, "'To See Ourselves as Others See Us:' The Rewards of Classroom Observation," in Christensen, Garvin, and Sweet, eds., *Education for Judgment*, 156–163; and Thomas P. Kasulis, "Questioning," in Margaret Morganroth Gullette, ed., *The Art and Craft of Teaching* (Cambridge, MA: Harvard-Danforth Center for Teaching and Learning, 1982), 38–48.

45. Alfred Benjamin, *The Helping Interview*, 2d ed. (Boston: Houghton Mifflin, 1974), 67.

46. Thomas Petzinger Jr., "With the Stakes High, A Lucent Duo Conquers Distance and Culture," *Wall Street Journal*, 23 April 1999, B1.

47. Irving J. Lee, *How to Talk with People* (New York: Harper & Row, 1952), 11. Italics in original.

48. Robert F. Bales, "In Conference," *Harvard Business Review* 32 (March/April 1954): 49. Italics in original.

49. Jayashree Mahajan, "The Overconfidence Effect in Marketing Management Predictions," *Journal of Marketing Research* 29 (1992): 329–342.

50. On pre-mortems, see Gary Klein, *Sources of Power* (Cambridge: MIT Press, 1998), 71–72; and Gary Klein et al., "Decision Skills Training," in *Proceedings of the 41st Annual Meeting of the Human Factors and Ergonomics Society* (Santa Monica, CA: Human Factors and Ergonomics Society, 1997). On prospective hindsight, see Deborah J. Mitchell, J. Edward Russo, and Nancy Pennington, "Back to the Future: Temporal Perspective in the Explanation of Events," *Journal of Behavioral Decision Making* 2 (1989): 25–38.

51. A. Barry Rand, executive vice president, Xerox Corporation, interview 25 February 1993.

52. Charles I. Gragg, "Teachers Must Also Learn," *Harvard Educational Review* 10 (1940): 30–47.

53. Richard Farson, *Management of the Absurd* (New York: Touchstone, 1996), 62.

54. Daniel Goleman, "All Too Often, the Doctor Isn't Listening, Studies Show," *New York Times*, 13 November 1991, C1, C15.

55. Quoted in Lee, *How to Talk with People*, 11.

56. David A. Garvin, "A Delicate Balance: Ethical Dilemmas and the Discussion Process," in Christensen, Garvin, and Sweet, eds., *Education for Judgment*, 301. Also see "Handling Q&A: The Five Kinds of Listening," *Harvard Communications Update* (February 1999): 6–7.

57. Lee, *How to Talk with People*, 6.

58. Gentile and Jick, "Bob Galvin and Motorola, Inc. (A)," 2.

59. Gragg, "Teachers Must Also Learn," 32–38.

60. Foushee, "Dyads and Triads at 35,000 Feet," 888.

61. Benjamin, *The Helping Interview*, ch. 7.

62. Quoted in Charles Handy, *The Age of Unreason* (Boston: Harvard Business School Press, 1989), 67.

63. Daniel H. Kim, "The Link between Individual and Organizational Learning," *Sloan Management Review* (fall 1993): 37.

64. They are not, however, sufficient. If an organization is made up of individuals who learn but has not developed the associated processes for capturing and retaining knowledge, it does not meet the litmus tests of chapter 1 and therefore does not qualify as a learning *organization*.

65. Farson, *Management of the Absurd,* 117.

66. Norman H. Mackworth, "Originality," *American Psychologist* 20 (1965): 60.

67. Quoted in *Leo Rosten's Carnival of Wit* (New York: Plume, 1996), 483.

68. Bales, "In Conference," 46.

69. Gary Klein, "Developing Expertise in Decision Making," *Thinking and Reasoning* 3 (1997): 337–352; and James Shanteau, "Psychological Characteristics and Strategies of Expert Decision Makers," *Acta Psychologica* 68 (1988): 203–215.

70. Karl E. Weick, "The Vulnerable System: An Analysis of the Tenerife Air Disaster," *Journal of Management* 16 (1990): 582.

71. Edgar H. Schein, "Management Development as a Process of Influence," *Industrial Management Review* (May 1961): 69–72.

72. George, *Presidential Decisionmaking in Foreign Policy,* 147.

73. Peter F. Drucker, "Managing Oneself," *Harvard Business Review* 77 (March/April 1999): 67–68.

74. Robert J. Sternberg, *Thinking Styles* (Cambridge, England: Cambridge University Press, 1997).

75. Bazerman, *Judgment in Managerial Decision Making,* 168–170; George, *Presidential Decisionmaking in Foreign Policy,* 58; Klein, "Developing Expertise in Decision Making," 347–348; Shanteau, "Psychological Characteristics and Strategies of Expert Decision Makers," 208; and James Shanteau, "Competence in Experts: The Role of Task Characteristics," *Organizational Behavior and Human Decision Processes* 53 (1992): 252–266.

76. March and Garvin, "Harvey Golub," 5.

77. Gardner, *Self-Renewal,* 97–98.

78. Benson P. Shapiro, Kash Rangan, and John J. Sviokla, "Staple Yourself to an Order," *Harvard Business Review* 70 (July/August 1992): 113–122.

79. This is one feature that distinguishes firms that are rapid decision makers (and also rapid learners) from those that move more slowly. See Kathleen M. Eisenhardt, "Making Fast Strategic Decisions in High-Velocity Environments," *Academy of Management Journal* 32 (1989): 543–576.

80. March and Garvin, "Harvey Golub," 1.

81. West and Garvin, "Serengeti Eyewear: Entrepreneurship within Corning Inc.," 7, 13.

82. For a discussion of the links between humility and scholarship, see Wayne C. Booth, "The Scholar in Society," in Booth, *The Vocation of a Teacher* (Chicago: University of Chicago Press, 1988), 73.

# Index

# About the Author

**DAVID A. GARVIN** is the Robert and Jane Cizik Professor of Business Administration at the Harvard Business School, where he teaches general management in the M.B.A. and Advanced Management programs. He has also taught in many corporate executive programs and has consulted with companies around the world on organizational learning and strategic change. He is the author or coauthor of eight books, including *Education for Judgment* and *Managing Quality*; twenty-five articles, including "The Processes of Organization and Management," "Building a Learning Organization," and "Quality on the Line"; and four videotape series, including *Working Smarter* and *Putting the Learning Organization to Work*.

Garvin is a three-time winner of the McKinsey Award, given annually for the best article in the *Harvard Business Review*, and a winner of the Beckhard Prize, given annually for the best article on planned change and organizational development in the *Sloan Management Review*. From 1988–1990 he served as a member of the Board of Overseers of the Malcolm Baldrige National Quality Award, and from 1991–1992 he served on the Manufacturing Studies Board of the National Research Council.